T0326820

Enculturing Law

Enculturing Law

New Agendas for Legal Pedagogy

edited by
MATHEW JOHN
SITHARAMAM KAKARALA

Tulika Books

Published by **Tulika Books**
35 A/1 (III floor), Shahpur Jat, New Delhi 110 049, India

© Mathew John and Sitharamam Kakarala

First published in India 2007

ISBN: 978-81-89487-32-4

The seminar on which this publication is based and the
publication itself were made possible by the financial support
of the Indo-Dutch Programme on Alternatives in Development
(IDPAD) – A Joint Programme on Development Research of the
Indian Council of Social Science Research (ICSSR), New Delhi
and Science for Global Development (WOTRO), The Hague.

Typeset in Sabon and Univers at Tulika Print Communication
Services, New Delhi; printed at Chaman Enterprises, 1603
Pataudi House, Daryaganj, Delhi 110 002

Contents

Preface and Acknowledgements

This collection of essays carries forward the debates that emerged at a seminar titled 'Enculturing Law: New Agendas for Legal Pedagogy' conducted at Bangalore in August 2005. The seminar was organized by the Centre for the Study of Culture and Society (CSCS) in collaboration with the National Law School of India University (NLSIU) and the Alternative Law Forum (ALF). It was supported by a generous grant from the Indo–Dutch Partnership on Alternatives in Development (IDPAD) – a joint programme on development research of the Indian Council of Social Science Research (ICSSR), New Delhi, and Science for Global Development (WOTRO), The Hague.

The seminar sought to address questions related to interdisciplinary pedagogy in the study of Indian law. Over the last twenty years, the emergence of many carefully branded 'National Law Schools' in various parts of the country has raised important questions related to the nature of legal studies in India. However, a large part of these concerns has been focused on improving standards in professional education, especially in the study of what is pejoratively called the 'black letter' law tradition. In this context, the 'Enculturing Law' seminar sought to argue a different approach by foregrounding the significance of law as part of a liberal education. In doing so, it also sought to foreground the intellectual and epistemic worth of the study of law at the intersection and through the commingling of different disciplinary traditions.

Of the twelve essays included in this volume, all except that of Datta-threya Subbanarasimha were presented at the seminar. Dr Subbanarasimha's essay was written as a response to the issues raised at the seminar, however, and engages with themes this volume addresses. The essays are divided into those that directly relate to legal pedagogy and those that deal with law as a social–legal phenomenon more broadly – that is, phenomena that present themselves for interdisciplinary scrutiny. Collectively, we hope the essays will indicate the possibilities for a differently oriented and truly interdisciplinary approach to the study of law.

We owe this volume to the generous support we have received from the Indo-Dutch Programme on Alternatives in Development (IDPAD). Sanchita Dutta at IDPAD has been especially helpful and supportive of our efforts at the seminar, as well as in publishing the present volume of essays. Friends at the Alternative Law Forum require special mention for their supportive yet lively criticisms of the present project. Shobha Raghuram of HIVOS Bangalore was highly encouraging and supportive of the project from the very beginning. Discussions with Arun Thiruvengadam on the history of the Indian debates on legal education have been extremely helpful. We are also grateful to the editorial team at Tulika Books for their excellent editorial assistance and for keeping us on track for the better part of the last year. Needless to mention, we remain finally responsible for errors that remain in the volume. Lastly, this volume would have been impossible without the support and help of our colleagues at CSCS, especially the enthusiastic support of Ashish Rajadhyaksha and Tejaswini Niranjana, and the untiring work of M.P. Nagaraj, administrative officer at CSCS.

Introduction

Mathew John and Sitharamam Kakarala

> When the arbitrary and traditional barriers between law and the humanities
> have been swept away, and the study of law takes its place as a department of
> liberal culture, a great step forward would have been taken toward making the
> university an institution whose art is, in truth, the art of social life, and whose
> end is fitness for social life.
>
> Edson R. Sunderland[1]

Writing in the early 1900s, Edson Sunderland reflects on what has been
an abiding theme for legal pedagogy across the twentieth century – should the
learning of law be confined to the study of legal form? Or, should legal learning
more broadly incorporate scholarship from the humanities disciplines as well? [2]
A problem with contemporary legal study has been the overwhelming resolution
of this tension in favour of a professional emphasis on the study of law. This
leads to a further range of related questions. Is there a significant reason to
separate law from other social sciences? Why do lawyers believe that the purpose of legal education is solely to create professionally competent lawyers and
nothing more? Has modern Euro–American legal thought always been a discipline autonomous of the other social sciences?

A cursory reading of the history of European legal studies indicates that
from its earliest moments in the medieval university, law has played a crucial role
in animating the development of scholarship in the humanities as a whole.[3] Thus,
the modern emphasis on professionalism raises questions on the status of law as a
site for scholarship on society and its challenges. Sunderland suggests that the narrow professionalism in the study of law was a result of historical accident and
professional conservatism, a conservatism that separated law from the social sciences. In his words:

> neither in England nor on the continent, did law and the liberal arts part com-
> pany by reason of any inherent incompatibility. The question of the value of
> law as a department of general education seems never to have been raised by the
> academicians or lawyers of medieval Europe. Accident separated them, tradi-
> tion perpetuated the division. . . .[4]

Identifying the reasons for the marginalization of the social sciences in the study of law is an extremely difficult task. However, we assume, like Sunderland, that despite the historical accidents that have resulted in this marginalization, there is much merit in studying law as part of broader social and cultural processes, and from the vantage point of other social science and humanities disciplines. The approach to law as a socially and cultural located phenomenon, however, has often had to contest legal orthodoxies in the legal profession as well as in the academy. In what follows we will discuss some of these contests in contemporary Euro–American legal thought and the ways in which they resonate with the concerns that bring together the essays in this volume. We will also look at the ways in which Euro–American debates tie into and resonate with similar debates on legal pedagogy in India. We hope, through this effort, to demonstrate the significance of interdisciplinary analysis to the study of Indian legal problems.

Resisting Legal Orthodoxy

The challenge to the narrow professional approach to law has come from a variety of sources. Some of these efforts have been by individuals,[5] while others have been more institutional and have had a systematic and significant impact on legal curricula. In this section we will briefly outline some of the prominent challenges to narrow visions of law and legal processes.

Sunderland's eloquent quote with which we began this essay represents a classic liberal opposition to the narrowness of professionalism. Sunderland elaborates this position in the following words:

> [The] world must have physicians, lawyers, engineers. Nowhere can such breadth of professional training be given as in the university, where a spirit of wide culture mitigates the tendencies toward professional conceits. But the world needs men more than lawyers, and citizens more than engineers. . . . The university, as a factor of modern life, ought chiefly to serve the great army of young people who expect to enter none of the professions, but wish to fit themselves to be intelligent and efficient members of the body politic.[6]

The liberal challenge to the myopic tendencies of professionalism is therefore cast in terms of preparing citizens for public life and therefore requiring more than just technical training.

A different kind of challenge was advanced by the approach that has come to be known as legal realism. Legal realism emerged as a response to the predominance of 'formalism', or the belief that law is an autonomous domain governed by scientific principles that could be ascertained through a close scrutiny of its principal sources, namely, court cases and judgements. Such an emphasis privileges doctrinaire casebook and black-letter methods of learning legal techniques and skills. The jurisprudential traditions of legal positivism provided formalism with its most formidable intellectual defence, arguing that law, a scientific system, should be understood from within and not from outside.[7]

Legal realism emerged as a direct challenge to this orthodoxy in legal pedagogy. It resisted law's claims to autonomy and proposed that law be viewed as a species of policy to be sourced and comprehended from the everyday practice of law; that is, it challenged the claim that law can be adequately understood by tracing the progress of doctrine. Legal realism drew heavily on empiricism and suggested that social-science methods, rigorously applied, were the best techniques available to comprehend and predict the functioning of legal institutions. Its significant contribution to legal thought lay in the implications of its challenge to legal formalism. In other words, if law was to be understood in its everyday functioning, then it followed that the manner in which rules were made operational relied heavily on the discretion of human agents in arriving at judgement in relation to these rules. Thus, legal realism contested the autonomy of law by pointing out that judges made law through discretionary acts of interpretation.

Realism had an enormous intellectual and institutional impact in the United States especially after the Second World War. In unmasking the autonomy claims of legal formalism, realism subjected legal institutions to empirical inquiry and thereby opened up fertile ground for new directions in legal thought and research. In understanding the everyday practice of law as matter of judicial policy, law became a political site where specific public policy objectives could be pursued. Thus, realism transformed law into social knowledge deployed in the service of state action.[8] However, the charge of realism was not just its conception of law as judicial policy, but also the range of interdisciplinary legal dialogues it facilitated.[9]

By far the most significant contribution of legal realism has been its role as the intellectual midwife to a series of 'critical movements' in law. These include intellectual movements ranging from the law and society movement,[10] the critical legal studies movement,[11] the critiques of legal anthropology and legal pluralism,[12] to feminist legal theory.[13] With the decolonization movements of the 1960s, law and development studies emerged as another of the critical schools of legal thought.[14]

Other scholarly approaches resisting the orthodoxy of formalism backed by narrow professionalism include the now sizeable literature on areas such as 'law and economics',[15] 'law and literature',[16] and 'law and history'.[17] Thus, the course of the twentieth century has seen a wide and impressive range of intellectual efforts challenging existing legal orthodoxies. However, despite these challenges in increasing numbers of law departments, law study associations, journals and courses, it is widely accepted that interdisciplinarity as a pedagogic approach to law continues to remain on the margins.

It is the continued marginalization of interdisciplinary approaches to legal studies that provides the backdrop for the present volume. Further, since a large part of the interdisciplinary work has emerged in the context of Western Europe and the United States, insufficient attention tends to be paid to building an interdisciplinary agenda that resonates with non-western concerns.[18]

However, non-western academic contexts themselves, like India for instance, have not demonstrated a significant capacity for foregrounding academic problems in law beyond legal orthodoxies. It is in this context that the essays in this volume foreground the intellectual significance of interdisciplinary legal study for India.

Legal Education in India
The Context of the Debate

Law has had an almost mythological status in the history of the Indian nation. Many leaders of the Indian national movement, like M.K. Gandhi, Jawaharlal Nehru and Sardar Patel, were lawyers and the study of law was probably an important avenue to secure entry into public life as well as social mobility, more generally. However, the commitment to legal education in India has been rather ambivalent. Here, we will run through the manner in which legal study has been approached in post-independence India, especially the ways in which Indian legal scholarship attempted to craft the study of law outside the orthodoxies of legal professionalism.

In an essay written in 1987, Rajeev Dhavan sombrely reflects on the instrumental approach taken to legal studies in India. Dhavan illustrates this instrumentality by pointing to a preposterous statement issued by the Ministry of External Affairs equating the professions of tailoring and law as subjects entirely unworthy of governmental support. Presumably, the government dismissed legal study as little more than vocational learning, and, needless to mention, tailoring and legal studies lost out to more nationally significant pursuits like science and technology.[19]

Much has changed for the study of law since the time Dhavan wrote his essay, the most significant amongst these changes being the widely acclaimed experiment instituting the National Law School of India University (NLSIU), in 1987. NLSIU has considerably changed the landscape of legal studies and it is now difficult to imagine an Indian government relegating legal education purely to the realm of vocational learning. However, despite the achievements and expansion of the NLSIU model to other parts of India, it continues to be difficult to assess whether legal education in India is more or less instrumental than it was when Dhavan wrote his essay. For instance, it is still difficult to answer questions of the following kind. How does one pick out the traditions of Indian legal scholarship that transcend a narrow and technocratic imagination? How vibrant are these intellectual projects? How have these projects found voice in pedagogic agenda and classroom method? In an attempt to answer these questions, this section draws up a potted history of Indian debates on legal education.

Debates on the state of legal education in India have for a long time been accompanied by a sense of unease and even crisis. In a plea going as far back as 1885, Justice Muthuswami Iyer calls for the development of legal study. He observes that law is hitherto studied in this presidency more as an art founded on certain arbitrary and technical rules than as a science which consists of principles laid down for the protection of human interests in various life relations. A college, therefore, where legal education is imparted on a scientific basis will be of great value to the country, and exercise a very beneficial influence on the practice of law as an art.[20]

After independence, the concern for the quality of legal education intensified. In one of the earliest studies on university education in independent India, the University Education Commission laments that, 'we have no internationally known expounders of jurisprudence and legal studies. Our colleges of law do not hold a place of high esteem either at home or abroad, nor has law become an area of profound scholarship and enlightened research.'[21] Though statements of this kind do not exhaust the concerns for legal education in India, they are nonetheless representative of the task that awaited the project of legal education in independent India.

After independence, the concern for legal education found expression through a number of commissions and studies backed and conducted by parties having a stake in legal education. Exhaustively representing the contributions of individual effort is both cumbersome and not very productive. Instead, it is more useful to identify the concerns that animated the thinking of legal educators over the years. The Report of the Curriculum Development Committee (CDC) in Law, published in 1989, attempts to do precisely this by historically classifying the discussions on the objectives, status and innovation in legal education into three phases. Phase I spans the period 1950–65, in which the principal concern was how best to transform legal education away from its colonial inheritance and to 'Indianize' it. Phase II covered the years 1965–1975, and was seen to be the period that emphasized the reorganization of curricula and pedagogy towards a professional legal education. Finally, in Phase III, running from 1976–88, the preoccupation was the 'modernization' of law curricula to increase its relevance to a society and state in the throes of transition.[22] Though the challenges identified with these various phases have been genuine concerns of legal educators, it is often difficult to strictly hold these concerns to the periods as marked out by the CDC. Hence, while working with the issues flagged by the CDC, it might be useful to present our concerns differently.

Legal Education Debates:
Concerns around Pedagogic Infrastructure
After independence concerns of creating a reasonable level of pedagogic infrastructure and an efficient teaching machine have dominated other issues. From the earliest studies and commissions on legal studies, issues such as the need for quality law libraries, the proliferation of part-time law teachers, poorly developed traditions of research, absence of standard textbooks, styles of learning by rote, questions on whether a law degree should last two or three years and

whether it should be pursued after or before graduation, and so on, have over-shadowed a substantial part of the discussion. For instance, the Law Commission, in its 14th report in 1958, devotes a chapter to legal education and makes, among others, the following suggestions to address the state of legal education in India:[23]

1. The pre-requisite for entrance into the LLB course should be graduation from a recognized university.
2. The duration of a law degree should be two years, during which the university should teach students the science of law and the principles underlying the various branches of law. Law graduates must possess a mastery over legal theory and legal principles.
3. Jurisprudence should be a compulsory subject, but, disagreeing with the earlier University Education Committee, the Law Commission suggested that Roman Law need not be taught as a compulsory subject.
4. Teaching of subjects like Taxation and Procedural Laws should be left to professional bodies.
5. Law is a social science, and it is imperative that it be taught in conjunction with other social sciences; interdisciplinary studies should be at the heart of legal education.
6. To improve teaching methodology, the lecture method was to be abandoned in favour of more extensive use of seminars, group discussions and tutorials.
7. The LLB degree should open different career options. However, those who wish to join the legal profession should have to undergo professional training organized by professional bodies like the Bar Councils.
8. The teaching of law should be confined to full-time institutions.
9. The Commission also urged the government to provide financial assistance to law colleges and universities to modernize legal education.

More than ten years later, A.T. Markose, in his 1972 keynote address to the Poona Conference on 'Legal Education in India: Problems and Perspectives' remarked that:

> we have achieved some improvements. We have a three-year LLB course which is tolerably functional. The monopoly of the monotonous lecture method has been broken. The practice of visiting professors has been recognized. The need for refresher courses and examination reforms has been accepted and university funds are now expended for them. An All India Law Teachers Association was established and is functioning. . . .[24]

Markose was of course reflecting on the achievements of an ongoing project. However, it is clear that putting together the building blocks or the infrastructure for quality legal education was still a significant concern of those worrying about the state of legal education. In fact, three years after the Poona conference, Upendra Baxi convened a review of legal education under the auspices of the University Grants Commission, stating that 'we must not make the mistake of moving forward from a point at which we are not at now'. In going on to describe the existing state of the problem, Baxi restates the difficulties as they had been identified for the better part of the previous twenty-five years. The problems he identifies include those associated with the massification of legal education, law education being pursued by most students as a part-time vocation, a large percentage of the teachers being part-time teachers and in many cases possessing just the bare minimum qualifications, poor library facilities, minimal evidence of innovative curricular experiments, demoralization of the teaching establishment due to the general difficulties of the field as well as the dubious academic practices by which departments are often run by administrations, and so on.

Despite the emphasis on the overwhelming difficulties of a context defined by extremely basic infrastructural and organizational problems, the years after independence also witnessed remarkable achievements in the field. Significant among these were the contributions of two to three generations of dedicated law teachers who built the foundations of Indian legal education.[25] Besides their significant contributions to pedagogy, many of these scholars have contributed immensely to institution-building in locations stretching from Delhi, Banaras, Kochi, Chennai, Jaipur, Pune, Nagpur, Chandigarh, to Bangalore and further. Many of them have also authored textbooks and treatises in fields such as Administrative Law, Constitutional Law, International Law and Labour Law. In their collective concern for legal education, this group of scholars and their body of scholarship did contribute, as Baxi rightly suggests, towards the Indianization of legal study. However, it is not obvious how the work of these scholars directed Indian legal scholarship away from its colonial inheritance, especially since the contemporary legal system is built on the foundations of a legal system left behind by 200 years of British rule – a concern of many contributors to this volume.

Another significant moment in this discussion on improving the infrastructure of legal study and research was the creation of the Indian Law Institute (ILI) in 1956. Functioning under the collective supervision of the Supreme Court, the Bar and parts of the teaching community, the Institute brought together generations of scholarship through what became a highly respected law journal and its annual surveys of different aspects of Indian law. In its half-a-century existence, ILI has encouraged young academics to develop research agendas, opened pedagogic possibilities through seminars on new teaching methods, provided opportunities for inter-generational interaction between scholars, provided a forum where aspects of Indian law could be subject to discussion between the Bar, the Bench and the academic community, put together one of South Asia's best collection of legal materials, and inaugurated new areas of (largely doctrinal) legal research. An equally important contribution of the ILI, along with other institutions like the Delhi University Law Faculty and the Banaras Hindu

University, was the key role they played in facilitating access to and interaction with foreign legal traditions and cultures. In the 1950s and 60s all three institutions, with the support of the Ford Foundation, hosted numerous foreign scholars, some of whom, like Duncan Derrett, Granville Austin and Marc Galanter, have made significant and authoritative contributions to the study of Indian law.[26]

A key outcome of the debates on quality educational infrastructure was the eventual establishment of the National Law School of India University in Bangalore in 1987. The Law School was mooted by the Gajendragadkar Committee Report, 1964, with the suggestion that

> if senior, well qualified and experienced teachers are attracted to such National Law Schools and are offered appropriate remuneration and are vouchsafed other essential facilities, it would be possible to revolutionize legal education on healthy lines without delay. Like law itself, the teaching of law would make progress by experimentation and the method of trial and error which can be adopted in the National Law Schools without external hindrance or impediment which will ultimately serve the purpose of bringing about a new pattern of legal education in this country.[27]

N.R. Madhava Menon, the first Director of NLSIU, attracted quality students and provided what has widely been accepted as a high standard of legal education. The success of the Bangalore Law School has also spurred similar experiments in various other parts of the country, and has more than actualized the Gajendragadkar Committee's call for at least four National Law Schools to be established in different parts of the country.

On Objectives: Justifying Legal Education

Though debates on infrastructure have been a significant concern of legal education debates in India, objectives of various kinds often drive such demands. These objectives need to be explored to get a more holistic sense of the concerns that have animated and driven the legal education project in India. At least two strands of argument can be discerned in the discussions on the objectives of legal education in India. The first is the classic concern – whether legal education should emphasize professional skills, or be more liberal and broad-ranging in approach. The second, on the other hand, is about social relevance or the role of legal education in social transformation.

Liberal Education or Professional Excellence?

Debates on whether legal education in India should emphasize a professional or a liberal orientation have assumed various forms over the last fifty years. The Law Commission Report of 1959, for instance, noted that legal education was unduly concerned with the business of dispensing information to potential legal practitioners, and insufficiently engaged with teaching law as a scientific and cultural subject. The Commission diagnosed this to be a reason why the Indian legal academy had not been able to produce mature and sophisticated jurisprudential thought. It further justified the need to emphasize liberal education since an overwhelming majority of the students who took to law study did not become practitioners of law but eventually opted for a range of other occupations. There are others who have also tried to justify a liberal slant to legal education by making reference to the student constituency in that it makes legal education relevant for them.

The Gajendragadkar Committee emphasized its idea of liberal legal education a little differently. Though the Committee noted that the primary goal of legal education was to produce legal professionals, it went on to suggest that the legal profession be understood in a broad comprehensive sense – that is, as an education that would take within its fold 'not merely practice in courts, but also law teaching, law research, administration in different branches where law plays a role'.[28] In other words, legal education should be viewed as a project that is oriented to the task of developing critical imagination and not merely given to engendering functional competence. Expressed negatively, Arthur von Mehron of the Harvard Law School contends that Indian legal education had not developed a 'rationally functional approach to the problems of law and the legal order', as the 'Indian legal education inevitably tended to evolve in patterns that emphasized rote memory. To impart information – not critical understanding – remained the goal of legal education.'[29] By significantly broadening the understanding of the lawyer, this account of liberal legal education sees it as one given to the preparation of the lawyer as a critical citizen.

Lurking behind the laudable concerns for broadening the approach to legal education, there have always been discussions about the kind of education that would ensure professional competence. These discussions range from arguments relating to the duration of a graduate legal programme to the methods best chosen for well-rounded legal teaching. The Gajendragadkar Committee argued that the duration of the law course should be three years after graduation[30] and taught in ways that diffused the centrality of the case law method. In its opinion, overemphasis on the case law method would overlook the fascinating stories of human relations which, it believed, were best told by understanding law from a sociological viewpoint.[31] In order to integrate approaches from a wide variety of disciplines like sociology, political science, history, economics and language into legal study, the CDC Report proposed that the basic legal course be a five-year multidisciplinary degree to be pursued immediately after the intermediate level.[32] Though there are obvious reasons to argue for an intensive five-year basic law programme, it has been far from easy to ensure that law schools (presumably those catering to the large number of part-time students) accepted this format. Thus, even Madhava Menon, who would later become a key advocate for the five-year law programme, was forced to accede to the opposition to this format when chairing the Committee of Legal Reforms of the All India Law Teachers' Association in its 1979 report.[33] As a compromise measure, the Committee suggested that the then existing three-year law course should be allowed to continue, with efforts being made to improve its content and methods according to a time-bound schedule. Still, colleges that had the infrastructure and capability were encouraged to experiment with the new pattern of the five-year law course. The Committee stated that the five-year course 'appears to satisfy academic demands more fully'.[34] Arguing for an integrated five-year programme was thus another way of incorporating a liberal imagination into the study of law.

Along with the structure of the academic programme, the other issue that eventually weighed in favour of a more professionally inclined legal education was the institutional body that would be the final authority regulating issues relating to the character and content of legal education. The Advocates Act of 1961 vests these powers with the Bar Council of India. Under Section 7(h) of the Act, the Bar Council is solely responsible for promoting legal education in India and to lay down the necessary standards in consultation with the universities imparting such legal education and the State Bar Councils. It is also empowered, under Section 7(i), 'to recognize Universities whose degree in law shall be qualification for enrolment as an advocate and for that purpose to visit and inspect the Universities'.

Such wide powers given to the Bar Council have aroused apprehensions in the teaching community, as the academic freedom to innovate legal studies is then vested solely with a professional body that is least concerned with the business of everyday teaching.[35] Section 10(2) of the Act partially addressed this concern, which stipulates that the Bar Council of India requires to set up a Legal Education Committee consisting of ten members, five being members of the Bar Council of India and five others who would normally be law teachers. Despite this it is clear that the institutional apparatus dealing with legal education is slanted towards its professional aspect.

On the Social Revolution

Finally, legal education has also been conceived in conjunction with platforms of development, social relevance or posed most sharply as with those of social revolution or nation-building. A clear early statement of this vision for legal education is:

> If society is to be adapted to the profound changes on the basis of social and economic life resulting from changes in the world conditions after the war, and in India, particularly after 1947, we feel it is mainly the lawyers that India must look to. The legal profession is called upon to take stock of this situation and to contribute to wide social adjustments. If it fails to do it, it will ultimately be eliminated from the revolutionary scene. . . . Their education, therefore, is of vital importance.[36]

The platform of social relevance found its contemporary champion in Upendra Baxi who, as the chair of two University Grants Commission committees, strongly advocated for a legal education oriented towards the task of social reconstruction and human development. This emphasis found expression in the statement of objects of the NLSIU, in whose conception Baxi played an important role. The statement of objects of the National Law School of India University Act, 1986, reads as follows:

> To advance and disseminate learning and knowledge of law and legal processes and their role in national development; to develop in students and research scholars a sense of responsibility to serve society in the field of law . . . in regard to advocacy, legal services, legislation, law reforms and the like; . . . To make law and legal processes efficient instruments of social development.[37]

It is only inevitable that the larger political battles in a society will find expression in the content and orientation of educational agenda. For instance, it is impossible to see how an education in law can be divorced from a keen understanding and even participation in the formulation and adoption of particular sets of governmental policy. However, there is good cause for caution in identifying educational agenda as the exclusive front for political agendas. Politics is about interests and interests that can even load themselves on to 'value-loaded' agendas like socialism, market freedom, identity struggles and so on. Therefore, as an educational mode it is also important to foreground the epistemological over the merely technical, pragmatic or political.

A Sociology of Indian Law?

Thinking about legal education in India in epistemological terms returns us to the questions we raised earlier. How does one pick out the traditions of Indian legal scholarship that transcend a narrow and technocratic imagination? How vibrant are these intellectual projects? How have these projects found voice in pedagogic agenda and classroom method? Our discussion of legal education debates in India indicates that the bulk of the existing discussion might not be entirely capable of rising up to the challenge posed by these questions. However, Upendra Baxi's scholarship stands out as an exception in this field. His comprehensive review of Indian socio-legal scholarship, titled *Towards a Sociology of Indian Law*, is an attempt to deal with precisely these questions.[38]

The challenge for a sociology of Indian law, according to Baxi, is to decide whether it should be 'policy or action-oriented or whether there ought to be more explicitly theoretical seeking to formulate normative theories about relations of forms of law with forms of social order and their evolution'.[39] Baxi resolved this tension by embracing the 'theoretical' but was faced with serious difficulty in elaborating the contours of a possible theoretical project. Baxi himself resolved this problem by a topographical move that mapped existing scholarship in the sociology of law[40] and, in so doing, presented the Sociology of Indian Law as an invitation to scholarship.

Sadly, however, Baxi's invitation has not produced a tradition of Indian legal scholarship at any level of vibrancy in contemporary Indian legal studies. The best of the graduate institutions, like the National Law Schools, have proved to be little more than reasonably efficient teaching machines, and the best of research institutions, like the Indian Law Institute, are in decay.[41] As Baxi himself has more than amply demonstrated, inspiration for such a project must necessarily draw on disciplines other than law and contexts other than India where the intellectual project in law is extremely instructive. Also, as more than a generation of interdisciplinary work has forcefully demonstrated, intellectual problems cannot be as easily formulated within the boundaries of conventional disciplines and must necessarily emerge at the intersection of various disciplines.[42] It is in this context that the present collection of essays assumes significance, as a contemporary effort to reiterate the call for vibrant intellectual projects in the study of Indian law.

The Essays

The contributions to this volume are concerned with two broad themes: pedagogic questions of and in law, and sites of interdisciplinarity. The essays that deal with the pedagogic questions in and of law are derived from cross-jurisdictional experiences and throw light on a number of similar concerns but divergent responses. They deal with a diverse range of themes, from re-imagining legal and institutional histories in non-western locations like India, to classroom experiences in Europe and elsewhere, to revisiting the colonial question in legal education processes. The essays that represent sites of interdisciplinarity, on the other hand, illuminate questions that are exclusively Indian. In the end, we believe, these two sets of writings will provide both hope and constructive leads for thinking about concrete possibilities in advancing the agenda of interdisciplinarity in legal studies.

Upendra Baxi's opening essay forcefully (and at times polemically) draws our attention to the problem of memory in constructing histories of legal education and institutions. He presents a number of ways to identify the cultural peculiarities and the socially specific measures by which educational practices and institutional performances can be analysed and evaluated. This argument acquires further theoretical significance especially in the contemporary Indian scenario wherein the yardsticks of measuring 'excellence' in legal education themselves are often borrowed measurements from dominant locations. Through his contestation, Baxi suggests an alternative framework of understanding and evaluating the contribution of past legal education and educators in India.

Reflecting on the tendencies of ignoring nuances and embracing sweeping generalizations in socio-legal analysis, Baxi points out that they lead both to distortions and violence. The only corrective, he suggests, is 'an incredible amount of labours of collective learning and sharing', for our 'shared ignorance concerning the evolution of teaching and research cultures is, indeed, immense'. Through such a caution, Baxi underscores the importance of rigorous empirical and ethnographic work on the functioning and failures of institutions and experiments at various levels. No attempt at 'enculturing law', he argues, can take place meaningfully outside the bounds of this reality.

Roger Cotterrell looks at legal scholarship's recent concerns with the complexity of law's relations with culture, argued from a socio-legal point of view. He points out the importance for legal studies today to have a comparative dimension, and to understand law in relation to culture or as a cultural phenomenon. Nonetheless, he notes that there are problems with culture as a legal concept (or a social-scientific one) since it has been notoriously vague. To deal with this problem he suggests an alternative route to map the importance of culture for law. This involves taking the notion of community seriously. Accordingly, he proposes a model consisting of four ideal types of community that cover the range of cultural situations on which the regulative umbrella of law could be brought to bear. He calls these forms of community (i) *instrumental* community, (ii) community of *belief or values*, (iii) *traditional* community and (iv) *affective* community. Various combinations of these communities, he suggests, comprise the cultural configurations that a contextually driven legal framework would be called upon to respond to. He suggests that a culturally rooted explanation of law would be one that responds to the appropriate call of the forms of community he outlines. A 'law and community' approach to legal study powerfully clarifies law's relations with culture, and gives a framework for comparative studies of law.

The essay by Tim Murphy grapples with the idea of a socio-cultural analysis of law by exploring the significance of 'critique' in law. Since critique (of law) is a genre or cultural practice, the consideration of its value and its limitations assumes significance. Murphy locates his notion of legal critique in the context where it played a significant role in the regeneration of the community that is represented by law. In the contemporary settings of at least Western Europe, the social resonance of law grounded in the cultural *experience* of a community stands replaced by new statistical positivities grounded in the empiricism produced by contemporary 'model'-driven social sciences. In his own words: 'what we see rather is a matter of identities and existences which are determined outside, not inside the law'. The law comes into contact with them precisely once we enter the sphere of rights talk. Inside this system of discourse, we conjoin rights with identities and existences fabricated elsewhere. Comprehending the task of critique in these complex circumstances forms the crucial analytic task that his essay outlines. This task is only further complicated when we throw in the variables of colonialism and the questions of cultural difference.

In an attempt to deal with the questions that culture and comparison raise for law, Patrick Glenn's essay contends with what he calls a hegemonic form of teaching law through the entire history of western legal education – that is, the teaching of only one law to the exclusion all others. Even though the teaching of state law replaced the teaching of the *ius commune*, from the eighteenth century, the dominant, controlling concept of western legal education has been that of the (national) legal system – a legal system which is inconsistent with the application of other law on national territory, incapable of conciliation with other laws, and inherently conflictual in terms of its relations with other laws. He notes that this form of studying law stands challenged today both internally, by the resurgence of non-state traditions, and externally, by various forms of transnational collaboration. Therefore, Glenn's essay is an attempt to respond to the challenge of plurality mounted against the study of law conceived as the study or operation of only one legal system. According to Glenn, from within a legal system the view is limited, since the system is exclusive, irreconcilable with other laws and conflictual in character. Therefore, to critique the system and make it respond to claims of alternative normativity, it is necessary to stand outside it and make it justify itself. In aid of this task, he offers the idea of legal traditions which allow one to see the national legal system as just one among many legal traditions available in a given jurisdiction.

Volkmar Gessner's essay discusses 'rule of law' debates and identifies three approaches underlying the vast literature, programmes and projects in the area. One approach, he claims, tries to show that modernization processes lead naturally to legal structures similar to what can be observed in western societies, and also that global structures will emerge on the same model. Another prominent theory, he says, often alluded to as justification for legalization, is Institutional Economics where rules and institutions are considered as mechanisms for effective avoidance of transaction costs. A third theory offered frequently as justification is Max Weber's process of legal rationalization running from traditional irrational forms to formal, bureaucratic forms of legal domination. Gessner argues that a particular kind of state-centred legalism presumed by all these approaches is not necessarily true of non-western societies, and, therefore, an understanding of legal culture against legal doctrine assumes significance. He then addresses the challenge of teaching the complexities of a legal culture in the context of a classroom of law.

Sitharamam Kakarala's essay scrutinizes the nature and evolution of human rights teaching practices, both within the stream of law and in the social sciences. Suggesting that the debates in human rights teaching are similar to that in law in general, Kakarala suggests that the essence of human rights learning, as demonstrated by the experience of various civil rights movements in India, namely 'taking suffering seriously', has rarely been translated into curricularization of human rights. By ignoring or underplaying such a crucial aspect, the higher learning institutions, he contends, tend to miss out on important opportunities which could forward their potential to evolve contextualized perspectives on rights and the trajectories through which they acquire their substantive meaning and circulate in everyday life. Unless the social movements' praxis is translated into pedagogic practice, human rights teaching, Kakarala argues, would continue to suffer from the problem of received knowledges.

Dattathreya Subbanarasimha sets himself the task of explaining how a teacher of law is to address the paradox of teaching principles of law passed on from the colonial encounter, which he knows to have been part of the colonizer's apparatus of violence. He addresses this problem by tracing the legacies of the intellectual encounter between the ideas of a 'modern' west and a 'traditional' non-west in the work of Max Weber, Émile Durkheim and Karl Marx, and the

ways in which theories of western modernity have found currency in the Indian
legal classroom. Through the specific case of Hindu Law, he demonstrates how
'modern' colonial legality absorbs what is commonly understood to be a com-
munity-generated form of social/legal regulation into the principle-bound framework of *stare decisis*. The challenge he leaves for contemporary legal academics
is to understand the impact of the distortions that modern British colonialism has
wrought on our understanding of Indian legal traditions, and how these distorted
understandings may be remedied 'by more intimate, first-hand ("local") knowledge of Indian social realities' – realities, he interestingly suggests, which are
already available to Indian law teachers.

Janaki Nair's essay, though dealing with colonialism, shifts the ground
of analysis from broad conceptual problems in the understanding of Indian law
to specific issues in Indian law. Nair historically reconstructs a legal case relating to events that transpired in a village called Isoor, in the erstwhile princely
state of Mysore. The event that she recounts took place in 1942 as part of Gandhi's
call during the Quit India movement, and resulted in sections of the village
declaring their independence from the British. An ensuing series of events led to
the killing of the local Amaldar and Sub-Inspector. As soon as this happened the
machinery of the state stepped in and the fledgling movement was quickly brought
to face colonial law through criminal proceedings, resulting in the eventual conviction of five of the numerous persons tried by the court. Nair's concern with
this case is that there seems to be no available account of the subtler cadences in
this case between the pure and simple case of criminality and that of the nationalist re-telling of the story which transforms it into one of police and state terror
unleashed on a people's struggle for independence. Caught between these narratives, the violence of the people of Isoor is persistently silenced. Disturbed by this
silence, Nair sets herself the burden of trying to recuperate the voices silenced
behind two overpowering narratives. Attempting to tease out the silenced voices
in this case, she uncovers the surrogate manner in which dominant groups in
Isoor managed their interests through subaltern groups who eventually could be
dispensed with and therefore bore a disproportionate burden for the happenings
at Isoor.

Tanika Sarkar provides another perspective to the discussion on the
making of colonial laws by taking on certain established ways of understanding
the colonial law-making process and suggesting alternative ways in which it can
be understood. Sarkar contends with the historiography of Indian personal laws
to show that important and influential studies (Chatterjee 1986, Sangari and
Vaid 1990) have not adequately reflected on the triangulated relationship between state, civil society norms and public sphere resources from which the modern arena for the creation and modification of personal laws was forged. She
elaborates on this triangulated relationship by following and reworking
postcolonial perspectives on law relating to widow immolation and widow remarriage. In her retelling of the story of legal reform, she looks at law as a
conversation among Indians themselves and with the state. Put differently, she

sees in the debates on reform of personal laws the making of the 'Indian sovereignty' that was to come, and the construction of the nineteenth-century Indian public sphere. With regard to this public sphere and public debate, the colonial state was remarkably ambivalent and often erred on the side of illiberal and conservative positions. Thus, for instance, the debate on *sati* was one that started with a mere regulation of the numerous incidents of *sati* in Bengal. It was then debated on the terms of scriptures reflecting the social conservatism of the likes of Manu. Finally, even in its proscription, it merely reflected the colonial state's belief that the ban had some form of general social acceptance. Thus, despite the conservatism of this discourse, ideas of right and equality were, according to Sarkar, a product of unintended legal excess rather than a planned trajectory towards progress and reform.

Oliver Mendelsohn's essay struggles with the contemporary sociological diversity of dispute resolution mechanisms that seem to coexist and actively vie for legitimacy with state authority. The search for a distinctly Indian character to these vibrant plural forms takes Mendelsohn into a study of Indological and colonial accounts of the distinctness of what might be an Indian notion of legality. The challenge that the Indological literature seems to pose is the divergence between what is supposedly the laws contained in the *Dharmasastras* and the customary forms by which communities actually governed their lives and their disputes. Drawing from Robert Lingat, Mendelsohn suggests that India's diverse customary legal forms, some of which he briefly describes, might be best understood by substituting a notion of legality with that of authority. Thus, it is the binding nature of authority over legality that Mendelsohn highlights which might provide answers to the diverse law-like forms obtaining in symbiotic and contesting relationships with contemporary Indian state law.

Dealing with another particular but contemporary legal issue, Flavia Agnes engages in a thick description of the campaign against a legislation banning Bar Dancing in Mumbai. Her paper presents an interesting account of the reflections of an activist group (Majlis, Mumbai) building a legal case for the rights and entitlements of the numerous Bar Dancers whose livelihood was under threat as a result of legislation that proscribed their source of livelihood. Her essay is an elaborate political economy of the Bar Dance phenomenon in Mumbai and a description of the difficulties in advocating such a case. Her paper is therefore an ethnography on a range of issues which include the manner in which various interest groups (especially poorer groups) interacted with the police, the internal divisions within NGOs fighting for the same constituency, and, most importantly, the extreme difficulty in working through issues like obscenity and morality and the challenge of fighting such notions when they overtly seem to obstruct the livelihood of marginalized groups like Bar Girls.

Ashish Rajadhyaksha's essay addresses a serious paradox about the issue of freedom of expression within the context of Indian cinema. Traditionally, the freedom of expression question has always been posed between the individual who is the source of the expression – the 'author' – and the state in determining the boundaries of proscription. The judicial scrutiny was limited to an enquiry into the validity of state action in limiting the freedom of the individual 'author', whereas the legitimate source of the state's authority in limiting individual freedom, namely the 'public', was always such as a mere recipient of the speech. Rajadhyaksha's essay takes on this third dimension, namely the 'public', as it emerged in the context of cinema, that is, the 'specator', and the new challenges it has posed to the traditional liberal–humanist jurisprudence of freedom of expression.

Taking the recent controversy surrounding the film *Fire*, Rajadhyaksha navigates through fascinating and diverse materials – ranging from prominent judicial decisions pertaining to expression within the context of cinema from 1947 till the *Fire* controversy, a number of reports of committees and commissions, and the academic scholarly literature – to emphatically suggest that the cinema context has transformed the 'public', which was seen as a mere recipient of speech, to 'spectators' who are not merely passive recipients but rights-bearing individuals and that there is sufficient judicial acknowledgement of this fact. Rajadhyaksha thus points to a potentially new area of study within contemporary Indian constitutionalism – namely the category of 'spectatorial rights' and its challenge to liberal–humanist jurisprudence of freedom of expression.

Conclusion

The collection of essays that has been put together in this volume contains a range of themes and, in a manner of speaking, it is only the *task* of outlining the many possible projects for research in law that holds it together. However, the disparate themes to which law lends itself indicates the complexity of building a legal research programme. It is a task that has no established disciplinary boundaries and is potentially vulnerable to a range of problems of a legal nature. Historically, the discipline of legal science, especially in India, has been notoriously lax in its attempts at grappling with problems outside the concerns of the practical, doctrinal or, at best, the normative. Formulating research problems, however, requires that this grip of both the doctrinal and the normative be broken in favour of the pursuit of research problems that the legal domain throws up for scrutiny. It is as an invitation to this pursuit that this collection forms a modest contribution.

Notes

[1] Sunderland (1906: 179–80).
[2] It is impossible to represent the contours and forms that this debate has taken over the years. Some of the significant debates in the early part of the century include the call by scholars like Max Weber and Roscoe Pound to understand law sociologically, and the challenge mounted by legal realism on formal approaches to law. More recently, the case for interdisciplinary studies has been made by many movements and formal academic associations – some of these include movements for law and history, law and society, law and development, and, more recently, law and literature, law and economics and so on. Of these, the law and society movement has been particularly active in fostering an interdisciplinary approach towards legal study and its

scholarship on various aspects of interdisciplinary study has been prolific. For a sense of the writing, see Friedman and Macaulay (1969); Abel (1980); Friedman (1986); Silbey and Sarat (1987); Campbell and Wiles (1976). The experience of the American Law and Society Association in particular, and the interaction of law and the social sciences, were comprehensively covered in the contribution of Garth and Sterling (1998); Stevens (2001). Also, for a detailed review of the recent debates on the growing 'disjuncture' between legal education and the legal profession in the United States, see Lilly (1995). For interdisciplinary legal scholarship in the Indian context, see Galanter (1987) and Baxi (1986).

[3] See, for instance, the work of Harrold Berman (1983) on the influence of law in the development of modern western learning.

[4] Sunderland (1906).

[5] For some illustrations of such efforts, see Leyh (1992) and Stevens (2001), especially Chapter 8, 'The Legal Culture and Legal Theory: The Social Sciences and all that'.

[6] Sunderland (1906: 180, 187–88).

[7] For an interesting assessment of the late nineteenth-century debates on formalism, especially the contribution of C.C. Langdell, Dean of Harvard Law School, 1870–1895, see Grey (1983).

[8] Ewick, Kagan and Sarat (1999: 1).

[9] Even today, interdisciplinary legal movements fashion themselves after legal realism. See, for instance, a programme of the University of Wisconsin Law School that calls itself New Legal Realism (http://www.newlegalrealism.org/) and is premised on a dialogue between law and other social sciences.

[10] The law and society movement is active both within the academia as well as in social action processes. The Law and Society Association in the United States was formed in 1964. Since then, a number of similar associations have sprung up in many other western countries such as Canada, the United Kingdom, Australia and New Zealand. A number of journals dedicated to law and society research and publication have also sprung up in many of these countries. While the law and society-related work has a long history in India and many other countries in the developing world, there appears to be no significant associational activity or systematic curricular interventions so far, save a few individual and sporadic interventions.

[11] The Critical Legal Studies Movement (CLSM) emerged as a radical left response in the background of the turbulent 1960s, which was marked by resistance and street protests across the west. It tried to popularize the slogan that 'law is politics'. Unlike the law and society movement, the CLSM began and largely remains an academic intervention that intended to bring critique to every level of legal education. However, civil rights litigation in the United States remains an important political process on the agenda of CLSM's radical political theorization of law (see, for instance, *Harvard Civil Rights–Civil Liberties Review*). Scholars associated with the CLSM include Roberto Unger and Duncan Kennedy, Austin Sarat, as well as British figures like Peter Fitzpatrick and Peter Goodrich.

[12] The intellectual work of anthropologists on law (anthropology of law) and legal scholars who adopted anthropological methods (legal anthropology) together contributed to create an impressive corpus of knowledge that deserves special mention. Legal anthropology has subjected an incredible range of subjects to scholarly scrutiny. These include the everyday perceptions of law by common people, the plurality of legal/normative systems, as well as ethnography of legal institutions and professions. Some of the important scholars who have conducted work in legal anthropology include Sally Falk Moore, Laura Nader, John Comaroff and Bernard Cohn. For an overview of the field, see Moore (2001).

[13] It is perhaps very difficult to specify a moment of origin for this school of thought as it was and is always intertwined with the concerns of feminist politics and movements. The post-Second World War histories of feminist legal theory could however be traced to the 1960s when the concerns of the women's movement were radicalized, where liberal feminist positions gave way to a more radical language of rights. Ever

since, hundreds of scholars and activists have contributed to the making of feminist legal theory. Contemporary concerns move beyond the classical concerns of 'gender' to issues of sexuality and sexual identity. Some of the prominent authors include Catharine MacKinnon, Andrea Dworkin, Martha Nussbaum, Carole Smart and Nicola Lacey. In the Indian context, the writings of Ratna Kapur, Flavia Agnes and Arvind Narrain are illustrative of the contemporary writing in this area.

[14] For a comprehensive review of the law and development movement till the late 1970s, see Snyder (1980). An interesting set of readings on the theme are compiled in Ghai, Luckham and Snyder (1988). Latin American scholarship is reflected in Karst and Rosenn (1977). The substantive contributions of this movement came from many prominent scholars in and on the developing world. Special mention must be made of Upendra Baxi, Yash Ghai, Issa Shivji, Kenneth L. Karst, Abdul Paliwala.

Recent trends and crises in law and development scholarship are captured in Adelman and Paliwala (1993); Trubek and Santos (2006); Rose (1998).

[15] Originally said to have begun at the Chicago Law School in the early 1970s, the school of thought is now a prominent and expanding branch of legal theory with a number of specialist departments/institutions emerging on the theme, both in the west and in the developing world. For an assessment of its contribution to legal theory, see Posner (1973); Oppenheimer and Mercuro (2005).

[16] Said to have originated as a part of legal realism (especially through the writings of Benjamin Cardozo), this is another branch of legal theory that has significantly grown from the early 1970s. It has contributed to the hermeneutic turn in legal theory. Many of the important contributions in this branch of legal theory could be found in Freeman and Lewis (1999).

[17] Historical approaches to law have taken place from diverse scholarly and disciplinary vantage points. In many developing countries, the interest in law and history is closely linked to studies in colonialism and nationalism. In the Indian context, there is a growing body of legal history produced by historians. An interesting example would be the legal essays of the Subaltern Studies collective.

[18] For instance, contemporary legal thought and imagination in most parts of the world are a product of the globalization of colonial law. Despite this, the colonial question has not been a major theme in interdisciplinary work. More recently, however, some third-world/southern scholarship has begun to look critically at the intellectual problems posed by colonial legal systems. Special reference should be made to the writings of Upendra Baxi, Anthony Anghie, Makau Matua and B.S. Chimni.

[19] Dhavan (1987).

[20] Cited in Law Commission Report (1958: 520).

[21] Cited in ibid.: 521.

[22] CDC Report (1989: 2–3).

[23] Law Commission Report (1958: 548–50)

[24] Markose (1973a: xxiv–xxv).

[25] Upendra Baxi draws up a list of two generations of law teachers. The first generation includes R.U. Singh, Anandjee, P.K. Tripathi, G.S. Sharma, A.T. Markose, M.P. Jain, T.S. Rama Rao, V.N. Shukla, S.S. Nigam, Lotika Sarkar, S.K. Agrawal, I.C. Saxena, Paras Diwan, T.K. Tope, Ajjappa, Shiv Dayal. The second generation includes S.P. Sathe, R.K. Mishra, R.V. Kelkar, S.N. Jain, Alice Jacob, G.S. Raghavan, V.S. Rekhi, P. Koteshwar Rao, R.P. Anand, Raj Kumari Agrawal, Rahmatullah Khan, B. Sivaramayya, K. Ponnuswami, M.C. Jain Kagzi and such others. See Baxi (1996: 35–39)

A third generation of law teachers could be added to this list, to include Upendra Baxi himself along with others such as Madhava Menon, Rajeev Dhavan, N.L. Mitra, B.B. Pandey, M.P. Singh, B.S. Chimni.

[26] Baxi (1996: 35–39).

[27] Report of the Committee on the Reorganization of Legal Education in the University of Delhi (1964: 34).

[28] Ibid.: 4–5.

[29] Von Mehren (1965: 1183).
[30] Report of the Committee on the Reorganization of Legal Education in the University of Delhi (1964: 8–9).
[31] Ibid.: 13.
[32] Thiruvengadam (2001: 32).
[33] Report of the Committee on Reforms in Legal Education in the 1980s (1979: 5).
[34] Ibid.: 9.
[35] Thiruvengadam (2001: 21).
[36] Report of the Bombay Legal Education Committee (1949: 5), cited in Thiruvengadam (2001: 9).
[37] Section 4(1) of the National Law School of India University Act, 1986 (Act 22 of Karnataka).
[38] Baxi (1986).
[39] Ibid.: 2.
[40] He resolved the sociology of law into eight themes, which include: 1. Studies on Classical Hindu Law; 2. Law and Social Change: The Colonial Experience; 3. Law and Social Change: Some Aspects of Contemporary Experience; 4. People's Law or Non-State Legal Systems; 5. Tribal Law and Justice; 6. Nyaya Panchayats; 7. Law and Social Control; 8. Adjudication under State Legal Systems. Baxi (1986: 3–4).
[41] Baxi (1996: 41–43).
[42] Wallerstein et al. (1996).

References

Abel, Richard L. (1980), 'Redirecting Social Studies of Law', *Law and Society Review,* 14 (3).
Adelman, Sammy and Abdul Paliwala (1993), 'Law and Development in Crisis', in Sammy Adelman and Abdul Paliwala, eds, *Law and Crisis in the Third World* (London: Hans Zell Publishers).
Anandjee (1973), 'Objectives of Legal Education', in S.K. Agarwala, ed., *Legal Education in India: Problems and Perspectives* (Bombay: N.M. Tripathi).
Baxi, Upendra (1979), 'Notes towards a socially relevant legal education: A working paper for the UGC regional workshop in law, 1975–77', in *Towards a Socially Relevant Legal Education* (New Delhi: University Grants Commission).
———(1986), *Towards a Sociology of Indian Law* (New Delhi: Satavahana Publications).
———(1996), 'On Judicial Activism, Legal Education and Research in a Globalizing India', Annual Capital Foundation Lecture (New Delhi: Capital Foundation Society).
Berman, Harrold (1983), *Law and Revolution: The Formation of the Western Legal Tradition* (Cambridge, MA: Harvard University Press).
Campbell, C.M. and Paul Wiles (1976), 'The Study of Law in Society in Britain', *Law and Society Review*, 10 (4).
CDC Report, *Report of the Committee on Reforms in Legal Education in the 1980s* (1979) (New Delhi: All India Law Teachers Assn Sectt).
Chatterjee, Partha (1986), *Nationalist Thought and the Colonial World: A Derivative Discourse* (London: Zed Books).
Dhavan, Rajeev (1987), 'Means, Motives and Opportunities: Reflecting on Legal Research in India', *Mod. L. Rev.*, 50: 725–49.
Ewick, Patricia, Robert Kagan and Austin Sarat (1999), 'Legacies of Legal Realism: Social Science, Social Policy and the Law', in Patricia Ewick *et al.*, eds, *Social Science, Social Policy and the Law* (New York: Russell Sage Foundation).
Falk, Sally (2001), 'Certainties Undone: Fifty Turbulent Years of Legal Anthropology, 1949–1999', *Journal of Royal Anthropological Institute*, Vol. 7.
Freeman, Michael and Andrew Lewis, eds (1999), *Law and Literature* (Oxford: Oxford University Press).
Friedman, Lawrence M. (1986), 'The Law and Society Movement', *Stanford Law Review*, 38 (3).
Friedman, Lawrence M. and Stewart Macaulay, eds (1969), *Law and Behavioral Sciences* (Indianapolis: Bobbs–Merrill).

Galanter, Marc (1987), *Law and Society in Modern India* (Delhi: Oxford University Press).

Garth, Bryant and Joyce Sterling (1998), 'From Legal Realism to Law and Society', *Law and Society Review*, 32 (2).

Ghai, Yash, Robin Luckham and Francis Snyder, eds (1988), *The Political Economy of Law: A Third World Reader* (New York: Oxford University Press).

Grey, Thomas (1983), 'Langdell's Orthodoxy', *University of Pittsburgh Law Review*, Vol. 45.

Jain, M.P. (1997), *Outlines of Indian Legal History*, fifth edition (Nagpur: Wadhwa and Co.).

Karst, Kenneth L. and Keith S. Rosenn, eds (1977), *Law and Development in Latin America: A Case Book* (Berkley and Los Angeles: University of California Press).

Khan, Rahmutallah (1973), 'The National Law School – A Proposal', in S.K. Agarwala, ed., *Legal Education in India: Problems and Perspectives* (Bombay: N.M. Tripathi).

Law Commission Report (1958), *14th Law Commission Report*, Vol. 1, (New Delhi: Government of India).

Leyh, Gregory (1992), 'Legal Education and Public Life', in Gregory Leyh, ed., *Legal Hermeneutics: History, Theory, and Practice* (Berkeley: University of California Press).

Lilly, Graham C. (1995), 'Law Schools without Lawyers? Winds of Change in Legal Education', *Virginia Law Review*, 81 (5).

Markose, A.T. (1973a), 'Key-note Address on the Seminar', in S.K. Agarwala, ed., *Legal Education in India: Problems and Perspectives* (Bombay: N.M. Tripathi).

—— (1973b), 'The Function of Post-Graduate Education in Law', in S.K. Agarwala, ed., *Legal Education in India: Problems and Perspectives* (Bombay: N.M. Tripathi).

—— (1973c), 'The Object of Legal Education', in S.K. Agarwala, ed., *Legal Education in India: Problems and Perspectives* (Bombay: N.M. Tripathi).

Menon, N.R. Madhava (1979a), 'Changes in the Law Curriculum – A Proposal', annexed to *Report of the Committee on Reforms in Legal Education in the 1980s* (New Delhi: All India Law Teachers Assn Sectt).

—— (1979b), 'Reforming Legal Education: Issues, Priorities and Proposals', annexed to *Report of the Committee on Reforms in Legal Education in the 1980s* (New Delhi: All India Law Teachers Assn Sectt).

Oppenheimer, Margaret and Nicholas Mercuro, eds (2005), *Law and Economics: Alternative Economic Approaches to Legal and Regulator Issues* (New York: M.E. Sharp).

Posner, Richard (1973), *Economic Analysis of Law* (Boston: Little Brown).

Report of the Committee on the Reorganization of Legal Education in the University of Delhi (1964) (Delhi: University of Delhi).

Report of the Curriculum Development Centre in Law (1989), Vols 1 and 2 (New Delhi: University Grants Commission).

Report of the Expert Panel on NLSIU (1996) (Bangalore).

Rose, Carol V. (1998), 'The "New" Law and Development Movement in the Post-Cold War Era: A Vietnam Case Study', *Law and Society Review*, Vol. 32.

Sangari, Kumkum and Sudesh Vaid, eds (1990), *Recasting Women: Essays in Indian Colonial History* (New Jersey: Rutgers University Press).

Sathe, S.P. (1989), 'Access to Legal Education and the Legal Profession in India', in R. Dhavan, N. Kibble and W. Twining, eds, *Access to Legal Education and the Legal Profession* (London: Butterworths).

Silbey, Susan S. and Austin Sarat (1987), 'Critical Traditions in Law and Society', *Law and Society Review*, 21 (1).

Snyder, Francis G. (1980), 'Law and Development in the Light of Dependency Theory', *Law and Society Review*, 14 (3).

Stevens, Robert B. (2001), *Law School: Legal Education in America from 1850s to 1980s* (New Jersey: Law Books Exchange Ltd.).

Sunderland, Edson R. (1906), 'Law as a Culture Study', *Michigan Law Review* 4 (3).

Thiruvengadam, Arun (2001), 'The Waning of a Magnificent Obsession: An Abridged Story of the History of Legal Education Reform in India' (unpublished manuscript on file with the authors).

Towards a Socially Relevant Legal Education (1979) (New Delhi: University Grants Commission).

Trubek, David M. and Alvaro Santos, eds (2006), *The New Law and Economic Development: A Critical Appraisal* (New York: Cambridge University Press).

Von Mehren, Arthur (1963), 'Some Observations on the Role of Law in Indian Society and on Indian Legal Education', *Jaipur Law Journal,* 13 (3).

——— (1965), 'Law and Legal Education in India: Some Observations', *Harvard Law Review,* Vol. 78: 1180–89.

Wallerstein, Immanuel *et al.,* eds, (1996), *Open the Social Sciences: Report of the Gulbenkian Commission on the Restructuring of the Social Sciences* (Delhi: Vistar Publications).

Contributors

FLAVIA AGNES is a practising advocate based in Mumbai, and is also with Majlis, A Centre for Alternative Culture and Right Discourse, Mumbai, India.

UPENDRA BAXI is Professor of Law at the University of Warwick at Coventry, UK.

ROGER COTTERRELL is Anniversary Professor of Legal Theory at the Department of Law, Queen Mary and Westfield College, University of London, UK.

VOLKMAR GESSNER is Professor of Law and Sociology of Law at the Law Faculty, University of Bremen, Germany.

H. PATRICK GLENN is Professor of Law at McGill University, Montreal, Canada.

MATHEW JOHN is currently a Doctoral candidate at the London School of Economics and Political Science, London, UK.

SITHARAMAM KAKARALA is the Director of the Centre for the Study of Culture and Society, Bangalore, India.

OLIVER MENDELSOHN is Associate Professor at the School of Law, La Trobe University, Victoria, Australia.

W.T. MURPHY is Professor of Law at the London School of Economics and Political Science, London, UK.

JANAKI NAIR is Professor of History at the Centre for Studies in Social Sciences, Kolkata, India.

ASHISH RAJADHYAKSHA is Senior Fellow at the Centre for the Study of Culture and Society, Bangalore, India.

TANIKA SARKAR is Professor of History at the Centre for Historical Studies, School of Social Sciences, Jawaharlal Nehru University, New Delhi, India.

DATTATHREYA SUBBANARASIMHA is Lecturer of Law at Christ College of Law, Bangalore, India.

The Pedagogy of Law

Enculturing Law?

Some Unphilosophic Remarks

Upendra Baxi

The Provocation

More than fifty years of postcolonial Indian legal education (at least in the chronological sense as something that occurs after decolonization) have merely 'modestly developed traditions of legal scholarship'. This is so because law teachers of yesteryear and also 'specialist' colleagues in other allied social science and humanities disciplines have 'by and large failed in building a research project in law with distinctly Indian problems and possibilities'. And the 'vice-like grip of doctrinal legal analysis' has rendered 'teaching and learning law' a 'self-referential enterprize in the interpretation of rules'; Indian legal scholarship, on this view of the matter, remains overwhelmingly exegetic and dismally doctrinal, content with 'commentaries' which merely 'chart the movement of doctrinal legal trends across various fields'. As a result, legal education in India has not been successful in going beyond meeting the minimal requirement of producing 'legal technicians' for a range of legal markets. Overall, 'legal education in India' has been unable 'to respond holistically and meaningfully to contemporary challenges'. It is with this provocation that the Law and Culture programme at the Centre for the Study of Culture and Society, Bangalore, convened the conference on 'Enculturing Law: New Agendas for Legal Pedagogy' from 11 to 13 August 2005.

The provocation is grave and sustained. It is grave because of the key assumptions it makes; it is sudden in its summons for 'building a research project in law with distinctly Indian problems and possibilities'. It is sustained because it (a) blights both Indian legal education and research without even suggestively exploring the historic patterns of research and writing, and (b) urges us to relate the specific vicissitudes of Indian legal education and research on the 'Global South' guided by an aspiration to create new patterns of critical solidarity through the specific practices of 'enculturing law'.[1]

In what follows, I explore some dialogue-friendly approaches to understand the provocation and to decipher the stated promise of the oncoming futures of Indian legal eduction. In the process, I offer some unphilosophic remarks on understanding the cultures *of* law.

Analytical Silences

What sense may we make of the perennial dichotomy between the 'doctrinal' and 'non-doctrinal?' Is 'doctrinal' ever devoid of 'non-doctrinal' and vice versa?[2] How may we essay an understanding of the relation between the two realms? Is the doctrinal an *asocial* consociation of juridical thought and judicial practice,[3] unresponsive to historical transformations? Is the non-doctrinal mode – here the empirical, contextual – always inherently redeeming? Are all legal doctrines necessarily dogmatic? To what extent (to recall Roscoe Pound's diction) does the 'technical' element in law remain at odds with its 'ideal' element? Is the 'ideal' less mystifying than the 'technical' element in law?[4] Is a critique of the 'doctrinal' directed only at the state law form or people's law formations as well? Or are we to read mélanges of legal pluralism as merely suggesting that the signature of the customary or community law formation is constituted by a lack of the doctrinal?

In any event, even within the state-centric conception of law, how may we understand the emergence of 'progressive' doctrines? This, in part, is a historical enquiry, but I raise the issue here in terms of the tasks of an analytic understanding of the condemnation of the 'technical'. To concretize, how may one consider salient legal doctrines: the doctrine of basic structure and essential features of the Indian Constitution, the Bhopal Case enunciation of the doctrine of absolute multinational enterprize liability, the varieties of estoppel doctrines (including promissory estoppel, legitimate expectations, and constructive *res judicata*), the doctrine of 'fair use' in copyright (or even copyleft), the doctrine of community property, the doctrine of 'creamy layers' invigilating the programmes and measures of affirmative action, the doctrine of standing that social action litigation in India transforms into cascading forms of participatory access in the domains of governance, rights, and justice?

Second, when may doctrinal analyses or textual exegeses become 'vice-like' in their 'grip?' There is simply no way to answer this question in any value-neutral way.[5] But for any critique of the doctrinal, it remains important to state what values may after all be at stake and this is a far more demanding enterprize than any stark contrasts may suggest. Value judgements, as we know, differ according to ideologically favoured/ingrained dispositions. Thus the neocon and neoliberal approaches celebrate in the contemporary global moment the sacrosanct nature of the doctrine of the 'free' market via a revival of near-absolute classical legal doctrines giving salience to rights to private property over the means of globalized relations of production, consumption, exchange and distribution. Critics celebrate as progressive legal doctrine formations that challenge and confront this new *doxa*. There is no doubt whatever that both camps agree in characterizing as regressive and violent, by way of retrospective judgement, and perhaps by the same token also somewhat ahistorically, some notable examples of the violence of legal doctrine.[6] There have existed (and even continue to exist) doctrinal approaches or traditions that justified and promoted slavery, colonization, genocide, apartheid, crimes against humanity, sex-based violence, state and non-state terrorisms.[7] Thus, some doctrinaire approaches to law may be said to be pernicious when they enforce a distinctive closure of legal thought and sensibility in ways that disable any imagination that enhances states of human well-being and of human freedoms. The 'vice-like' grip imagery suggests scope for its other, the 'virtuous' doctrinal reading of the law, its processes and purposes, unless, of course, all that is 'doctrinal' must always remain ethically irredeemable. But were we to regard the closure as necessarily dialectical, as do historians of social evil and legal wrong, closure does indeed occur but never in ways that altogether forbid acts of interpretive insurgency. Repressive legal doctrines invite impertinent gestures of interpretive infidelity. One may even go as far as to suggest that the stronger the 'vice-like grip', the greater remains the incipient tendency toward social struggles against the injustice and violence of the law. We may not ever fully understand the 'grip' from outside struggles to loosen its shackles.

I make here no defence of repressive legal doctrines but only wish to suggest that any serious concern with legal education and research becomes insensible, even quixotic, when the 'doctrinal' stands thus altogether derided and denied. The practices of subaltern resistance and critique of the doctrinal law (outside the realms of fully-fledged practices of philosophical anarchism or legal nihilism) favour at the end of the day different doctrinal regimes in diverse genres such as provided by human rights, capabilities, well-being and flourishing, and people-oriented reworking of governance-imbued notions about 'the rule of law'.

However, because even the virtuous legal doctrinal regime must sustain the force-monopoly of state law, we stand presented with the need to distinguish (to invoke Robert Cover's germinal distinction) between jurispathic and jurisgenerative forms of violence,[8] or the 'foundational' and 'reiterative' violence of the law (as Derrida names this).[9] On this perspective of the ontological and epistemological violence of the law itself, the 'vice-like grip' necessarily infects all forms of law, whether pre or postmodern.

Third, are teaching and learning law 'self-referential' enterprizes in the interpretation of rules'? This raises a basic epistemological, and not merely jurisprudential, problem. We learn when 'teaching' John Austin, Hans Kelsen, H.L.A. Hart, Ronald Dworkin, among others, that this entire talk about the authority of the law as an ongoing enterprize necessarily remains self-referential. Hans Kelsen demonstrated a long time ago that the juristic performance of the acceptance/ presupposition of the *grundnorm* as being 'by and large' efficacious is a necessary condition for all legal thought or theory; otherwise, we invite an infinite logical regress of any posited ground of the obligation to obey not just the law but indeed any rule formation. Gunther Teubner, in our own time, has reiterated the paradox of self-referentiality as an inevitable grounding for the authority/ authorization, or self-founding of 'modern law.'[10] He insists that 'the paradoxes arising from self-reference are not an end-point, but the starting-point for further evolution'.[11] No Indian law teacher pursuing the enigma of the Basic Structure doctrine so happily unleashed by the Indian Supreme Court in *Kesavananda Bharathi*, would here disagree.

Fourth, the indictment suggested by the rolled-up images of 'contemporary challenges' to which the past formations of India legal education/research have been unable to respond 'holistically and meaningfully' raises a crowd of definitional questions: What are, or how may we proceed to construct, these 'challenges' and from *whose* and *what* perspectives? What does it mean to say 'holistically and meaningfully'? This raises also a larger question: which other form of education may have done so?

Fifth, there is the issue of these 'challenges' formed in terms of 'legal markets' whose needs for technical services are met by doctrinal legal education. Is the issue here one of market regulation or reform, inviting then a re-examination of the assumptions concerning the relationship of legal education and research to the practice of law or one pertaining to the creation of radically different markets for legal services? How may we understand the emergence of the new markets in relation to national and cross-national 'Old' and 'New' social movements? Or, as some of us in the unlovely past of Indian legal education and research sought to achieve, does this name the problem of creating services for social justice markets both within and outside legal education and the profession?[12] And how might transformative pedagogies distance themselves from some fake pluralisms now relentlessly pursued by global hegemons in terms of 'good governance' and 'alternate dispute resolution'?

The Problematic Sphere of Doing 'History'

There are many histories of Indian legal education and we lack adequate narratives of them. Serious pursuit of these histories of legal learning is one important programmatic contribution that our dialogue may make. This is a task fraught with many imponderables. In this section, I look at some difficulties in developing general histories of legal education. I use the notion of general history as signifying patterns of institutional development of the certificatory/credential and other related regimes of legal education. If by 'history' we signify, with William Twining, 'an exercise of construction and imagination commensurate with the complexity of human experience',[13] this names the beginnings of the task, not its endings. At issue is the relative autonomy of the calling and craft of the historian of legal education. How far can we capture the distinctively 'legal' in human 'experience'? We all too readily flounder on the Scylla of 'experience' and the Charybdis of the distinctively 'legal.' 'Experience', as a category of understanding, remains problematic as we know from the travails of the inaugural contrast that Oliver Wendell Holmes sought to install between the roles of 'logic' and 'experience' in the life of law.[14]

But the complexity of legal and ethical experience (to borrow the title of the felicitous work by F.S.C. Northrop) forbids the reduction of the distinctively 'legal' entirely to the domain of the politics of desire produced by state law and its province and function. Put another way, the gifts of understanding brought to us by many traditions of pursuing legal pluralism may no longer be forfeited in the grasp of the distinctively 'legal'.[15] The institutional histories of law, understood both as state and people's law formations[16] and their propensities for violent domination, as well as forms of coequally violent and passive resistance to this, ought at least to guide conceptions of specific histories of legal education in terms of 'effective histories' (to steal a phrase from Foucault) of the law's 'effects – of its violence as well as knowledge – upon those who come up before it or are otherwise affected by it'.[17] This means at least that general histories of legal education may not be kept apart from the social histories of the law itself and as furnishing ensembles of means and techniques for social control.

Almost everywhere, not just in India, entrenched conceptions of teaching law celebrate the visions of the law's autonomy and integrity and the 'law' necessarily conceived as a state law formation. The resilience of these conceptions has troubled innovators of legal education everywhere. How may we best proceed to understand the contribution of pluralist perspectives to the histories of learning law? Indeed, how may we essay a historical understanding of the many-sided pluralisms of the state's law formation, on full view, for example, in the 'colonial' and 'postcolonial' articulation of state differentiation, especially the inherent tendency towards the autonomization of judicial power? State law speaks to us with a forked tongue. A reductionist view of state law poses some threshold difficulties even for a state-centric understanding of the institutional development of legal education and its varied, and often incommensurate, social impacts.

The struggle to preserve a non-reductive understanding of state law stands more or less fully archived in the positivist and naturalist, as well as sociological and semiotic contributions to legal theory or jurisprudence. Taking this understanding as a historic 'given', there is still some merit in recalling the early Roberto M. Unger's valiant endeavour at the construction of a post-Weberian understanding of four dimensions of the autonomy of law: the institutional, the methodological, the professional and the troublesome 'substantive' autonomy.[18] And in the narratives of the Law's Empire, Ronald Dworkin posed the issue of autonomy as one of law's integrity in a constant struggle to distinguish between 'legislation' and 'adjudication'.[19] In contrast, Stanley Fish derides almost fully the claims of law's desire for autonomy.[20] I desist foregrounding here the similar torment that haunted US and Scandinavian Realists, though not without lamenting the fact that the contributions of the latter have as yet to be fully revisited, in particular the corpus of Carl Olivecrona, A. Hagerstrom and Alf Ross, that in various ways depicted the magical realism of state law. I mention all this, necessarily in passing, to suggest the modes in which even modest claims of law's autonomy stand contested from within entrenched curricular and pedagogic conceptions. I suspect further that all this also guides us to an understanding of the inherent and conflicted pluralisms of state law formations. May we then not ask how we retrieve specific Indian and Global South understandings of law in their everyday teaching and patterns of writing? What processes of creative mimesis have addressed these tense pluralisms of state law formations?

Further, if one was to understand pluralism not as a substantive domain of multiplicity of laws but as 'castes of mind', or as histories of mentalities, how may we imagine the tasks of doing general histories of legal education? At one level, such histories surely ought to explore the interaction between the 'state' and 'people's law' formations; in this respect, 'enculturing law' means learning and studying law as a composite 'couture of many cultures' always entailing the traffic of ideas, sensibilities, beliefs and values between the state and people's law (the latter no longer to be regarded as that curious epistemic bag lumping together the diverse 'customary,' 'communitarian', 'personal' and other 'non-state' social beliefs, behaviours, and conducts). How may legal education histories tell stories concerning the relations of support and antagonism between state law and people's law cultures in distinctive patterns of violent social exclusion as well as some of benign inclusion? In what senses have patterns of legal education articulated markers of both continuity and discontinuity in the relations of struggle for hegemony and social facts of symbiotic existence among the differing realms of law? How may we tell stories about imparting law within the curricular and pedagogic 'mix' of the state and *faute de mieux* the 'non-state?'

Even more is involved in terms of the histories of received and imposed as well as rebellious pedagogies. What constituted the origins and resilience of the received pedagogies? How may we understand and archive at least two kinds of reception: of the taught traditions of the common law and the modernizing tradition derived from US acculturation?[21] How indeed may we trace the histories of epistemic rivalries thus entailed, both in terms of their neo-colonial grasp over the future of Indian legal education and research and of a wider location presented by the histories of the 'making of South Asian studies'?[22] What presence or voice may we concede to the formative role of the civil law tradition?[23]

A more fundamental issue, then, stands posed in terms of unravelling biographical and institutional histories of the 'givers' and 'takers' of the received pedagogies and how the reception managed to inhibit the flow of the dissenting voices within the Anglo–American taught traditions. As far as I know, the 'givers' constituted a white male elite of prestigious Anglo–American law schools; neither the learning arising from the then nascent critical legal studies traditions nor from feminist critique of the law nor from critical race theory ever reached Indian shores. What has reached are the contrasting models of common law and case method-based approaches to legal learning that transferred forms of law teaching into a form of 'madness', fetishizing understandings of the law.

Any genuine comparative excursus will also cure Indian legal scholarship of the excessively court-centric understanding of state law forms, which came to India via the dynamism of the Ford Foundation modernizers' penchant for 'case method' legal learning. This no doubt made an important contribution in weaning studies of law from a treatise-based, doctrinal understanding of law. But it also, in part at least, induced what has been termed as the scholarly 'love' of common law tradition, law reports constituting 'case madness' which translates in a 'mad lawyers' discourse'. This 'softening of the brain' constitutes, in the wounding words of Peter Goodrich, a form of 'biblio-spongiform encaphalopopathy'.[24] The histories of metropolitan Indian legal education (if only because the 'reforms' never wholly percolated to the *mofussil*) as forms of enduring psychiatric illness, or the crises of downright 'lunacy' and institutionalized trauma, have yet to be archived. On this register, we no longer pursue the programmes of clinical legal education but rather regard some forms of legal education as themselves clinically iatrogenic.

It is just as well that 'rebellious' pedagogic practices remained almost wholly indigenous. Nowhere, in the histories of the 'givers', exist any precedents for the type of feminist critique of the law launched by the Open Letter to the Chief Justice of India authored by four law teachers in regard to the Supreme Court of India's misogynist performance in the Mathura rape case[25] that in fact generated a sustained, many-sided movement against the patriarchal violence of Indian law. No precedents exist in that world for the inaugural contribution made by legal academics in democratizing access to justice via the radical transformation of constitutional standing for activists that sought to initiate judicial protection of the rightless peoples of India.[26]

However, it also needs saying that these do not by any means exhaust the impact of related courageous praxes originating outside the law schools. For example, it is simply unconceivable that the Total Revolution Movement launched by Jayaprakash Narain in the 1970s has left no trace on teaching, learning and writing about the 'law'. Much the same may be said concerning narratives of similar 'exogenous'-looking Indian Green, feminist, animal rights, identity, and the distinctively Indian human rights and anti-corporate, anti-globalization movements. The sad fact is that we have failed to construct an archive both of the narrative histories of linkages and a reflexive history of law-teaching practices.

The historic identity of Indian law teachers as communities of organic knowledge producers lies submerged within some lifeless narratives of the encounters between the 'receivers' and the 'givers'. In sum, we have failed to theorize, even as we acted against miserable productions of subjectivities constituted by contemporary Indian law and jurisprudence, the production of Otherness. I salute in this context the Alternate Law Forum, and especially Arvind Narrain and his colleagues in the movement for bringing back to our attention the Indian law's shaping of 'despised sexualities' (to evoke a phrase from Nancy Fraser). Surely, any 'rebellious' legal pedagogy needs to address the complex and contradictory practices of subjection through the governance of sexuality, made now more insistent by the varied and tormenting histories of the National Population Policy.[27] Likewise, we surely need recourse to adaptive histories of messages from critical race theory, unfortunately submerged by the constitutionally mandated waffle concerning the curious constructions of the 'Scheduled Tribes' ascribed in dominant caste metaphors as *adivasis* (aboriginal peoples) or *girijans* (the forest peoples.)

Bringing Back the Learners?

The reductive lumping of 'law students' or legal learners mystifies. These are human beings with infinitely varied social, educational, economic and 'ethnic' backgrounds, including the millennially deprived learners of the law, peoples living with disabilities,[28] the sexually constituted subjects of the law, and the constitutionally colonized rightless masses of impoverished rural and urban Indians. Elite theories (especially of the now fully entrenched National Law School prototypes) homogenize, in several modes, the actually existing learning communities, their needs, and aspirations. Regardless, the question remains: how may historical narratives bring the learners back in?

The cherished aspirations of 'enculturing law' stand impoverished when we speak only, or overwhelmingly, in the barbaric idiom of globalization of all law teachers as semi-autonomous service providers and students as collective customers of pedagogic and curricular histories. These one-dimensional modes block *in limine* any creative understanding of the different gender, race and class subject positions of 'teachers' and 'learners' alike. How may we take account of the different histories of the recipients of legal learning? Put crudely, what imageries of these recipients may have evolved over time in legal education? A while ago, I sought to popularize Paulo Friere's notions concerning' the 'banking conception' of law teaching in India where the teacher becomes a 'depositor' and the students emerge as 'depositaries';[29] yet monolithic narrative modes remain the sovereign violent norm in attempts to understand Indian legal education and research, *as if* there existed *no* diversity, or histories of Otherness, in teaching, learning, researching and writing the 'law.'

Let alone legal education, even general histories of education in India have yet to produce historic narratives that at the very least distinguish between the 'old' and 'new' 'professionalisms'.[30] Likewise, these remain almost a million miles from any understanding of the patterns of violence of legal and other forms of education to which Celia Haig-Brown brought to our attention in her classic work.[31]

I have in view here not just histories of law teaching but also those of legal learning by generations of our students. If the switch-over from 'teaching' to 'learning' 'the law' is ever to occur, we need at least to share the concrete interactional ways in which some Indian law students have actually challenged the *doxa*. Any attempt at developing critical South solidarities must at least remain conversant, or if inconversant, complicit, with the diverse ways of constructing the Law's Empire.

Yet histories of learning the law direct attention towards an understanding of the ways in which the 'learners' may have shaped 'teaching'. Whatever may be our evaluative stances concerning postcolonial legal education, constructed by the orders of both inclusion and exclusion, it is a global social fact, even truth, that the ideologically conflicted, politically messy and perhaps historically inefficacious programmes and measures of affirmative action for the Scheduled Castes and Tribes have brought millennially denied peoples to the roles of both professional learners and teachers.[32] I know from my own experience as a law teacher in India (and many Indian colleagues I hope will testify to this) how startlingly this infusion has challenged even our self-styled, reflexive pedagogies.

I was born anew as a law teacher several times over in one lifetime when some students (at the Delhi and Jawaharlal Nehru Universities) whom I urged to read Nehru's famous tract *Discovery of India* returned to me with the question: 'What, and whose, India did Nehru thus after all discover, even invent?'

Other Sites of Legal Learning

We surely need to grasp the complicated relation between state formation practices and patterns of legal education. Legal education under the university system auspices occurs as an aspect of (what Michel Foucault termed as) the exercise of constituting 'certificatory sovereignty' contrasted with production, circulation, and consumption of non-certificatory/non-credential forms of institutionalized knowledges about the law. These include a range of university-based educational initiatives not directed at providing credentials for entry into legal practice. These non-certificatory programmes of learning the law occur at various sites celebrating the role and function of liberal legal education in the university such as:

- Humanities and social science learning
- Various programmes of the Open Universities and, within the 'closed' ones, the distance, adult and continuing legal education programmes which seek to promote some aspects of learning the law
- Legal learning promoted in management and technology institutions, exemplified in India by the Indian Institutes of Management and Indian Institutes of Technology
- Post-certificatory legal education programmes and off-campus based learning systems, in many regions in terms of continuing education of legal professionals and the judiciary.

But such programmes may prove to be too constricting a range of non-certificatory legal learning modes. I have in view here four such ventures: first, the ILO-inspired worker education programmes; second, the often antagonistic state and civil society programmes directed at the promotion of legal literacy; third, the grassroots people's education programmes that provide quotients of critical legal learning in strategic, even opportunistic, uses of legal knowledges enabling the 'wretched of the earth' to move centimetre-by-centimetre towards amelioration of their states of human rightlessness; and fourth, the various *programschriften* pursued by militant movements for the destruction of extant regimes of lawful illegalities, in turn fostering new legal utopias or hypertopias.

May I suggest that we endeavour to understand somehow the extraordinary complexity of relation/non-relation between and across these diverse sites of certificatory and non-certificatory programmes of legal learning or indoctrination? Should not our quest for new, even radically different, critical legal pedagogies lead us to enlarge our understanding of the 'histories' of legal education to the relations between credentialist and beyond-the-certificatory realms of reason and passion for legal education in India as elsewhere? In essence, we need to reconfigure Professor William Twining's illuminating contrast between the figurations of Pericles and the plumber.[33] In doing histories of legal education in India, we may well extend this metaphor in an age of globalization of law which invites the servants and savants of Indian legal education to now merely become Macaulay-type educationist servitors of corporate globalization.

Politics and Legal Education

The relationship between college and university education and power politics has been a subject of constant concern for students of education in India.[34] Party affiliations and political patronage often outlive any serious commitment to ideological politics which demonstrably affect the everyday life of teaching and learning in Indian universities. The issue of the medium of instruction has fanned many a violent upstaging of political career, both inside and outside Indian campuses. Long dormant conceptions of 'value education' (from the 1948 Radhakrishnan Report to the 1999 S.B. Chavan Committee Report) have been frequently exploited to promote specific regime aims and styles. Political perceptions concerning the role of education in 'nation building' have generated cycles of often noxious party and cadre-based interventions in educational processes and university leadership. Regime styles that actively install and promote factional politics within university education also thrive from languages of accountability in institutions of 'higher education'. Even the entirely constitutionally justified and valid promotion of policies of educational reservation for the millennially deprived classes has been pursued in some explosively traumatic modes by political leaders, whose faith in affirmative action and loyalty to equity in access to education remains, to say the very least, rather opaque. State funding has been used to discipline and punish Vice Chancellors who dare to assert conceptions of university autonomy. Various national governmental regimes have developed onerous procedures limiting the potential of scholarly mobility for cross-national dialogical enterprizes, and research concerning so-called 'sensitive' issues defined at will by a reigning minister or bureaucrat. Considerations inimical to the functional autonomy of universities and visions of academic excellence have often presided over the making of university educational regimes.[35] College and university managements thus, overall, favour and foster the plenitude of Gresham's Law. Even the otherwise enchanted realms of management and technological institutions of learning have not escaped capricious governance styles. Campus violence, in the main fostered by militant student union outfits of political parties, is often regime-sanctioned. This unfortunately includes staff and student politics concerning even issues such as sex-based campus harassment.

In this overall frame, it is remarkable that the life of the mind has still managed to survive the fallouts of everyday campus politicking, fomented by political regimes; this, as it were, constitutes a modern miracle. All this testifies, though in a different context, to Foucault's motions concerning the dialectic of the politics of certificatory sovereignty. This fragmentary narrative is in part intended to achieve some understanding of the travails of education in the Global South and to provoke some radical disagreement concerning the ways that fashion more benign narratives of the relationship between state power and university education in India.

The question, for the present purposes, concerns the ways in which party politics may be said to have affected the itineraries of legal education. This is a vast theme and I can offer here only a few random remarks.

To start with, despite high-minded periodic concern voiced since the 14th Report of the Indian Law Commission in the 1960s, and the subsequent takeover by the Bar Council of India of the power to recognize law degrees for purposes of legal practice, undergraduate legal education has remained an ethical orphan, neither fully owned or adopted by the state executive power within the federal system nor by the University Grants Commission of India.[36] The various state governments, aside from some flagship institutions often known as government law colleges, and indifferent support to postgraduate departments in law, have disowned any financial responsibility for undergraduate legal education.

Even before the advent of neoliberal policy regimes in India, legal education was owned by and practiced in law colleges run by charitable trusts and societies managed mostly by industrialists. State governments funded commerce and arts colleges, but not law colleges. I accidentally reached an understanding of the political animus behind this invidious treatment in a running argument with the government of Gujarat during my term as the Vice Chancellor of South Gujarat University (1982–1985); the then Chief Minister (who himself, like most leading Indian politicians, had a law degree) was brutally frank in his assertion that the government serves the public interest in the best manner by not being implicated in the production of legal competencies that challenge and disrupt state/regime/governmental performance. Behind the façade of the argument suggesting the lack of adequate state resources, the reality of state abstention articulated a libidinal anxiety, even fear, of state managers and political classes. I am unable to say, without further research, how widespread this symptom is across the Indian states. But I believe that a close study of the arguments advanced by many states in a social action petition by Professor S.P. Sathe that finally prompted the Supreme Court of India to end this discriminatory regime may well sustain an across-the-board generalization.[37]

I may only suggestively invite here some attention to the rather tantalizing differential between the colonial and postcolonial governance of Indian legal
education. The colonial 'rulers' viewed the production of legal competencies and
knowledges as an aspect of the repertoire of skills and competences needed for colonial 'governance'. In contrast, at least some postcolonial 'rulers' curiously regarded such production as fostering anti-governance cultures! How may we understand and narrate all this, especially given the statutory role and functions
assigned to the Bar Council of India to invigilate standards of legal education, a
role already stymied at birth, as it were, by elevating the politics and pathologies
of the Indian Bar as the presiding deity over the future of legal education? Indeed,
how may we ever fully understand the new political passion embracing a mad
rush for the reproduction of National Law School-type legal education?

The Conference statement is right, no doubt, in raising concerns regarding the second wave of reprivatization of production of legal knowledges and
competencies and in asking us to critique 'the content that academic programmes
must now assume'. How may we understand the new forms of reprivatization
that mime and even cannibalize the initial 'ideals' governing the National Law
School Universities? Unlike the privately run law colleges that minted millions
by admitting large masses of students at affordable fees, the National Law School
Universities of India, and kindred institutions, now perhaps generate remarkable
revenue surpluses by levying high fees on the chosen few.[38] Unlike the privately
run law colleges of yesteryear which only performed perfunctory legal education, the latter day counterparts insist on quality legal education, with full-time
faculty, residential campuses and recruitment of students at school-leaving age.
These brand equity National Law School prototypes continue the itinerary of
fulfilment of the vision of some US founders of 'modern' legal education. But is
this necessarily the best progress narrative that historians of Indian legal education have to offer?[39] In any event, while I fully recognize the implicit orders of
correlation thus posed between globalization and legal education, I also believe
that the tasks ahead are not exactly or eminently well served by funerary ora-
tions on the end of the nation state genera.[40]

How far have the practices of power politics shaped the practices of
teaching law? Have political regime changes impacted on legal education and
research? Have these impacts been strong and, at times, decisive? Put another
way, one may ask: how have political practices and regime styles 'encultured
law'?

Some profiles are clear enough: many law teachers and student leaders
remain openly affiliated to leading political parties, and so do the leading lawyers who constitute the leadership of the state and central Bar Councils with the
power to affect the standards of legal education. Further, political affiliations
animate many attempts at the 'modernization,' and now 'globalization' of Indian legal education as well as the production of Indian legal scholarly performance. However, it is difficult to draw any sustained inferences from these facts
about any structural relation between party politics and legal education histo-

ries. Perhaps we need to explore the unexamined political dimensions of curricular change and pedagogic reform.

It is in this context that I may perhaps indulge in some anecdotal material. For a long time, Indian law schools organized the teaching of 'personal law' frankly named as Hindu and Muslim Law. The modernizing wave of curricular changes replaced this organization by renaming units of instruction as Family Law I and II. It was this renaming that led some Law School curriculum committees (known as Committees of Courses), regardless of my protests, to so organize the curricular content of these two courses as to altogether marginalize the instruction in Islamic law. I am in no position to say that this signified any early form of 'saffronization' of law teaching; nor am I able to say how far Islamic jurisprudence is given the dignity of discourse in certain law-teaching regions in the present times. But, overall, the way 'personal law' is taught matters a great deal to the future of Indian constitutional secularism. Equally important is the denial of difference entailed in such curricular offerings: nowhere (outside perhaps the North-East) is instruction in indigenous people's law offered; there is virtually no instruction in Parsi law or Zoroastrian jurisprudence, nor in the Christian and Judaic systems. Indeed, one may go through a distinguished career in law teaching and studies without even a nodding familiarity with these systems of jurisprudence.

Curricular changes rarely reflect any sustained concern with the practices of violent social exclusion (outside the jurisprudence of affirmative action.) Very few course offerings exist, for example, concerning people living with disability, sexual exploitation at the workplace in disorganized labour markets, child labour, other slave-like labour practices, trafficking in human beings, the rights of unorganized and migrant labour. The Delhi Law School pioneered courses and readings in an umbrella course called Law and Poverty; at no time in my twenty-three years of teaching did the enrolment exceed, on an average, 6–8 students per year! The idea that this course offering be made a compulsory subject remained subject to violent opposition. The related suggestions that we arduously assembled in the 1994 UGC Curricular Development Centre Report that I was privileged to lead, have obviously failed to leave the soundproof rooms in which some contemporary leaders of Indian legal education flourish.

Perhaps all this suggests that the dominant patterns of curricular change and even modernization remain heavily affected by some implicit class, caste, and gender biases. We need to systematically explore histories of legal education and research to demonstrate the tenacity of these biases. Only then may our dialogic search for enculturing law serve its stated ends in some measure.

To return to the theme of histories of legal education, all I can say here is that an incredible amount of labour of collective learning and sharing remain necessary, for, at the very least, furnishing the raw material for projects aiming at some order of descriptive realism concerning Indian legal education. Our shared ignorance concerning the evolution of teaching and research cultures is, indeed, immense. We need to know how cultures of teaching and research have

developed over the decades; we need to retrieve from oblivion, the profiles of
some of the pioneers of legal education reform and of those who encouraged
generations of law teachers to undertake research and to publish. We need to
know the reasons why some curricular and pedagogic innovations succeeded in
some law schools but failed altogether in others. Further, we also need to grasp
the patterns of relationship between undergraduate and postgraduate studies and
doctoral studies and advanced research in law. The stories of learning/unlearn-
ing experiences of Indian law students should also form a crucial aspect of our
enculturing law talk. Because most contemporary law teachers were once at the
receiving end of 'pedagogies', we must begin by sharing experiential notes, without waiting for any lush Foundation funding for information-retrieval of generations of our present-day 'victims'. Put another way, no doing of 'histories' of
legal education and high-minded talk concerning 'enculturing law' may achieve
any self-assigned purposes outside the frame of the *ethic of listening* celebrated
by Corradi Fiumara.[41]

'Enculturing' Law

Because the 'law' always stands culturally embedded, the question always is: what elements in the construction of Otherness in the 'old' may be
problematized, which may be modified and carried over, and which wholly
dis(re)membered in the construction of the 'new' and how might the telos of that
'new' be constructed after all? These are difficult questions concerning the dialectical play, even war, between what Raymond Williams named as the 're-
sidual,' 'dominant' and 'emergent' cultures (conceived both in terms of the cultures *of* law and law *as* culture.)

Before we begin the pursuit of 'enculturing law', we ought to ponder a
paradox. How is it that the relatively unencultured legal professional in India,
poorly educated (at least in terms now fully legislated by the National Law
School mindsets) in the colonial times, these pleaders and *vakils*, these half-
baked, forensic creatures, were actually able to torment the British Raj legalities
(as Bernard Cohn so often fully brought to view)?[42] How may we ever understand the social fact that the 'premodern' and poorly educated lawyers in the
Indian independence struggle achieved so much to transform the unBritish rule of
law (to borrow a phrase from Dadabhai Naoroji) into what now parades as some
paradoxes of postcolonial Indian law and jurisprudence? And how may we
understand that a similar breed likewise has continued to contribute enormously
to the protection of rights and preservation of human liberties in postcolonial
India?

How may we further fully understand, in view of the 'modesty' of achievement of Indian legal education and research, the fact that faceless district lawyers still led judges in nine Indian High Courts (themselves also products of
'modest' Indian legal education) with such eminent success to deny the sovereignty of the dreaded security legislations during the 1975–76 Emergency Rule
by resurrecting the elementary rights of personal liberty?[43] Which faceless dis-

trict lawyers contributed so vigorously to the solidity of the practices of Indian constitutional secularism by maintaining since 1950 an extraordinary regime of stay orders over the Ayodhya Ram Mandir/Babri Masjid for over four long decades, which was disrupted, with catastrophic and barbaric effects, by the subsequent products of 'modernized' legal education? How may we fully understand the enormous contribution made by plain and relatively 'unencultured' and 'ordinary' lawyers to the fashioning of the profoundly litigious Indian cultures of democratic ordering? In contrast, though this requires further empirical exploration, I do wish to suggest that that most 'encultured' law products of the National Law School prototypes now serve better the causes of globalized lawyering than the future of human rights in a globalizing India.

How may we 'enculture' law outside the ways of a historically sensible and sensitive grasp of that which already precedes us when we begin to think of the present moment? What fidelity to histories, or at least the craft of historical narratives, may any search for relocation of legal education and research owe to the past successes and failures in imaging their role in a changing society? Further still, we need to ask whether formal, both pre-postmodern and postmodern, legal education matters *at all and for whom?*

Notes

1 The conference call statement is available at http://cscsban.org/html/EnculLaw.htm

2 Incidentally, this was the very issue I opened up in my *Socio-Legal Research in India* (ICSSR Monograph 12, 1973) and was variously responded to (notably by Professor S.N. Jain) in a special number devoted to legal research methodologies of the *Journal of the Indian Law Institute* 23 (1982).

3 This in turn raises several questions concerning the doctrinal element arising from other 'authoritative legal materials,' a notion by which Roscoe Pound invited our attention to decisional materials other than the judicial, an arena that Ronald Dworkin subsequently differentiated in terms of the domain of principles and policy. See U. Baxi (2003).

4 By 'ideal', Pound (1958) meant to suggest not merely the 'mental pictures' or the images of a 'good' legislator and a judge (and of other lawpersons) but also 'the end or the purpose of law as social control – what we are seeking to bring about by adjustment of relations and ordering or conduct' by 'systematic application of force of politically organized society'.

5 This perhaps overstates the matter. Perhaps, the 'values' of a good doctrine or doctrinal development may be measured simply in analytical or formal theory terms such as clarity of enunciation, internal conceptual consistency and even as 'integrity' in a Dworkinian sense in terms of crafting the best possible narrative 'fit' of interpretive change. Even on this register, it is not clear how the legislator may proceed to propound and install doctrines or at least translate these as initially crafted by the judge-jurist combine.

6 See Fitzpatrick (1992, 2001); Goodrich (1995); Nottir (2005); Tuit (2004); Mamdani (1996); Young (2001).

7 See especially, Mamdani (2003); Robertson (1999); Rummel (1997); Power (2002).

8 Cover (1983).

9 Derrida (1992, 2002).

10 Max Weber demonstrated that the production and substance of 'belief systems' concerning the authority of law remain historically and sociologically diverse, and often incommensurable. See generally Cotterell (1997) and more recently Sarat (2004).

11 Teubner (1999).

[12] I deal more fully with the problem of conversion of human rights movements into human rights markets in Baxi (2002a: Chapter 7).

[13] Twining (1994: 191).

[14] See Hurst (1964a, 1964b). Further, no reader of Gadamer (2005) or of Koselleck (2002) may fail to return to doing legal history with the hermeneutic complexity of 'experience. See more recently Schinkel (2005).

[15] See Griffiths (2002); Baxi (1985).

[16] Baxi (1982).

[17] Goodrich (1995).

[18] Unger (1976). But also see Unger (1996).

[19] Baxi (1990).

[20] Fish (1994).

[21] See Krishnan (2005).

[22] See the fascinating narrative in Assyag and Benet (2005).

[23] Duncan Derrett has archived for us the histories of interaction between varieties of Indian colonizers and the Hindu law. Joseph Minattur was the only Indian legal scholar to retrieve for us the legal history of French law and jurisprudence in Pondichery. My research reveals an unhappy lack concerning the working of Portuguese law in India. As far as I know, Professor Krishna Mohan Sharma's article in an *American Law Review* (apologies for this non-specific citation) remains the only available indicator of an attempt to understand civil law enclaves within an Anglicized Indian legal tradition. And the specific contributions of Professor Charles Alexandrowicz (from Krakow) who nurtured for well over a decade the Department of International Law at Madras University and Conrad Dieter (Heidelberg) are unfortunately rarely mentioned.

[24] All this incidentally reminds me of my very first address at the Hyderabad Conference of the Association of Indian Law Teachers (1974) where I sought to contrast two forms of legal consciousness in India: the *All India Reporter* and the everyday consciousness of the law's multifarious workings.

[25] See Baxi, Sarkar, Kelkar and Dhagamwar (1979); P. Baxi (2004).

[26] See Baxi (2000a, 2000b); Sathe (2001).

[27] See Baxi (2000c) and Baxi (2002b).

[28] I still recall with horror how, as a Dean of the Delhi Law School, I had to wrestle with the Controller of Examinations over a mindless application of the rule that disallowed a visually disabled student from enrolling at an examination simply because he had failed to comply with a notice, pasted on the notice board, concerning the relevant last dates for application! Indeed, it never occurred to the University that some folks may not be able to read the pasted notifications! I similarly had to struggle against the University legality concerning the recourse to helpers for visually disabled or differentially abled students, who required the services of an amanuensis, under the regimes that enacted a suspicion of unfair academic practices by people living with disabilities. I tried, as the Vice Chancellor of Delhi University, even amidst the resource crunches generated by the then Finance Minister Manmohan Singh, to provide for Braille library services as well to provide a quotient of reservations for the differentially abled law students in particular and students generally. I thus focus piquantly on the situation of the 'peoples living with disabilities'.

[29] Baxi (1979: 9–10). It is refreshing indeed now to read the debate over three contrasting conceptions of legal education in the United States: the 'midwife' conception contrasted with the 'universal filling station' imagery (where legal education recipients tank up the knowledge that they will need later) and the 'sports coach' conception in which a law teacher may impart to the player the sport skills that he or she needs best. See Woodhouse (1993).

[30] See, as regards this distinction, Sachs (2003).

[31] Haig-Brown (1998).

[32] All this happened long before the unfortunate Ford Foundation transferral of the American agendum of pursuing 'diversity' in Indian legal education, and this flourishes happily despite this.

[33] Twining (1966–67: 396).

[34] Lloyd and Rudolph (1972) should still guide our understanding of the relation between party politics and university education.

[35] Incidentally, I recall with some poignancy that many Vice Chancellors, including V.V. John, thus resorted to a 10+2+5 legal education with a single-minded view to avoid the presence of rowdy law students on the campus! A singular educational innovation stood as a moment of de-militarized styles of campus governance!

[36] It does not as a rule fund undergraduate legal education (outside the auspices of national universities) though it occasionally provides matching resources for some development projects and enables some national coordination through its panel on legal education.

[37] See the reflections in Baxi (1996).

[38] The explosive issue of 'capitation' fees, that has affected many sectors of professional education (see Kaul 1993) has not in any severe mode visited the high investment from students and parents that National Law Schools, and their prototypes, now pursue with such eminent success.

[39] I must here fully acknowledge my own failure in the pursuit of the vision of the National Law School at Bangalore, with which I remained heavily pregnant for 13 years allowing a caesarian surgery, after all, by Madhava Menon. It is indeed interesting that Jayanth Krishnan in his recent survey of 'modernizing' legal education finds of interest only two arcs of transition: the Ford Foundation auspices and its astonishing revitalization by Menon, for which he deserves credit. See Krishnan (2005).

In the process remain wholly ignored even a bare mention of alternate imageries of the socially relevant legal education which animated five national workshops under the auspices of the University Grants Commission in 1975–76, its massive Curriculum Development in Law Report, 1993, the landmark seminar at the University of Dharwar on teaching jurisprudence, the ICSSR recognition of law within the ambit of social science research production and the several workshops in social science research methods – all of which I was singularly privileged to initiate and lead. This interregnum is important, even decisive because here, altogether summarily presented, it:

- breached the Ford Foundation-induced models of curricular and pedagogic transformation
- transformed understandings of teaching of jurisprudence and Indian legal history
- aspired, and, with some success, accomplished, empirical and sociological explorations the Indian constitutional and legal development
- enabled recognition of legal studies as worthy recipients of sociological research funding
- reshaped, overall, legal education – pedagogy, curricular reform, and research landscapes
- encouraged student-based legal learning directed to initiatives for law reform and imaginative delivery of legal aid and services to the 'poorest of the poor' and in the process launched a critique of unconstitutional and anti-constitutional governance policies and practices.

[40] See regarding this Baxi (2006: Chapters 8, 9). Also see, in a comparative context of the travails of legal education in the era of neoliberalism, Thornton (2005) and Cownie and Bradney (2005).

[41] Fiumara (1990). See also Todd (2003); Ellsworth (1997); Fraser (1997) and hooks (1994).

[42] Cohn (1965).

[43] Though denied in fullness by the infamous habeas corpus Shiv Kant Shukla Supreme Court Bench. See Baxi (1989).

References

Assyag, Jackie and Vernoique Benet (2005), *Remapping Knowledge: The Making of South Asian Studies in India, Europe, and America (19th–20th Centuries)* (New Delhi: Three Essays Collective).

Baxi, Pratiksha (2004), *The Social and Juridical Framework of Rape in India: Case Studies in Gujarat*, Doctoral dissertation, Department of Sociology, Delhi School of Economics.

Baxi, Upendra (1979), 'Towards a Socially Relevant Legal Education', in *A Consolidated Report of the University Grants Commissions Workshops on the Modernization of Legal Education* (New Delhi): 9–10.

—— (1982), *The Crisis of the Indian Legal System* (New Delhi: Vikas).

—— (1985), *Towards a Sociology of Indian Law* (New Delhi: ICSSR/Sathvahan Publications).

—— (1989), *The Indian Supreme Court and Politics* (Lucknow: Eastern Book Co.).

—— (1990), 'On the Problematic Distinction between "Legislation" and "Adjudication": A Forgotten Aspect of Dominance', *Delhi L. Rev.*, No. 12: 1–15.

—— (1996), 'Judicial Activism, Legal Education and Research in a Globalizing India', Capital Foundation Annual Lecture (New Delhi).

—— (2000a), 'The Avatars of Judicial Activism: Explorations in the Geography of (In)Justice', in S.K. Verma and Kusum, eds, *Fifty Years of the Supreme Court of India: The Grasp and Reach* (Delhi: Oxford University Press and Indian Law Institute): 156–209.

—— (2000b), 'Bringing Judas Back to the Last Supper: The Tasks of Republican Criminology in the Service of Globalization', in Rani Dhavan Sankardass, ed., *Prison and Punishment: Indian and International Perspectives* (New Delhi: Sage): 261–343.

—— (2000c), 'Gender and Reproductive Rights: Problems and Perspectives for the New Millennium', UNFA Lecture, 6 September.

—— (2002a), *The Future of Human Rights* (New Delhi: Oxford University Press).

—— (2002b), 'Sense and Sensibility in the New Indian Population Policies: A Human Rights Oriented Critique', *Seminar*, No. 511.

—— (2003), 'A Known but an Indifferent Judge: Situating Ronald Roscoe in Contemporary Indian Jurisprudence', *International Journal of Constitutional Law*, No. 1: 557–89.

—— (2006), *The Future of Human Rights*, second edition (Delhi: Oxford University Press).

Baxi, Upendra, Lotika Sarkar, Ragunath Kelkar and Vasudha Dhagamwar (1979), 'An Open Letter to the Chief Justice of India', *Supreme Court Cases (Journal Section)*, No. 4: 17.

Cohn, Bernard (1965), 'Anthropological Notes on Disputes and Law in India', *American Anthropologist*, 67(6): 82–122.

Cotterell, Roger (1997), *Law's Community: Legal Theory in Sociological Perspective* (Oxford: Blackwell).

Cover, Robert (1983), 'Foreword: Nomos and Narrative', *Harvard Law Review*, No. 97: 62.

Cownie, Fiona and Anthony Bradney (2005), 'Gothic Horror? A Response', *Social and Legal Studies*, No. 14(2): 277–85.

Derrida, Jacques (1992), 'The Mystical Foundation of Authority', in Drucilla Cornell, Michel Rosenfeld and David Gray, eds, *Deconstruction and the Possibility of Justice* (London: Routledge): 3–67.

—— (2002), *Acts of Literature* (London: Routledge).

Ellsworth, E. (1997), *Teaching Positions: Difference, Pedagogy and the Power of Address* (New York: Columbia University Teachers College Press).

Fish, Stanley (1994), *There's No Such Thing as Free Speech and it's a Good Thing Too* (New York: Oxford University Press).

Fitzpatrick, Peter (1992), *The Mythology of Modern Law* (London: Routledge).

—— (2001), *Modernism and the Grounds of Law* (Cambridge: Cambridge University Press).

Fiumara, Corradi (1990), *The Other Side of Language: A Philosophy of Listening* (London: Routledge).

Fraser, Nancy (1997), *Justice Interruptus: Critical Reflections on the 'Postsocialist' Condition* (New York: Routledge).

Gadamer, Hans-Georg (2005), *Truth and Method* (London: Continuum).

Goodrich, Peter (1995), *Oedipus Lex: Psychoanalysis, History and Law* (Berkeley: University of California Press).

—— (1995), 'Twining Tower Metaphors of Distance and Histories of the English Law School', *U. Miami Law Review*, No. 49: 901.

Griffiths, Anne (2002), 'Legal Pluralism', in Reza Banker and Max Travers, eds, *An Introduction to the Law and Social Theory* (Oxford: Hart Publishing): 289–310.

Haig-Brown, Celia (1998), *Resistance and Renewal: Surviving the Indian Residential School* (Vancouver: Tillicum Library).

hooks, bell (1994), *Teaching to Transgress: Education as the Practice of Freedom* (New York: Routledge).

Hurst, James Willard (1964a), *Justice Holmes on Legal History* (New York: Macmillan).

—— (1964b), *Law and Economic Growth: The Legal History of The Lumber Industry in Wisconsin 1836–1915* (Cambridge, MA: The Belknap Press of the Harvard University).

Kaul, Rekha (1993), *Caste, Class, and Education: Politics of Capitation Fees Phenomenon in Karnataka* (New Delhi: Sage).

Koselleck, Reinhardt (2002), *The Practice of Conceptual History: Timing History, Spacing Concepts* (Stanford: Stanford University Press).

Krishnan, Jayanth (2005), 'Professor Kingsfield Goes to Delhi: The Ford Foundation, and the Development of Legal Education in India', *William Mitchell College of Law: Legal Studies Research Working Paper Series,* Working Paper No. 3.

Mamdani, Mahmood (1996), *The Citizen and Subject: Contemporary Africa and the Legacy of Late Colonialism* (Princeton: Princeton University Press).

—— (2003), *When Victims Become Killers: Colonialism, Nativism and the Genocide in Rwanda* (Oxford: James Currey Publishers).

Norrie, Alan (2005), *Law and the Beautiful Soul* (London: Glasshouse Press).

Pound, Roscoe (1958), *The Ideal Element in Law: Tagore Law Lectures* (Calcutta: University of Calcutta).

Power, Samantha (2002), *A Problem from Hell: America and the Age of Genocide* (New York: Basic Books).

Robertson, Geoffrey (1999), *Crimes Against Humanity: The Struggle for Global Justice* (Harmondsworth: Penguin).

Rudolph, Lloyd and Susanne Rudolph (1972), *Education as Politics in India: Studies in Organization, Society, and Polity* (Cambridge, MA: Harvard University Press).

Rummel, J.S. (1997), *Death By Government* (New York: Transaction Pub.).

Sachs, Judyth (2003), *The Activist Teaching Profession* (Buckingham: Open University Press).

Sarat, Austin, ed. (2004), *The Blackwell Companion to Law and Society* (Oxford: Blackwell).

Sathe, S.P. (2001), *Judicial Activism in India* (Delhi: Oxford University Press).

Schinkel, Andres (2005), 'Imagination as a Category of History: An Essay Concerning Koselleck's Concepts of *Erfahrungsraum* and *Erwartungshoriznot*', *History and Social Theory*, No. 44: 42–54.

Teubner, Gunther (1999), 'Dealing with Paradoxes of Law: Derrida, Luhmann, Wiethölter' (on file with the author), relying in part on Koschorke, *Die Grenzen des Systems und die Rhetorik der Systemtheorie*, in Koschorke and Vismann, eds, *Widerstände der Systemtheorie: Kulturtheoretische Analysen zum Werk von Niklas Luhmann* (Berlin): 49–60, 56.

Thornton, Margaret (2005), 'Gothic Horror in the Legal Academy', *Social and Legal Studies*, 14(2): 267–76.

Todd, Sharon (2003), *Learning From the Other: Levinas, Psychoanalysis, and Ethical Possibilities in Education* (Albany: State University of New York Press).

Tuit, Patricia (2004), *Race, Law, Resistance* (London: Glasshouse).

Twining, William, L. (1966–67), 'Pericles and the Plumber', *Law Quarterly Review*, 83.

—— (1994), *Blackstone's Tower: Discipline of Law* (London: Sweet and Maxwell).

Unger, Roberto Mangberia (1976), *Law in Modern Society* (New York: The Free Press).

—— (1996), *What Should Legal Analysis Become?* (London: Verso).

Woodhouse, Barbara Bennett (1993), 'Mad Wifery: Bringing Theory, Doctrine, and Practice to Life', *Michigan Law Review*, No. 91: 1980–81.

Young, Robert (2001), *Postcolonialism: An Introduction* (Oxford: Blackwell).

Culture, Comparison, Community

Social Studies of Law Today

Roger Cotterrell

Culture

What can an English legal theorist and legal sociologist, with an almost entirely European social and legal experience, hope to contribute to a realistic discussion of legal studies in a country with a profoundly different culture – for example, India? The challenge is to try to find a way of bridging cultures through legal and social theory, legal and sociological scholarship. It is also to find a way of talking about culture that is neither vague and merely impressionistic (like a tourist), nor misleadingly dogmatic so that complex communal ways of life are labelled 'cultures' as if they were monolithic and uniform, and irreducibly different from other cultures. On the one hand, there is a danger in using the concept of culture in a way that assumes an inevitable similarity between people who are different in important ways. On the other, the danger is in assuming an irreducible difference between the 'other' and 'us', when, in fact, much may be shared and bridges of understanding can be built that make culture highly 'porous' – open to cross-influence, mutual learning, recognition of commonalities and inter-group translation of experience, beliefs, aspirations and attachments.

This paper's aim is to outline a theoretical framework that might be helpful in addressing some of the complexities of culture in the social studies of law. It presents ideas about culture, comparison and community in law at a fairly high level of abstraction. But my hope is that these ideas are broad and sensitive enough to have some local resonance, and that they may be criticized and tested to explore their applicability for legal studies in specific national contexts, in particular the context of the current development of legal education and scholarship in India.

These ideas reflect a strong interest in comparative legal studies and comparative legal history, but they cannot entirely escape the predominantly English common law experience that has shaped them. Nevertheless, limitations of experience and perspective face anyone engaging in comparative cultural studies of law. One can try to be aware of these limitations and make them explicit; one can try to transcend the parochial without discarding local insights. In other words, the aim should be to protect the integrity of the 'method of detail'

– the method of close, first-hand participation and observation – from being absorbed (losing its richness and precision) into the broad, general view. But it should also be to try to understand (reinterpret, contextualize, evaluate, deepen) the former in terms of the latter.

All of us inhabit cultures that, in part, we are aware of. But, in part, insofar as culture forms us and makes us who we are, we are not conscious of it. To understand culture, it is necessary somehow to step outside ourselves, observing ourselves participating in life. Up to a point, this is possible. Observation and participation cannot ultimately be separated. We necessarily observe the situation in which we participate, while we participate in it (like a lawyer who, arguing a case in court, watches the judge and other participants and gains useful knowledge from observing their behaviour); and we often participate in order to observe. This may be a virtual participation (as in the empathetic understanding that a Weberian sociologist needs in studying social action) or it may be actual participant observation, which all of us do all the time if we are curious about social life.

The point is that cultural translation is very difficult, but not impossible. In getting to grips with culture (which, this paper will argue, is a crucial aspect of legal studies today), there is no sharp line to be drawn between observation and participation, insiders and outsiders, internal and external viewpoints.[1] The concept of culture becomes dangerous when it is used to draw those lines of demarcation, presenting them as fixed rather than as infinitely fluid and dependent on standpoint and perspective. In other words, culture should not be treated positivistically, as a 'thing' or a 'social fact' in Émile Durkheim's sense.[2] One of the hardest challenges for legal studies today is to decide how to deal with the idea of culture, integrating it into legal thinking but avoiding the kind of reification that treats culture as monolithic, a causal factor in itself,[3] or an explanation of legally relevant behaviour (as, for example, in the use of 'cultural defences' in criminal law and other legal fields).[4] Later in this paper, some suggestions will be made as to how this problem can be avoided.

But is culture really important in legal studies? Legal positivists have long tended to assume that it is not. Law, in their view, may derive both its coercive power and its legitimacy from its link to the state (or, in the Austinian version, the sovereign), and the question of state authority is seen as one for political theory; otherwise law is to be understood as a system of norms or rules that regulate their own creation (Hart, Kelsen) – law is portrayed as normatively autonomous and self-standing. So the argument goes, an understanding of the various aspects of culture may not be important to an understanding of law. If culture relates to law, it is, in a typical legal positivist view, a professional culture: the culture (in this case the professional values, traditions, allegiances or interests) of legal officials (especially judges and lawyers) who accept a rule of recognition, or the existence of a basic norm. But even in western countries, where an assumption of law's isolation from culture has long had currency, this assumption is becoming increasingly untenable. Law is now seen, even in lawyers' doctrinal writings (not just the writings of legal sociologists or legal anthropologists) as related to culture in many ways.

The following are a few examples. Comparative lawyers invoke the concept of legal culture in referring to the fact that it is not only rules that must be compared between legal systems but also ways of 'doing' law – practising, invoking and developing it. If law is changing more quickly than ever before in many countries, the forces behind legal change need to be understood. Culture may, in the view of an increasing number of comparative lawyers, be a good concept to adopt in addressing these matters. The study of rules alone may give little real assistance in understanding law in flux.

At the same time, the literature on globalization often suggests that law moves easily from country to country, and across national boundaries. In much of this literature, law is seen as the 'camp follower' of transnational economic and financial development.[5] Law is often assumed to be straightforwardly instrumental in character; a mere technical device. In this context, ideas of legal culture (for example, relating to the organization of transnational professional legal practice)[6] are sometimes convenient in referring to the socio-legal conditions that facilitate globalization. But legal culture can also refer to local ways of practising, using and thinking about law that operate as factors of resistance to globalizing trends and the harmonization of law.[7]

Culture is important also, in western countries, as a legally relevant idea in considering the legal challenges and possibilities of multiculturalism, in issues such as the recognition of polygamous marriages in monogamous cultures;[8] varied practices of marriage and divorce;[9] the legal recognition of minority religious or traditional practices;[10] the use of 'cultural defences' against criminal and civil liability, as mentioned earlier; and the protection of 'cultural heritage'.[11]

I have not defined 'culture' here. The examples given earlier suggest many different meanings of the term – and that is this paper's first major theme. *Culture does not refer to a single idea that is analytically useful in legal studies.* This does not mean that culture is unimportant – quite the opposite. It is vitally important as a matter for legal scholars to take into account. But it refers to many disparate elements – different kinds of social bonds and experiences. They need to be separated analytically.[12] Otherwise, in talking about culture, we are sometimes talking about religion or other belief systems; sometimes about traditions and customs that may be entirely secular; sometimes about material culture (levels of economic well-being and technological development); and sometimes about emotional ties (for example, to nation, to kinship group, to communal goods such as music and other arts, to shared memories, etc.) as well as emotional hostilities (to 'other' nations, races, religions, ethnic groups, etc.). It is impossible to make much progress in relating law and culture systematically without separating these different elements that may pull against, as much as reinforce, each other.

Comparison

Before considering how this separation of the elements of culture might be achieved, it is important to say more about changes in legal studies in general that are making the relation of law and culture increasingly significant. One important consequence of these changes is surely that comparative legal studies are becoming much more central to legal scholarship.

Comparative law as a scholarly field has served many functions[13] but its dominant practical roles in western countries have been as a technical aid to improve national law, as a servant of efforts to unify or harmonize law between nations, or to aid legal communication between them, especially in the interests of facilitating commerce. The dominant idea in much comparative legal scholarship seems to have been to seek similarity in law, to get rid of obstacles in the form of legal difference that hamper legal interaction between modern nation states. Alan Watson's influential writing on legal transplants relates, in part, to this orientation. For him, comparative law is concerned with studying how particular legal systems develop by borrowing legal ideas from other systems.[14] The focus is on integrating legal ideas in unified legal systems, not on recognizing differences between laws in different systems.

Some recent writers such as Pierre Legrand and Vivian Curran have, however, advocated that comparative law should recognize, respect and even protect difference.[15] What kind of difference? There seems no obvious reason to celebrate difference in positive law as such. For the new 'comparatists of difference', the focus is on recognizing, even celebrating *cultural difference*, focused on law. Thus, legal culture becomes, in this kind of comparative legal study, a central idea – referring vaguely to the entirety of ways of practising and thinking about law in a certain environment. It seems to point to the range of values, traditions, allegiances and collective interests that surround and inform law in a particular time and place. Legrand, however, talks of legal culture in terms of *mentalités* – outlooks, ways of thought, legal world-views – a notion that seems to retain the usual imprecision of the term culture, but may not indicate the full range of matters which, as seen earlier, this term can address.

Why is comparative law becoming central to legal scholarship? Firstly, globalization, though hard to define uncontroversially, is an experienced reality of increasingly transnational ties, influences, pressures, opportunities and dependencies affecting law in many countries. Even if law is merely a technical instrument, a camp follower of globalization, the building of globalized technical law and the adapting of local legal variation to transnational demands for uniformity may require comparative legal expertise, if regulatory problems arising from the diversity of local legal conditions are to be avoided. Law, as a kind of technology, designed in a particular locale, may not work in the same way in a different setting under different conditions. 'Officials' expected to make the technology work in the new locale may find it hard to operate without adapting it (or, at least, without an intelligible translation of the makers' instructions for use).

Secondly, however, the links already suggested between law and culture show that law is more than mere technology. Globalization creates situations where law is an object of struggle, a prize to be fought for in cultural wars centred around globalization. Multinational corporations, nation states and the 'itinerant armies of transnationalism' in commerce, finance, intellectual property and other fields, devote much attention to ensuring a favourable legal climate for the pursuit of their projects abroad. For the foreseeable future, that involves drawing on certain kinds of comparative legal expertise. At the same time, law expresses in various ways traditions, values, beliefs, interests and allegiances that often pit themselves, at least implicitly, against the strategies and purposes of the 'armies of transnationalism'. Otherwise, they link themselves to *different kinds* of transnationalism from those most familiarly associated with primarily economic globalization.

At the very least, law, in many national contexts, confronts opposing aspirations and demands that reflect its diverse cultural reference points. As population flows make ethnic and religious diversity commonplace in nations that once thought themselves unproblematically homogeneous, the need to think of law and culture pluralistically makes comparative legal studies important.[16] In Anglophone legal theory, feminism, critical race theory and other developments symbolize the fact that the professional interpretive communities of lawyers are becoming much more diverse, especially in countries like Britain and the United States.

What all of these indications add up to is the recognition that neither legal systems nor societies can be thought of as unified and integrated in the way that western legal thought has often assumed. A comparative legal perspective is no more than the systematic recognition that law is always fluid, pluralistic, contested and often subject to contradictory pressures and influences from both inside and outside its jurisdiction; that it reflects an always unstable diversity of traditions, interests, allegiances and ultimate values and beliefs. If the comparative perspective on law was once a view of the exotic legal 'other', or of the 'external relations' of one's own law with the law of other peoples in other lands, now it is a view of transnational legal patterns and of the cultural complexities of law at home. We live in conditions where the law of the nation-state must respond to a great plurality of demands from different population groups within its jurisdiction. At the same time, it must respond to powerful external pressures. Legal thought in national contexts is being fragmented *from within* in a new 'jurisprudence of difference',[17] and globalized *from without* by demands for transnational harmonization or uniformity.

Comparative law today is thus concerned with both seeking similarity (legal harmonization or unification) and appreciating difference (between legal ideas, practices, systems and experiences). *Similarity* is often sought on the level of positive law and with the assumption that law is an easily transferable or changeable technical instrument. The problem of adaptation is seen essentially as a technical, juristic one. But, as suggested earlier, this assumption is often mistaken. It is justified, if at all, only for problems of regulation that are essentially instrumental in character, yet constitute merely part of law's focus. Positivist or functionalist approaches, which have dominated unification or harmonization movements among comparatists, are appropriate mainly to the analysis of law intended to facilitate essentially instrumental relations (e.g. contract, commercial law). They may lack the resources to address regulatory problems bearing on some other aspects of culture. It is dangerous to assume universally that even instrumental relations are *entirely* free of complexities requiring comparative cultural analysis. This assumption in legal analyses may arise in part from a parallel one in some economic analyses: from the view that only (relatively homogeneous) transnational economic elites are relevant in considering the primary conditions of local economic well-being, and that local economic life in general will merely follow the lead of these elites.

On the other hand, when comparative law seeks to appreciate legal *difference* – usually explicitly invoking ideas of culture or legal culture to do so – it runs up against a problem that this paper has already identified: that culture is not a single thing, that it is a vague term referring to a broad range of aspects of the social. It lacks analytical utility and rigour. So, there is no alternative but to break culture down in some way into elements that can be treated rigorously for the purposes of legal analysis and socio-legal inquiry. The next section of this paper considers how this might be done.

Community

In December 2004, in Britain's second largest city, a play staged at the main theatre caused riots. The Asian playwright Ash Kotak wrote: '*Behzti* (meaning Dishonour in Punjabi), the play that caused violent clashes between Sikh protesters and police in Birmingham at the weekend, was closed yesterday. With its scenes of rape and murder taking place within a Sikh gurdwara (or temple), Gurpreet Kaur Bhatti's production offended a vocal conservative group within the [Sikh] community. . . . The playwright should only have to answer to his or her conscience. . . . But the play comes at a particularly sensitive time when religious people from all quarters feel threatened – both by what they perceive as the moral breakdown of society and by others' accusations of religious fundamentalism'.[18]

The writer of the play, a British Sikh herself, critical of aspects of life among Sikhs in the UK, especially those affecting women, was forced into hiding by death threats after the play's opening. The issue of respect for religion was prominent in public discussion of the play and its consequences. So also was freedom of speech, treated as a fundamental value of British society as a whole. Reports dwelt on the sensitivities of minority groups, and also on tensions between different generations of the British Sikh community and between conservative/traditional and progressive/modern sections of it. Meetings were organized between community leaders and concerned artists to discuss freedom of expression. Leading theatres across Britain backed proposals to host readings of the script to demonstrate support for the author's right of artistic expression.[19]

One feature of the public debates around this painful episode is particularly relevant to this paper: the very weak identification of the various *constituencies* or communities involved. There was much talk of the Sikh community, but also a hazy recognition of fundamental divisions within it. There was, in the debates, the implication of a national community united in support for the value of free speech, as well as a more professionally concerned theatrical community. There was the hint of a feminist constituency, perhaps within the Sikh community but perhaps including some Sikh women along with others of different faiths or none. Ash Kotak's report, quoted above, implies the existence of a community of religious people, from all quarters, with a stake in society's moral well-being; and also the idea of society itself (unspecified in nature or scope), which may or may not be threatened with moral breakdown. Is 'community', which is invoked so often in these debates, no less opaque, vague and slippery a concept than 'culture'?

Used in this way, the answer is clearly yes. It is unsurprising that nothing conclusive emerged from all the newspaper coverage and discussion between various groups after the Birmingham disturbances. Not merely did the constituencies remain undefined, but (partly as a result) the issues remained not clearly distinguished so that they could not be addressed systematically. Some issues were about values and beliefs (the integrity of the Sikh religion, the value of free speech); but there were also questions about gender relations (raised by the play) and about traditional allegiances and customary ways (the changing character of the Sikh minority; the place of minority groups generally in British society). In addition, there were economic and professional interests at stake (the concerns of theatres, actors and playwrights to be able to pursue their work profitably). No doubt other matters could easily be identified.

But, with significant adaptation, the concept of community could be used in a more rigorous way, separating the various kinds of issues and groups indicated. Just as a culture should not be thought of as a 'thing' in positivist fashion, neither should a community. Community is better seen as indicating a web of understandings about the nature of social relations. It 'exists as something for people to think with' in making sense of social relations and their place in them.[20] But these understandings are part of social relations themselves, not separate from them. They constitute (i.e., they form, give shape and meaning to) social relations in different ways. Community entails that social relations have positive meaning for the participants in them, so that people in these relations experience a sense of bonding and mutual interpersonal trust of some kind. Social relations of community have some continuity and intelligibility for those who participate in them, and this ongoing character of the relationships can be identified also by other people who are outside them.[21]

Some socio-legal theorists, notably Georges Gurvitch, have gone to great lengths in categorizing numerous kinds of social relations of community (he calls them forms of sociality) expressed through law or addressed by law.[22] But legal theory needs to classify only a *minimal* number of types of community. These can then be considered practically in the contingent ways they combine in actual social life. Isolating this small number of irreducible types of community enables us to ask whether each of them has some special features that law necessarily addresses differently.[23] Do different types of community entail different types of legal regulation, or different challenges for law? In general, I think, the answer is yes.

Following this approach, it is possible to distinguish just four abstract types of community: instrumental community, community of belief or values, traditional community and affective community.[24] The Birmingham Sikh protests case revealed a *community of belief* among the religious believers involved, as well as among other categories of people united by their common commitment to ultimate, overriding values of free speech. It also showed the power of *tradition* which, in some respects, united the Sikh minority, but in other respects divided it generationally. *Traditional* community refers to social relations based on common experience, environment, history, language or customs. *Instrumental* community is the community formed by people engaged in common or convergent projects or purposes, often economic, but not necessarily so. In the Sikh case, it is represented in part by the common concerns of those engaged in theatrical work to be able to present plays and perform them. *Affective* community is community based on purely emotional ties (or, sometimes, hostilities). Negatively, it may be a type of community based on dislike or hatred of others. Positively, it is based on affection for those with whom one identifies. In socio-legal analysis, it is likely often to be the 'wild card', the focus of social forces that are hard to predict, define and control, such as those shaped by pure prejudice.

A warrant for separating these four types of community lies in a direct adaptation of Max Weber's sociology. Weber identifies four basic types of social action,[25] irreducibly distinct from each other and comprehensive; he claims that they underlie all social patterns, structures and institutions. The four types of community directly reflect Weber's types of action. But, like them, they are ideal types – pure concepts or ideas designed to aid analysis, rather than observations of empirical reality as such. So, the types of community are not necessarily to be found independently of each other in reality. They are combined in many ways in the actual patterns of social association in which people live. These combinations can be called *networks* of community.

How can this idea of community help practical legal inquiry? First, a law-and-community approach frees socio-legal inquiries from the old paradigms of 'law and society' or 'law in society'. Unfortunately, for lawyers and most sociologists, 'society' has come to mean mainly the politically organized society of the nation-state. But transnational law, now developing in many forms, must relate to social environments (networks of community) that extend beyond or across nation-state boundaries. Equally, pluralistic views of law and culture, discussed earlier, suggest that law needs to be related systematically to diverse social groups and networks in national societies. These groups and networks are linked by aspects of common culture, but by using the typology of community, it becomes possible to break down the elements of culture into bonds of shared beliefs or values, bonds formed around common projects, bonds of shared history, customs or experience and bonds of emotional allegiance. The immensely complex webs of culture are woven from these distinct and sometimes conflicting elements.

Thinking in terms of law and community is not inevitably conservative or reactionary. Instrumental community almost always looks towards change, achievement and development. It aims at building something new. Traditional community, by contrast, looks towards roots, stability, the familiar, the tried and tested, the customary or the habitual. Affective community, based on pure feelings of attraction or repulsion, is often volatile (Weber thought purely affectual social action was not susceptible to rational interpretation). Communities of belief or values can be revolutionary or reactionary, evangelical or fundamentalist, open or dogmatic, tolerant or censorious, stable or unstable. This variety combined in different ways in the types of community also suggests that the regulatory problems of community are likely to vary considerably from one type to another. It also suggests that networks of community (combining these types) will often show *contradictory* regulatory requirements or demands.

Much more work would be needed to identify in a theoretically adequate way the different regulatory challenges posed by these different abstract types of community.[26] Nevertheless, it is possible to make tentative suggestions – exploratory or indicative rather than comprehensive – about relations between modern state law and the four types of community.

There seem good grounds for suggesting that of these four types, *instrumental community* is usually the easiest to regulate legally. Law regulating common or convergent projects, for example, business enterprises and transactions, trade and financial institutions and other economic networks, is usually itself instrumental in character. It often addresses narrowly defined social relations, limited in scope (focused only on the project, deal or enterprise). Sometimes these relations are strictly limited in duration too, lasting only until the project is completed or the deal is fulfilled. Law in this setting may well be the 'camp follower' of globalization: seen as relatively unproblematic and effective because strictly limited in social aim and scope. Certainly, comparatists usually see commercial or contract laws as the types of law easiest to harmonize or unify or transplant.[27]

On the other hand, systems of values or beliefs are notoriously difficult to define conclusively and so to make the object of direct legal regulation. Thus, *community of belief* is legally problematic. The integrity of religious doctrine is, for example, always at risk from diverse interpretations and schisms. It can be conclusively defined only when it has authority structures at least as strong as, and probably stronger than, those of state law (for example, expressed in terms of the 'infallibility' of certain religious leaders in making rulings or issuing interpretations or edicts). State law, as such, can only make rules that *imply* ultimate values; that is, it can create structures of rules that can be plausibly interpreted as collectively expressing these values. But there will usually be room for debate, and, because the debates focus on beliefs or values that are objects of commitment, disagreements may become bitter or violent. Even if almost everyone, for example, supports the sanctity of human life as an ultimate value, people may disagree as to whether an unborn foetus is such a life, or whether there is a point at which this value no longer holds when quality of life has deteriorated beyond a certain point (as in cases of patients in a permanent vegetative condition).

This does not mean that state law can or should have no concern with supporting certain values or beliefs. The problem is to recognize the limits in which it can do this and the wisdom of avoiding legal pronouncements on some value controversies. At the same time, it is necessary that, in complex, pluralistic modern societies, law should, on the one hand, firmly defend the right of communities of belief to exist and flourish and, on the other, no less firmly defend as 'universal' the values of personal human dignity and autonomy that are essential for all individuals of whatever creed (or none) to co-exist peacefully and with mutual respect.[28] Human rights law is especially relevant, today, to these kinds of legal tasks. But the types of community do not correlate neatly with juristic classifications of law.

Traditional community was associated above with a focus on roots, custom and familiar ways. Bonaventura De Sousa Santos[29] speaks of 'rights to roots' as well as 'rights to options' as being demanded in the contemporary world. Globalization makes some people and organizations more mobile than ever; they may be established in one country or several, invest in other countries and own property or trade in yet others. For these actors, rights to options (unfettered movement) are a priority. But many people – the majority of the world's population – are not easily mobile in this way. Law is faced with demands to protect conditions of co-existence in which people find themselves living, whether by choice or not: traditional locales, practices and understandings, common languages, shared heritage and collective memories, and physical and social environments. Law's most basic task in this context (performed usually mainly by criminal and tort law) is to prevent the personal frictions that arise as a result of mere proximity to others.

In some respects, this is relatively simple law. Like law protecting and promoting instrumental community, law protecting basic conditions of co-existence has a limited, narrowly defined, even straightforward social task. It is surely no surprise that the most basic aims of criminal and tort (delict) law are not strange to most citizens in many countries. On the other hand, the legal conditions of basic co-existence are becoming increasingly complex and contested: local communities seek to defend their local environment against the ravages of commercial exploitation or pollution from outside. Conversely, global environmental concerns (for example, about rain forests or endangered animal species) are pitted against local needs to exploit natural resources in order to provide a means of livelihood or to increase local prosperity. The specific dilemma for law in relation to traditional community is not so much how to devise means to protect rights in this community as how to define the *arenas* of co-existence. In one sense, these arenas are expanding with globalization – people are increasingly aware of world-wide common concerns with physical security and with the ecological health of the planet. At the same time, distinctive local environments seem more precious as global forces foster a bland uniformity in the conditions in which people live.

Of all the types of community, *affective community* may be the hardest to regulate by state law. Social relations based purely on emotional attachment (or rejection) are very difficult to analyse in legal terms, since law requires precise rules and binding definitions of the meanings of actions and situations. For example, lines between consensual sexual intercourse and rape, between invited intimacy and assault, between attraction and repulsion, are clear in theory, but in practice may be established and moved in ways that law is powerless to rationalize. Law directed against racism or religious intolerance may be faced with levels of bigotry that it simply cannot counter with reason or with normal sanctions. In regulating social relations powerfully shaped by emotion, law seems often to work by indirection, addressing not the unfathomable relationship itself but action resulting from it or demonstrable conditions of domination or vulnerability created through it.

Conclusion

A law-and-community approach gives basic theoretical resources for analysing law in social contexts today. It marks fundamental distinctions between types of social relations that occur throughout all fields of social life; that is, distinctions that are fundamental for understanding the tasks, capabilities and limitations of regulation. On these distinctions, particular juristic and sociolegal analyses can be built.

The social universe to which law relates cannot be thought of simply as 'society', a unified, monolithic, politically organized society whose boundaries are those of the nation-state. Law is now called on to express the aspirations and provide the security of nation states; of nations within states; of nations without states (for example in the challenge that Palestine poses for international law); of states and nations within larger unions (for example, the European Union). Law is required equally to address the aspirations and regulatory demands of transnational networks of business and finance; of ethnic groups, adherents of particular religions, carriers of endangered traditions and ways of life, populations in threatened environments, globally mobile entrepreneurs, social movements of many kinds; and of slowly emerging global networks of community united in their concern for the future of the world. Such aspirations and demands, in total, are beyond the capacity of any currently existing legal order to bear. Nevertheless, they form what will be an agenda for legal studies on a global scale in future. The problems exist, awaiting solutions.

This paper has tried to suggest that culture is fundamentally important to law. In large part, this is because invoking the idea of culture hints at many of these agenda items. Comparative study of law is the means by which legal scholarship must gradually expand its horizons to come closer to accepting this huge agenda. But, despite the legal significance of culture, culture cannot become a legal concept adequate to the theoretical tasks involved. A law-and-community approach, as sketched here, may be a necessary means of working towards theory that can help in distinguishing and organizing the regulatory tasks that the future agenda of legal studies will have to address.

Notes

[1] For general discussion see Cotterrell (2006: 30–31, 59–60).

[2] Durkheim (1982).

[3] As Haring (1949: 29) puts it, '"culture" never does anything to anyone. Whatever happens culturally to human beings in societies is done directly or indirectly by other human individuals'.

[4] See Renteln (2004).

[5] Cf. Barber (1993: 119): 'Law has always been the destitute camp follower of the itinerant armies of transnationalism.'

[6] See especially Dezalay and Garth (1996).

[7] See, for example, Legrand (1999).

[8] E.g., Shah (2005: Chapter 5).

[9] E.g., Murphy (2000: Chapters 4 and 5).

[10] E.g., Shadid and Van Koningsveld (2005); Freeman (1995).

[11] For fuller discussion and other examples see Cotterrell (2006: ch. 6).

[12] The idea that culture as a 'vague abstraction' (Radcliffe-Brown 1940: 27) should be broken down into more precisely specified components to make it amenable to rigorous conceptual analysis is far from new: see e.g. Haring (1949). However, this paper's concern, focused on juristic and sociolegal approaches to culture, is specifically with the need to develop concepts useful for distinguishing and analysing different kinds of regulatory problems that culture may present.

[13] For an indicative summary see Cotterrell (2006: 130).

[14] Watson (1993).

[15] Legrand (1999), Curran (1998). In Jacques Vanderlinden's (2002: 166) view, the task of comparatists is to 'try to "understand" the Other, in space and time, as deeply as they possibly can'. Legrand (2006: 30) writes of comparatists' responsibility to '*sustain* otherness' (emphasis in original).

[16] Demleitner (1999).

[17] Cotterrell (2003: Chapters 8 and 9).

[18] Kotak (2004).

[19] Dodd *et al.* (2004).

[20] Cohen (1985: 19).

[21] Cotterrell (2006: 68, 70–72).

[22] Gurvitch (1947: Chapter 2).

[23] This might be seen as a socio-legal correlate of normal methods of juristic analysis, involving the separating and narrowing of issues in order to deal with polycentric problems.

[24] Cotterrell (2006: Chapter 4).

[25] Weber (1978: 24–26). Weber's types of social action are 'instrumentally rational', 'value-rational', 'affectual' and 'traditional'.

[26] For some exploratory studies see Cotterrell (2006).

[27] Bonell (1995), Levy (1950).

[28] On this theme, see Selznick (1992: Chapter 4), and Cotterrell (1999: 201–4).

[29] Santos (2002: 177, 296).

References

Barber, Benjamin R. (1993), 'Global Democracy or Global Law: Which Comes First?', *Indiana Journal of Global Legal Studies*, Vol. 1: 119–37.

Bonell, Michael Joachim (1995), 'The UNIDROIT Principles of International Commercial Contracts', in R. Cotterrell, ed., *Process and Substance: Butterworth Lectures on Comparative Law 1994* (London: Butterworth): 45–74.

Cohen, Anthony P. (1985), *The Symbolic Construction of Community* (London: Routledge).

Cotterrell, Roger (1999), *Emile Durkheim: Law in a Moral Domain* (Stanford: Stanford University Press; Edinburgh: Edinburgh University Press).

—— (2003), *The Politics of Jurisprudence: A Critical Introduction to Legal Philosophy* (Oxford: Oxford University Press; London: LexisNexis).

—— (2006), *Law, Culture and Society: Legal Ideas in the Mirror of Social Theory* (Aldershot: Ashgate).

Curran, Vivian Grosswald (1998), 'Cultural Immersion, Difference and Categories in US Comparative Law', *American Journal of Comparative Law*, Vol. 46: 43–92.

Demleitner, Nora V. (1999), 'Combating Legal Ethnocentrism: Comparative Law Sets Boundaries', *Arizona State Law Journal*, Vol. 31: 737–62.

Dezalay, Yves and Bryant G. Garth (1996), *Dealing in Virtue: International Commercial Arbitration and the Construction of a Transnational Legal Order* (Chicago: University of Chicago Press).

Dodd, Vikram, Tania Branigan and Charlotte Higgins (2004), 'Arts and Community Leaders to Discuss Freedom of Expression', *The Guardian*, 22 December.

Durkheim, Émile (1982), *The Rules of Sociological Method and Selected Texts on Sociology and its Method*, translated by W.D. Halls (London: Macmillan).

Freeman, Michael (1995), 'The Morality of Cultural Pluralism', *International Journal of Children's Rights*, Vol. 3: 1–17.

Gurvitch, Georges (1947), *Sociology of Law* (London: Routledge & Kegan Paul).

Haring, Douglas G. (1949), 'Is "Culture" Definable?', *American Sociological Review*, Vol. 14: 26–32.

Kotak, Ash (2004), 'Not In Our Gurdwaras: My Generation of Asian Writers Has Reason To Provoke', *The Guardian*, 21 December.

Legrand, Pierre (1999), *Fragments on Law-as-Culture* (Deventer: W.E.J. Tjeenk Willink).

—— (2006), 'Antivonbar', *Journal of Comparative Law*, Vol. 1: 13–40.

Levy, Ernst (1950), 'The Reception of Highly Developed Legal Systems by Peoples of Different Cultures', *Washington Law Review*, Vol. 25: 233–45.

Murphy, John, ed. (2000), *Ethnic Minorities, Their Families and the Law* (Oxford: Hart).

Radcliffe-Brown, A.R. (1940), 'On Social Structure'; reprinted in Adam Kuper, ed., *The Social Anthropology of Radcliffe-Brown* (London: Routledge & Kegan Paul, 1977): 25–41.

Renteln, Alison Dundes (2004), *The Cultural Defense* (New York: Oxford University Press).

Santos, Bonaventura de Sousa (2002), *Toward a New Legal Common Sense: Law, Globalization and Emancipation*, second ed. (London: Butterworth).

Selznick, Philip (1992), *The Moral Commonwealth: Social Theory and the Promise of Community* (Berkeley: University of California Press).

Shadid, W. and P.S. Van Koningsveld (2005), 'Muslim Dress in Europe: Debates on the Headscarf', *Journal of Islamic Studies*, Vol. 16: 35–61.

Shah, Prakash (2005), *Legal Pluralism in Conflict: Coping with Cultural Diversity in Law* (London: Glass House Press).

Vanderlinden, Jacques (2002), 'Religious Laws as Systems of Laws: A Comparatist's View', in Andrew Huxley, ed., *Religion, Law and Tradition: Comparative Studies in Religious Law* (London: Routledge Curzon): 165–82.

Watson, Alan (1993), *Legal Transplants*, second ed. (Athens, Georgia: University of Georgia Press).

Weber, Max (1978), *Economy and Society: An Outline of Interpretive Sociology*, translated by E. Fischoff *et al.* (Berkeley: University of California Press).

Cultures of Criticism

Tim Murphy

The Orient does not endure the kind of inconsiderate critique, either of itself or of others, in which all European progress is grounded. The very critique of what exists, of the state and nature, of God and human beings, of principles of faith and prejudices – this power of making distinctions, which embraces every-thing, calls it into question, doubts it, and investigates it, is a basic element of European life, without which that life is unthinkable.[1]

Karl Loewith

What does it mean to be critical? And what is the value of criticism? Is criticism something other than, more than, discussion, debate, the exchange of views? 'Critique' and the critique of law must be seen as a genre or cultural practice. But 'critique' needs to be disaggregated. The core of the idea is not a method or process. Rather, it is an attitude, a way of challenging 'what is' and the techniques used necessarily depend on how 'what is' is assembled.

The law school and its professors have served as the producers and guard-ians of orthodoxy. The same may be equally true in other disciplines, though I suspect that in legal studies there have long been particular pressures which work in this direction. The heterodox can thus be subversive rather than innovative; from time to time this will require their works to be anathematized. And the discipline, if we should call it that, has had in recent years a distinctive character of (selectively) orthodoxizing the once critical. Human Rights is the best current example in western law schools. That this happens is concealed by the illusion which results from the agonistic character of the orthodox academy: because it is already the home of thrust and parry, how can it be accused of 'dogmatism'? Perhaps to be critical in this environment, and to be heard to be critical, demands at very least a certain stridency of tone and this explains the necessity of the language of combat for the promoters of heterodoxy. Moreover, to the extent that US Americans assume that they take their law more seriously than most, perhaps these 'struggles' and the dramatic self-presenting which accompanies them, are even a way of enacting the social drama for the next generation of the elite.

But practices of criticism are located within cultures – intellectual, moral, legal, political. Whether Loewith's claim, with which I began, is true is less important than what it implies. Those who work in Western universities often complain that 'Asian' students – and potential staff in a hiring or recruitment context, for example – are (too) subservient.[2] 'Critical' or 'independent' thought is said to be something they often find difficult, being accustomed to be deferential (or respectful) to their teachers. This is one symptom of criticism being something culture-bound itself.

Of course, what culture 'is' is a complicated question in its own right. Is it something national, regional or local? Is it gendered? Is it ethnicized, and if so (since multiculturalism is often modernspeak for what used to be called multiracialism), what are the implications? To resort to culture, in other words, may be to introduce a range of new problems which far from shedding light on the original one serve only to obscure it. What is 'Indian' or 'Chinese' or even 'Japanese'? What is 'European'? Loewith seems to know what he is talking about, but does he?[3]

In the current context of supposed globalization, this is especially difficult. We all speak the language of human rights, we inhabit a universalized world with a lingua franca of democracy and the rule of law (in this context, India is frequently hailed in political rhetoric as Asia's oldest democracy). But do we all mean the same thing, and how do we tell if we do, and in any event *should* we all mean the same thing?

I address some of these issues by working through the following genres: (i) Mirrors for Princes and Admonishment of Rulers; (ii) Self-Criticism; (iii) 'Modern' Critique: Dogmatism and Criticism; (iv) Science, Social Science and Anti-Science as Criticism; (v) 'Neo-cons' and Critique. The concluding section examines the limits of culturalism and re-examines the familiar distinction between transcultural universals and cultural particularisms.

Mirrors for Princes and Admonishment of Rulers

Mirrors are essentially instruction manuals for rulers, codes, dos and don'ts. They presuppose institutions of rulership (rather than democracy, for example)[4] and, in that sense, they offer a mirror in which a ruler (or more loosely anyone with 'power') can see himself as a ruler and obtain a clear sense of his rights and responsibilities and of the opportunities and dangers which confront and surround him. Occasionally, but only occasionally, for 'him' we can substitute 'her', but these female rulers are still 'princes' in this scheme of things.

Admonishments of rulers often involve ritualized occasions in which criticism is addressed to rulers. These presuppose the existence of codes for rulers, a framework in terms of which a ruler's performance can be assessed and critiqued. These frameworks can be irrational to modern critical eyes. In China, it is commonly said, earthquakes and other natural disasters were 'signs' that the Mandate of Heaven had been withdrawn from the then-ruling dynasty. They justified peasant revolts and a more general abandonment of support or at least tolerance for the regime in place. We are beyond such superstitions perhaps: Harold Wilson, British Prime Minister in 1966, called an election after England won the World Cup. We now call this the 'feel-good factor'. There is little room (or need) for Weberian concepts of legitimacy in all this.

Both examples are, in a sense, legalistic. But to ask the Prince to respect the laws and/or to uphold and enforce them (or to provide mechanisms for these tasks) is often only one aspect, and not the foremost, of these genres. Often, terms like morality, virtue, order (or orderliness) are more central, and law is a distinctly secondary feature. States of exception, the duties of rulers in emergencies, can, and commonly do, override such narrow concerns.[5] In a society of rulership, analogies can work both up and down: fathers can be conceived as princes or princes as fathers of families: either way, morality, in a broad sense, can overwhelm the minutiae of the law.

All of these long-established genres can hit the rocks when it is rulership itself which comes into question. In an aspiring, emergent or actual democracy[6] when rulers become (public) servants, one ends up unsure what service means or what the public whom they serve is supposed to be.

Is there a cultural dimension here? Perhaps we should just say that there are cultural differences which flow from established but different styles of rulership.[7] This may also affect the way in which transitions towards and subsequent practices of democracy can and/or do take place.[8] We should also be aware of the influence of culture upon rulership, but here we need to distinguish cultural schemes which are internal to rulership systems from those in circulation in the wider societies over which rulership claims to exert its command or influence.[9]

Self-Criticism

I used to think that this genre was closely caught up with the particular metaphysics of Christianity. Now I am not so sure. To be sure, the malign influence of Christianity has colonized the minds of much of the world – but not, in general terms, in China. But Confucianism, never mind Marxism (with or without Chinese characteristics), seems to endorse a confessional mode, a mode of self-rectification, which cannot be explained by means of the Christian landscape of the soul and its teleology and eschatology.

Self-criticism presupposes what Bourdieu called a *doxa*, an understanding, often formulaic, of 'how things are'.[10] It often includes, as well, an eschatology – a doctrine of how things must/will end. Since eschatology is often muddled up with teleology, a common basis for self-criticism is interference with the 'natural' processes of history – being a blockage on the path to progress or diverting history's natural flow. The *doxa* in the background which makes all this possible, which sometimes demands these self-immolating acts, provides a songsheet against which individuals or groups can register and proclaim their deviations from the truth (the true way). Epistemology (how we know what is true) is unnecessary in this situation.

The institutionalization of this is commonly in the show-trial. 'Show-trial' means quite precisely that the trial becomes a public theatre. It tells us something about legal processes that this mechanism has been widely found to be valuable, even legitimate. But again, this is not the exclusive mechanism through which self-criticism works. Mea culpa can operate through the penitential system of Catholicism; through 'apologies to the House' in the British parliamentary system and its imitators.

European traditions (I use this term merely geographically) abound with these themes at different times (although 'we were wrong' is not exactly shouted loudly in the current triumphalism). The rooting out of heresy was an enthusiastic if sporadic project of the Middle Ages.[11] After the Second World War, in the European theatre, denazification became a primary strategy for those with nothing better to do.[12] Whether or not one would say 'sorry' was and remains a pivotal issue, as the post-war career of Heidegger, for example, illustrates. But what is the meaning of this 'sorry'?[13] China expects Japan to say 'sorry' for what it did in Nanking (now Nanjing). What difference would this 'sorry' make? For all the important FDI flowing from Japan and the reciprocal importance of trade between the two countries (helping among other things to revive the Japanese economy) 'sorry' in this context, seems to be the hardest word.[14]

'Modern' Critique: Dogmatism and Criticism

Dogmatism presents a wide landscape. The core idea is that of religion and the core critical stance is the Enlightenment attitude encouraged by Kant.

This mode of critique imposes no limits upon itself. The need to escape from dogmatism remains, although we have new dogmatisms. Critique now takes the form of 'theory', which is ironic given the origins of critique in a scepticism about metaphysical claims. What is the purpose of this stance of critique, what are its methods if any and what are the presuppositions of any methods which might be used?

Two come to mind without difficulty: the critique of dogmatism in any form; the critique of law specifically for betraying its claims or pretensions to equality and universalism in relation to those within its zones of application.

A good example of the latter is this:

> But what rule of law? What rule of law where the law did not even remotely issue from the will of the people; where Indians, denied the right to vote for most of the duration of British rule, were allowed, during its last thirty years, only a restricted franchise which took decades of struggle and incalculable amounts of physical and spiritual pain to increase from three percent of the adult population to fourteen percent? What rule of law where the 'law,' during the first hundred years of the raj (out of a total of one hundred and ninety), was merely a body of executive orders, decrees, regulations; where, during the next three quarters of a century, all legislative institutions at the central and provincial levels of government were composed either entirely of officials and official nominees or the latter supplemented, for a relatively short period at the height of British constitutionalist magnanimity, by a handful of Indians elected on the

basis of restricted franchise? What rule of law where even the devolution of power left all strategic decisions for the governance of the country as a whole to a central executive made up of a Viceroy nominated by Whitehall, his own nominees recruited from the colonial bureaucracy and a handpicked minority of pliant Indians and Europeans? What rule of law where the execution of the laws, made for the people but not by them, was all too often characterized by double standards – one, until the end of the nineteenth century, for the whites and the other for the natives, and during the remainder of British rule, one for the administrative elite, British and Indian, and the other for the rest of the population?[15]

There are so many contexts in which this mode of critique could be employed. Whether the context permits this employment is another question where once again the question of power and the question of culture become circular.

We need to recognize that power shapes culture rather than the other way round. The way power organizes itself shapes how people think about what is possible or acceptable or normatively correct. This does not mean that 'society' is determined by 'government'. Society must be viewed as an autonomous (semi-autonomous if you must) field. Structures of power determine or influence to a significant extent their metaphysics, imaginaries and so on. This is why revolutions are in these respects not revolutions but rather processes or cycles of the dispossession and repossession of power and influence and property. (We also need to recall the degree to which government and structures of power can determine what otherwise look like cultural or ethnic identities.[16]) What determines power structures is open to argument but what should be beyond argument is that they are open to contingency and path dependency. Culture arrives quite late on this scene if by that we mean a phenomenon which is identifiable and can be interrogated as to its own determining role so far as anything else, including law, is concerned.[17]

Science, Social Science and Anti-Science as Criticism

The problem with science is its capacity to access reality. This is its limit, not its error. This limit simply means that its results are provisional and open to revision. The legacy of dogmatism is more likely to reside in anti-science. But the critique of science as well as of science as the critique of itself (of what then becomes myth) are both rooted in Enlightenment structures. However, each warrants a closer (if necessarily brief) discussion.

The issues which arise here are at first sight peripheral to the current theme of 'enculturing law'. But the whole theme of critique in general, the sense of its possibilities, as well as the meaning of culture itself, are entangled with the moves which scholars and others make in this area. Kant was right to seek to disentangle science from morality and aesthetics, or at least this was an intelligent move given the circumstances of his time. Even absolute rulers, on Kantian criteria, could not object to science and its discoveries, insofar as science and technological progress could be strongly linked.[18] This is also to say that science migrates, after Kant, from an alliance with theology (as natural theology) to an alliance with technology, from which the spiritual was supposed to be banished.[19] When we enter this phase of critique, we encounter what could be called the 'feel-good' factor – the dream of making the world, or, more precisely, human society, a better place without (too much) pain.[20]

Science once presented a way of contesting the dogmatisms of religion. This style of critique may still have resonance in some parts of the world, and not just in the so-called developing parts of this world.

The relevance of this to the theme of 'enculturing law' is twofold. First, issues or conflicts in law and science arise with increasing frequency and how science is to be positioned in this equation may well not be culturally neutral. Take, as an example, the question of homosexuality. Is this a cultural or scientific question, and even if it is scientific, is this independent of culture?

The second zone of relevance concerns the social sciences. Here what is central is the discipline of economics. Scientificity and what this epistemic model really entails is central. Adam Smith opened up what we would now call a debate about what traditional governmental techniques could achieve (or not). Scientific economics seeks to enumerate and calculate the flows of people and things through the world. As such, it is easily exposed to critique. Whether this has to take the form of ideological critique is another matter.[21]

Neocons and Critique

'Critique' has been linked, as I have tried to stress, with a particular set of ideas about material progress, societal development and political participation which arose in the rather specific context of state formation in the west. More recently, although only quite recently, these themes have been unrolled as global themes, and concepts once developed to analyse or moralize about particular western states have also been shouted around, like 'global civil society'.

Of course, there is no reason why other societies should not aspire to these ideals if 'ideals' is what they are. Freedom is one thing: it means, essentially, leaving people to get on with living their lives (the interminable philosophical discussions of this theme simply suggest how difficult it is in modern circumstances to accept the idea that government should not care, should not try to shape culture). But if freedom in the sense of being left alone is one thing, the capacity of people to deal with their situations is another. This becomes the responsibility of the government. Incapacitated peoples need to be 'empowered'.

The 'neocon' label derives as we know from contemporary developments in the politics of the US although it has spawned satellites or derivatives elsewhere. In the current so-called liberal world order, this mode of thinking surely counts as critical in the sense that it raises questions, challenges orthodoxies, asks why and so on. It may seem part of the current (but in my view probably ephemeral) US orthodoxy, but the whole basis of this mode of critique is to attack what it takes to be the liberal *doxa* and replace it with a new *doxa* which is at the same time not very dogmatic. However, there are broadly two forms this type of critique can take.

The first, and most articulate, is the kind of critique asserted most lucidly by Hayek in his famous work *The Road to Serfdom*.[22] In a country like India, this should be readily understood. This does not make Hayek right but thematically available as a mode of critique.

Hayek's argument involved a romanticized or unachievable sense of the rule of law and the concept of minimal role of the state which it advocates – provision of traffic lights, but no economic planning – is something which governments have found it impossible to adopt. Currently, this is widely deployed in discussions of China and the limits on its progress.

The second mode can be associated with Carl Schmitt, and could be called romantic conservatism, although such a label would blur the acuity of the critique and bury the questions which it raises.

Both Hayek and Schmitt were twentieth century figures. In each case, we can identify precursors. Adam Smith prefigures Hayek in some respects, to the extent that we can compare mercantilism and socialist planning (a comparison which cannot, however, be stretched too far). There are limited comparisons which can be drawn, too, between Weimar Germany and the immediate post-revolutionary situation in France, regarding Schmitt and, one might add, Leo Strauss.[23]

The neocon perspective takes on a new edge once it is thought that the judiciary has 'gone soft' or become 'liberal'. This is very much the case in the mediatized politics in Britain, especially after the introduction of the Human Rights Act, but it also is relevant in the United States. If critique used to be conducted in the name of equality, now it tends to focus on precisely these projects (and they are seen as projects, on the assumption that individuals in society will never be equal).

The Limits of Culturalism: Transcultural Universals and Cultural Particularisms

Enculturing law cannot be discussed without raising this problem of cultures and universals. But which side is meant to be a critique of which? For us, is there no escape from the starting point in the debates which are located or entrenched in science? Are there human universals independent of culture? What is hardwired? And how do we get from these kinds of questions to the normative questions about whether certain rights or freedoms should be universal or whether any universalist claims are just updated instances of Western imperialism?

At this point, there is a danger within Western (and not just Western – see the Asian values) literature[24] of losing touch almost completely with reality. One example is the way in which, in recent years, the term 'cosmopolitanism' has entered the field as some normative ideal. With it comes a lot of rather empty but well-intentioned noise about international law.[25] Behind all this, if only as a discursive device to confer academic depth, is the shadow of Kant.[26] International conferences, sustained by cheap international travel, bring only a slender segment of the world 'together'.

In what the West now considers to be its tradition, the law cares about individuals.[27] In marital breakdowns, individual children must have their best interests addressed. In the criminal law, criminal defence lawyers fight for their clients, exploiting every loophole if that will be of help. In sentencing, the judge looks carefully at the individual defendant and on one view should tailor his/her sentence to that individual.

One can affirm the sacredness of individual rights even while acknowledging the deficiencies of judicial decision-making. As a regulative ideal, the individual serves to hold together freedom, self-determination, self-respect and respect for others, and to the extent that these remain ideals to be realized, the progress of the realization of the individual *qua* individual serves as a measure of progress itself.

This concern for the individual is indeed clear among modern North American and European lawyers, especially in their traditional and 'flagship' locale of the courtroom or adjudicative scene. In this domain, probability still bears its old meaning, connecting directly with terms like authority, credit (as in belief), etc. Historically, this legal vision was once the shape of a general social theory, the imprint of which is still visible in, for example, the juxtaposition of the individual and society which we find in Durkheim.

Both sides of this polarity are right. More or less everyone in the so-called international community signs up to universal values. On the other hand, more or less everyone in this same community agrees that making these universal values concrete requires sensitivity to the local situation.

I wish to make a different point and draw attention to a different kind of universal, which takes us beyond values. What gets overlooked in these dreams and fantasies is that this universaling legal scheme of society sits alongside something quite different and to lawyers something often quite disturbing.[28] The key to this other world is that it is the world of the aggregate, not of the individual. If this world is equated with money – with financial numbers – I must insist that this is only one form that the aggregate can take.

Modern government, politics and administration are now largely uncoupled from these legal schemes of the social and operate with the new positivities of the modern social sciences as their horizon. It is here that we find the indicators of performance and the genesis of tasks for government to address and 'solve'. Law becomes external to government – a mere tool or instrument and legislation its dominant mode. Law in the form of adjudication is no longer how government is conducted or how society is known. Indeed, the legal system itself becomes potentially a target of the same performance-driven managerial impulses which come to animate government in the modern age. The point is not that these modern truths articulated in economics and sociology and statistical sciences are more generally 'true' than what went before them or than what is generated in and by the law itself today. The point is rather that a new and quite different way of being 'true' has emerged, a new mode of deployment of the distinction between true and false, and therefore a new way of assessing success and failure.

The world of the aggregate is the world of the superorganism.[29] Behaviour in a society of ants becomes one kind of thought-vehicle for the human world as well.[30] (Indeed we know that the human world is no longer an exclusively human world and that bacteria and machines probably have more of a future ahead of them than we do).[31]

The true 'new world order' is an order of models, simulations, virtualities, projections, estimates and guesstimates, a world of the 'as if' which can only be 'experienced' on paper, in files, on screens. This is why another distinction is important – between experience and empiricism. What this distinction draws attention to is the difference between a world in which one could base truth (and the critique of claims to truth) on what was given to the senses, and our world in which truth is a matter of positivities whose 'truth' guaranteed only by methodology and procedure. In 'our' world, what might be called operational truths – the facts of the world which we know and which serve as the distant horizon of our lives – are largely executive summaries of complex texts, bottom-lines of complex sets of accounts, or to use a different metaphor, the graphical user interface dependent on and fronting up all manner of computer algorithms which most users do not understand.

What results in this situation is something rather strange: the detachment or uncoupling of our experience as people who live and die from the 'reality' of the world in which we live. Of course, the world is the world and there is not much we can do about it except have arguments about it, so by 'world' what I really mean is 'society'.[32] And a further point: our experiences are no longer innocent or our own but 'colonized' by a range of experts in 'subjectivities'. We no longer own ourselves.[33]

This problem is even more acute in legal systems which make extensive use of juries or untrained judges who do not identify with 'The Law'. Modern forensic evidence now places perhaps impossible demands on the common sense of many juries. So too, perhaps, do various aspects of modern organizational behaviour. Finally, one might add that something else changes when modern cost and management accounting principles and practices are applied to either law firms[34] or to court systems themselves. Or, when even those sections of governmental activity concerned with the legal system buy into this life on the screen, the language of organization theory and the positivities of modern social science in formulating their tasks and defining how their achievements are to be assessed.

If we adopt an outsider perspective, what we see rather is a matter of identities and existences which are determined outside, not inside, the law.[35] The law comes into contact with them precisely when we enter the sphere of rights talk. Inside this system of discourse, we conjoin rights with identities and existences fabricated elsewhere. *How* they are fabricated, and why, raise interesting historical and sociological questions.

Critics of my position point to, for example, anti-discrimination laws, and say that I overlook the fact that modern law is also about empowering people (and not just individuals – it is said that I also overlook the significance of class actions). In my view, what these examples tend to show is that adjudication becomes a new ethical space or conscience of society increasingly preoccupied with such issues.[36] This leads to a new situation of impoverished citizenship, political participation and, more importantly, political responsibility and leadership. A plurality of issues and problems are cleared off the desks of the political system and repackaged as 'legal issues for the courts'. Decisions as a result are made irresponsibly and unaccountably by judges and opinion-formation in society is replaced by the 'expert' in agonal production and circulation of the opinions of lawyers. Attempts to dignify this state of affairs with the mantle of a jurisprudence of principles seem to me dubious. However, the moral absolutism involved here, while clearly feeding from the deep reservoir of universalism left to modern legalism by Judaeo–Christian thought, also curiously mirrors in its abstraction the distance from common sense experience, everyday life and mundane discourse which we find equally characteristic of the positivities generated within the modern social sciences.

The nature of the memory of the law will vary from culture to culture. It is certainly part of the cultural history of state formation in the west, although the nature of this memory and the illusions which accompany it vary depending on the differences between the common law or Anglo–American and civil law or French/German legal traditions.

East and Southeast Asian countries, including China, while having their own legal traditions, adopted the (German) civil law model, I assume in emulation of Japan (which in any event imposed it on some countries like Korea). The older Chinese legal tradition is probably linked to a set of memories which most want or have wanted to repress.[37] But what is the meaning of these transplantations of codified law? In terms of my present theme, it creates the perhaps misleading impression that the adoption of western-style law signals the adoption of western values, or at least that it signals the western idea of the value of the individual.

At the same time, 'the West' has the idea that 'the East'[38] is attuned to a different philosophy. We do not need to call this 'Asian values' although many political leaders have. But, in general, the sentiment in the west is that the legacy of Confucianism is deep and that in this mode of thought the individual is subordinated to a wider set of duties and relationships and that the legal valorization of the individual should take second place to the need to resolve disputes in a way which will restore harmony. Socialism with Chinese characteristics was just one spin on this deeply rooted structure of feeling and thought encompassing most of 'the Orient'.

This 'Orient' is a funny place, encompassing so much of the world's population, and therefore so many of the world's cultures. It never really included the India that was embraced within the fold of the Empire.[39] The Orient was somewhere else, somewhere other than India. Or perhaps we need to say that in the western imaginary there were at least two Orients – the despotisms of East Asia with which the west principally sought to trade, and the collapsing despotisms of South Asia which required, eventually, 'empire' if it was to be governed. 'India', and the post-independence states which replaced it, could acquire the benefit of the English language and of English civilization more generally – public schools for the indigenous elite, even the benefit of a university education in England. Even at the end of empire, a certain comfort could be derived from the assumption that the Nehru family spoke English at home. What could not be achieved in inscrutable China – hence, there, the insistence on extraterritoriality – could be achieved in 'India': the transmission of the universal values of the rule of law and, in due course, democracy. Guha's critique, quoted above, argues powerfully that we should not take this at face value. The British Empire left a legacy of ideas about how to govern, as did the French, especially in Africa (arguably, Indochina was too inscrutable for this to happen there, although Vietnam has French-style civil law). But how deeply did these European states penetrate the societies they sought to govern, especially when we look beneath the local elites of these societies?

I would conclude with a paradoxical assertion: the colonial system, as applied to large and complex societies like those who inhabited the Indian subcontinent, involved devoting (limited) governmental resources to the question of understanding the societies being governed (not in a disinterested sense!). This led to a range of cultural dislocations. The British 'third way', the intrusion of an alien power, created divisions. The cultural legacy, as a consequence, was something of a void, an empty space. In particular, following partition, what was Indian? What was Pakistani? Answers to these questions have had to be found, or are in the process of being found. Modernization, globalization and the project of identity formation go together. This conjuncture points to an ambivalent or ambiguous culturalism and does not provide a secure foundation for universalization. Instead, we have a legacy of divisions and rivalries – ethnic, religious, cultural, ideological.

One of the legacies of empire is the return of the colonized to the colonizer's territory and the ongoing issue of how such groups are to be slotted into the societies of the 'mother country'. This term used to be in common use but now sounds rather strange. And this is at the centre of the current global problem: are post-imperial states mother countries? Are their societies? If not, why not? Many 'western' societies are now having to rebrand themselves as 'multicultural'. Few of them know what this means or whether it means anything.

Notes
[1] Loewith (1995).
[2] Sen (2005).
[3] Goswami (2004); Varma (2005); Hong and Murray (2005); Ching (2001). For a critique of negritude, it is still worth consulting Hountondji (1983). For Europe, a provocative discussion is Geary (2002).

[4] There are some interesting exceptions. See Kaufman (1997). For a typically robust approach to the 'Culture' question, see Sperber (1996).

[5] This is the area which Carl Schmitt has made famous and has continued to attract much attention, not least because of the frequency with which emergencies 'arise': see Schmitt (2004); McCormick (1997); Balakrishnan (2000); Cristi (1998); Kennedy (2004); Scheuerman (1999); Agamben (2005). For extended discussion of Neumann's contemporary critique of Schmitt, see Scheuerman (1994). For the continued resonance of the passions Schmitt aroused, among older German scholars at least, see Habermas (1998). Habermas' engagement with Schmitt is also germane to the issues of universalism and particularism which I discuss below and which have received a particular inflection in the intellectual and cultural context of Germany and its modern history.

[6] I do not really know what this is although on this subject there is no shortage of literature.

[7] Blanning (2002).

[8] Lloyd (1996, 2005).

[9] Just a few examples: Burke (1992); Srohm (1988).

[10] Bourdieu (1977).

[11] Hepworth and Turner (1982); Ginsberg (1980) captures the inquisitorial and confessional mode very well.

[12] Cf. 'Letter [from Karl Jaspers] to the Freiburg University Denazification Committee (December 22, 1945), in Wolin (1993); Annan (1996); Overy (2001).

[13] Clearly, self-criticism is often a ritualized response to criticism. One could see these as point-counter-point moments of certain institutionalized political forms. Check the index entries to self-criticism in Fitzpatrick (1999); Dutton (2005); Bakken (2000).

[14] Guha (1997: 66–67).

[15] Torpey (2000); Chua (2003).

[16] Interesting discussion can be found in Chartier (1991).

[17] Although the egalitarian implications of railways were not always welcomed: see Faith (1994: 58ff).

[18] The obvious contrast is with Hume (1998).

[19] Luhmann (1989); Luhmann (1998).

[20] I will skip the usual references to Marx. More pertinent today are Ormerod (1998); in more agitprop mode, Keen (2001).

[21] Hayek (1944).

[22] Masseau (2000) and Masseau 1995).

[23] de Bary and Weiming (1998); Bell and Chaibong (2003); Wei-Ming (1996).

[24] Without attributing these views to him, see the analysis in Koskenniemi (2005), especially the epilogue.

[25] Especially 'Perpetual Peace', in Reiss (1991).

[26] See also my 'Durkheim in China' in Freeman (2006: 107–18).

[27] For the religious (Judaeo–Christian) basis of this, see Murphy (1997: Chapter 2).

[28] I say 'legal'; one observes something similar in some branches of political theory, in electoral politics, and in mass-media-shaped or informed common sense. This is why my argument largely bypasses the issues of democracy and democratization, and certainly doesn't invoke democracy as a solution to all our problems.

[29] Hamilton (1995).

[30] I make no comment about Indian cities, but the experience of the streets of Ho Chi Minh City or Can Tho' might encourage westerners at least in the appropriateness of the ant colony analogy. Resnick (1997) provides stimulating perspectives.

[31] See especially the writings of Latour (1999). Exactly the same process is at work at the sub-individual or micro-human level. One could link the implosion of the unitary or solid individual in some modern sensibilities to the evolving architectures of psychology and psychoanalysis. One could also stress the new significance of genetics and the genetic reduction of the organism.

[32] In Luhmann's sense. See Freeman (2006: 107–18).

[33] Interesting here are Dineen (1999). See also Healy (1993); Berg and Mol (1998).

[34] Though perhaps this is less new in the US than in the UK, see Linowitz (1994).

[35] I have tried to address some of these issues at length in a regrettably hard-to-find essay: 'One of Us? Politics, Difference and Affirmative Action' (1995).

[36] See Murphy (1997: Chapter 8).

[37] As in the Ming and Qing codes.

[38] India, and even Pakistan, are largely excluded from this assumption or prejudice on the basis that they are thoroughly impregnated with common law values and modes of thinking. The biggest challenge in some parts of the farmer Empire (e.g., Malaysia) to this rather complacent attitude is the rise of Sharia law.

[39] For recent discussion of this embrace, see Dirks (2006).

References

Agamben, Giorgio (2005), *State of Exception* (Chicago: University of Chicago Press).

Annan, Noel (1996), *Changing Enemies: The Defeat and Regeneration of Germany* (London: HarperCollins).

Bakken, Borge (2000), *The Exemplary Society: Human Improvement, Social Control, and the Dangers of Modernity in China* (Oxford: Oxford University Press).

Balakrishnan, Gopal (2000), *The Enemy: An Intellectual Portrait of Carl Schmitt* (London: Verso).

Bell, Daniel A. and Hahm Chaibong, eds (2003), *Confucianism for the Modern World* (Cambridge: Cambridge University Press).

Berg, Marc and Annemarie Mol (1998), *Differences in Medicine: Unraveling Practices, Techniques, and Bodies* (Durham: Duke University Press).

Blanning, T.C.W. (2002), *The Culture of Power and the Power of Culture: Old Regime Europe 1660–1789* (Oxford: Oxford University Press).

Bourdieu, Pierre (1977), *Outline of a Theory of Practice* (London: Routledge and Kegan Paul).

Burke, Peter (1992), *The Fabrication of Louis XIV* (New Haven: Yale University Press).

Chartier, Roger (1991), *The Cultural Origins of the French Revolution* (Durham: Duke University Press).

Ching, Leo T.S. (2001), *Becoming 'Japanese': Colonial Taiwan and the Politics of Identity Formation* (Berkeley: University of California Press).

Chua, Amy (2003), *World on Fire* (London: William Heinemann).

Cristi, Renato (1998), *Carl Schmitt and Authoritarian Liberalism: Strong State, Free Economy* (Cardiff: University of Wales Press).

de Bary, William Theodore and Tu Weiming, eds (1998), *Confucianism and Human Rights* (New York: Columbia University Press).

Dineen, Tana (1999), *Manufacturing Victims: What the Psychology Industry is Doing to People* (London: Constable).

Dirks, Nicholas B. (2006), *The Scandal of Empire: India and the Creation of Imperial Britain* (Cambridge, MA: Harvard University Press).

Dutton, Michael (2005), *Policing Chinese Politics: A History* (Durham: Duke University Press).

Faith, Nicholas (1994), *The World the Railways Made* (London: Pimlico).

Fitzpatrick, Sheila (1999), *Everyday Stalinism. Ordinary Life in Extraordinary Times: Soviet Russia in the 1930s* (Oxford: Oxford University Press).

Freeman, Michael, ed. (2006), *Law and Sociology* (Oxford: Oxford University Press).

Geary, Patrick J. (2002), *The Myth of Nations: The Medieval Origins of Europe* (Princeton: Princeton University Press).

Ginzburg, Carlo (1980), *The Cheese and the Worms: The Cosmos of a Sixteenth-Century Miller* (London: Routledge and Kegan Paul).

Goswami, Manu (2004), *Producing India: From Colonial Economy to National Space* (Chicago: University of Chicago Press).

Guha, Ranajit (1997), *Dominance Without Hegemony: History and Power in Colonial India* (Cambridge, MA: Harvard University Press).

Habermas, Jürgen (1998), *A Berlin Republic: Writings on Germany* (Cambridge: Polity Press).

Hamilton, W.D. (1995), *Narrow Roads of Gene Land*, Vol. I: *Evolution of Social Behaviour* (Basingstoke: W.H. Freeman).

Hayek, F.A. (1944), *The Road to Serfdom* (London: Routledge and Kegan Paul).

Healy, David (1993), *Images of Trauma: From Hysteria to Post-Traumatic Stress Disorder* (London: Faber & Faber).

Hepworth, Mike and Bryan S. Turner (1982), *Confession: Studies in Deviance and Religion* (London: Routledge and Kegan Paul).

Hong, Keelung and Stephen O. Murray (2005), *Looking Through Taiwan: American Anthropologists' Collusion with Ethnic Domination* (Lincoln: University of Nebraska Press).

Hountondji, Paulin J. (1983), *African Philosophy: Myth and Reality* (London: Hutchinson).

Hume, David (1998), *Dialogues concerning Natural Religion* (second revised edition; Hackett).

Kaufman, Gerald (1997), *How to be a Minister* (second ed., London: Faber & Faber).

Keen, Steve (2001), *Debunking Economics* (London: Zed Books).

Kennedy, Ellen (2004), *Constitutional Failure: Carl Schmitt in Weimar* (Durham: Duke University Press).

Koskenniemi, Martii (2005), *From Apology to Utopia: The Structure of International Legal Argument* (Cambridge: Cambridge University Press).

Latour, Bruno (1999), *Pandora's Hope: Essays on the Reality of Science Studies* (Cambridge, MA: Harvard University Press).

Linowitz, Sol M. (1994), *The Betrayed Profession: Lawyering at the End of the Twentieth Century* (Baltimore: Johns Hopkins University Press).

Lloyd, G.E.R. (1996), *Adversaries and Authorities: Investigations into Ancient Greek and Chinese Science* (Cambridge: Cambridge University Press).

—— (2005), *The Delusions of Invulnerability: Wisdom and Morality in Ancient Greece, China and Today* (London: Duckworth).

Loewith, Karl (1995), *Martin Heidegger and European Nationalism* (New York: Columbia University Press).

Luhmann, Niklas (1989) *Ecological Communication* (Cambridge: Polity Press).

—— (1998), *Observations on Modernity* (Stanford: Stanford University Press).

McCormick, John P. (1997), *Carl Schmitt's Critique of Liberalism: Against Politics as Technology* (Cambridge: Cambridge University Press).

Masseau, Didier (1995), *Heinrich Meier, Carl Schmitt and Leo Strauss: The Hidden Dialogue* (Chicago: University of Chicago Press).

—— (2000), *Les ennemis des philosophes: L'antiphilosophie au temps des Lumieres* (Paris: Albin Michel).

Murphy, Tim (1995), 'One of Us? Politics, Difference and Affirmative Action', in Jan Broekman, David Kennedy, Jacques Lenoble, eds, XIII *Current Legal Theory Special Issue 2: The Rhetoric of Reconstruction. Architectural Moves beyond Interpretation*: 21–52.

—— (1997), *The Oldest Social Science?* (Oxford: Oxford University Press).

Ormerod, Paul (1998), *Butterfly Economics* (London: Faber & Faber).

Overy, Richard (2001), *Interrogations: The Nazi Elite in Allied Hands* (London: Penguin).

Reiss, Hans, ed. (1991), *Kant: Political Writings* (Cambridge: Cambridge University Press).

Resnick, Mitchell (1997), *Turtles, Termites, and Traffic Jams: Explorations in Massively Parallel Microworlds* (Cambridge, MA: MIT Press).

Scheuerman, William E. (1994), *Between the Norm and the Exception: The Frankfurt School and the Rule of Law* (London: MIT Press).

—— (1999), *Carl Schmitt: The End of Law* (Lanham: Rowman and Littlefield).

Schmitt, Carl (2004), *Legality and Legitimacy* (Durham: Duke University Press).

Sen, Amartya (2005), *The Argumentative Indian: Writings on Indian History, Culture and Identity* (London: Penguin).

Sperber, Dan (1996), *Explaining Culture: A Naturalistic Approach* (Oxford: Blackwell).

Srohm, Paul (1988), *England's Empty Throne: Usurpation and the Language of Legitimation 1399–1422* (New Haven: Yale University Press).

Torpey, John (2000), *The Invention of the Passport: Surveillance, Citizenship and the State* (Cambridge: Cambridge University Press).

Varma, Parva K. (2005), *Being Indian: Inside the Real India* (London: William Heinemann).

Wei-Ming, Tu, ed. (1996), *Confucian Traditions in East Asian Modernity: Moral Education and Economic Culture in Japan and the Four Mini-Dragons* (Cambridge, MA: Harvard University Press).

Wolin, Richard, ed. (1993), *The Heidegger Controversy* (London: MIT Press).

Legal Systems, Legal Traditions and Legal Education

H. Patrick Glenn

Western Legal Education

The most dominant characteristic of western legal education, in the millennium of its existence, has been its hegemonic nature.[1] This may appear surprising, since education is generally seen as benign and even beneficent, but legal education has historically been the single most important technique in the transformation of western societies. At the time of the twelfth-century 'Renaissance' in Europe, legal education was used to transform thinking about social organization and the new, 'rational' lawyers were the primary instrument in overturning the old folk and religious ways, opening the way for secular authority. So, western legal education was hegemonic in the first instance, effecting a transformation of Europe. It did so in developing the methodology, which it has maintained over the last millennium, of teaching only the single law – *ius unum* – which facilitated hegemonic objectives. Europe was largely governed, in terms of wealth and daily activity, by feudal law, but feudal law was not the law taught by the system of legal education. In European law faculties, and the statement is as true for those in England as for those on the Continent, the law which was taught was the remodelled Roman law which acquired the name ius commune. This was a law of private property, consensual obligations, successions and actions, and was largely antithetical to the lives that most people lived. For better or for worse, the law professors undertook the task of overturning the law of the society, and did so very well. The professional instruction in the English Inns of Court was less ambitious and closer to home, but conformed to the overall model of teaching only a single law, that of the Royal courts.

Western legal education thus distinguished between law fit to be taught and law not fit to be taught. Law not fit to be taught had essentially no place in the curriculum, whatever might have been its importance for the society involved. Moreover, there were reasons of the highest order for not opening the law school curriculum to different models of law. The Empire was interested in the law of the Empire, not other laws, and the Church saw its law as necessarily universal in character. Active comparison with other laws, in the teaching process, would necessarily detract from these universalist objectives.[2]

The reaction to the teaching of a law unresponsive to local need and

circumstances eventually came, in Europe, and it resulted essentially in the elimination of teaching of *ius commune* or Roman law. In its place, as a law meant to
be entirely responsive to local need and circumstance, was substituted the law of
the state, completely divorced from any universalist objectives and entirely terri-
torial in character (though incorporating substantial portions of Roman law).
The law taught thus changed radically, from the nineteenth century (in France,
there were governmental inspectors charged with ensuring compliance with the
new curriculum), but the underlying, hegemonic character of western legal education remained. In western law faculties, only one law is taught – originally ius
commune, but for the last two hundred years the law of the state. The teaching
remains essentially hegemonic, since in the circumstances of today's world, the
graduate of a western-style law school has no knowledge of law other than the
one law which has been taught. The law graduate inevitably approaches every
new legal problem, wherever it is encountered in the world and whatever the
context, from the perspective of the single law which has been learned, and with
the implicit understanding that it is acceptable to think only in terms of a single
law. With some good will and basic knowledge of the circumstances of the world,
there will be some receptivity to the law of others, but no knowledge of that law
or of the methods of conciliation in different laws.

At the beginning of the twenty-first century, this is still an accurate description of legal education in western-style law schools. There have been courses
developed in international law (itself a western construction as a means of the coordination of western state structures imposed on the rest of the world), philosophy of law (concentrating entirely on western legal philosophy), comparative
law (concentrating on classifying or describing national legal systems, again as
western constructions, and profoundly unsuccessful in pedagogical terms) and a
further range of optional, under-attended and marginal courses which depend
more on the personal interests of individual professors than on any coherent
policy of legal education.

Since the overthrow of ius commune (indicative, however, of the possibility of major curriculum change) and the turn to state law, western legal education has been profoundly influenced by the notion of the national legal system.
State law is taught as a system, and this has profound consequences for what is
taught and the manner of its teaching. The teaching remains hegemonic, in concentrating almost exclusively on a single source of law, but theoretical justification is provided by the argument that law is best thought of in systemic terms.
This requires that some attention be paid to the concept of a legal system as an
obstacle to curriculum reform and the 'enculturing' of legal education.

Legal Systems

Contemporary legal positivists treat state law as a fact. It has been formally enacted, in structured and systemic form, and it has engendered, in the
language of Herbert Hart, a social fact of obedience (at least in the best of
circumstances).[3] Kelsen spoke of the necessary 'efficiency' of the national legal

system.[4] State law would thus represent a fundamental legal reality which legal education could not ignore. In the most developed and internally consistent positivist thought, it is maintained, and even argued strenuously, that the state legal system gives rise to no obligation to obey the law.[5] It simply exists as fact, and facts cannot give rise to obligations. So long as it is factually efficient, however, people will tend to obey it, realizing that disobedience may attract sanctions for targeted behaviour, even if one cannot speak of obligation.

This fundamental, factual, character of the national legal system would be its great strength, in contrast to other claims of normativity. It would justify the ongoing exclusivity of instruction in state law. Yet there are a number of other features of the national legal system which contribute in a more specific fashion to the grip which the concept of system presently maintains on western-style legal education.

First, the notion of a legal *system* is one which necessarily entails exclusivity. A system, according to the theory of systems, is a bounded cadre within which the elements of the system are in interaction. Within the cadre of the system, there are, therefore, only the elements of the system which form a non-contradictory field of meaning, and the legal system is, therefore, incompatible with other forms of law on the same territory. The national systems would thus have eradicated the plurality of laws which existed (taught or not) in particular territories in Europe. Hart specifically states that '[t]he legal system of a modern state is characterized by a certain kind of *supremacy* within its territory and *independence* of other systems. . .'.[6] Kelsen speaks of the relations between 'norm systems' as being either those of independence or subordination, such that co-existence implies subordination.[7] Joseph Raz has explained that '[a]ll legal systems . . . are potentially incompatible at least to a certain extent. Since all legal systems claim to be supreme with respect to their subject-community, none can acknowledge any claims to supremacy over the same community which may be made by another legal system'.[8] Teaching of law other than state law, in a western law school, must, therefore, necessarily be peripheral, since it is not law, or law not fit to be taught. This is well-reflected in most law school curricula and degree requirements.

Second, the notion of a legal system is incapable of reconciliation with other laws. The system purports to be exclusive, but even in the face of other laws which would somehow, inexplicably, be present in the territory of state law, the state system is incapable of being reconciled with such other laws. In the language of the explanatory statement for this conference, teaching and learning of law has thus remained 'a self-referential enterprize'. This follows from the fundamentally factual character of the legal system. As something which simply exists, it is unaccompanied by normative information which would address the question of when and whether it should yield to non-state law. It has no flexibility, no possibility of self-effacement, no possibility of co-ordination with law other than itself. It cannot be argued with. It simply sits there, a very large, dumb animal which displaces all else in its physical area. This is evident also in the reaction of the lawyers of the system to systemic criticism. They usually simply ignore it, and this explains the impervious character of the core curriculum of western-style law faculties. Systemic criticism, or the alternatives which other laws or the social sciences would provide, can be ignored because so long as the legal system exists, as a fact, it necessarily displaces all other normative claims and can be worked within. In the language of Niklas Luhmann, the legal system is 'operatively closed'.[9] Confirmation of this is found also in the resistance of lawyers of the system to any idea that legal systems exist *as a matter of degree*.[10] In spite of the existence of states in varying degrees of failure in the world, and in spite of widespread corruption in most national legal systems, theoretical positivists are steadfast in their insistence that legal systems either exist or do not exist, and that there can be no degrees or variation in the state of their existence. Degrees of existence of systems would require explanation; the social fact of obedience would be put into question; normative explanation would be required; and the legal system would lose its fundamental factual importance. So the legal system cannot be required to explain or justify itself, given its simple existence. Since it cannot be required to justify itself, it cannot be allowed to develop normative justification for reconciliation with other laws and necessarily, in certain circumstances, yielding to other laws. The fact of its existence provides no reasons for doing so.

Third, to the extent that some factual circumstances actually cross the boundaries of states and national legal systems, state law deals with such problems in terms of largely geographical criteria of whether or not state law applies. Once again, there are no degrees of application, or questions of substantive justice, but rather an essentially conflictual reading of the relations of the laws of the world. This is why the notion of conflicts of laws became so important in the nineteenth and twentieth centuries, since the relations between exclusivist constructions can only be conflictual when the two constructions come into contact. In the Indian dance of Kuchipudi, conflictual relations are expressed as closed fists, which do not strike one another or other objects, but which are rather slowly brought into contact with one another. There is no room to manoeuver; one fist or the other must give way. In contrast, notions of reconciliation and interdependence are indicated, again by the hand gestures of the dance, as two hands approaching one another so that the extended fingers intertwine. Here there is room and reason for reconciliation. We learn from Indian dance that relations between peoples and things need not be conceptualized in a mutually exclusive, conflictual manner, and that there are other possible conceptual constructions than those of national legal systems. This, however, involves going outside the system, yet in a way which is not destructive of it, since there are never any revolutions in law, as opposed to politics, and legal change is always gradual in character. This brings us to the concept of legal tradition and its relation to that of the legal system.[11]

Legal Traditions

The notion of tradition has been the object of great vilification in the western world. Edward Shils concluded that it was not only *the* tradition of the *ancien régime* which the 'enlightenment' sought to eliminate, but the concept of tradition itself.[12] This would leave the field free to contemporary rationality, to modernity, and then to postmodernity. This is still how the popular, western world largely conceives itself but there are now indications of the theoretical recognition that the western tradition is one of many, and that there is need for the reconciliation of them all.[13] The western tradition is one which calls itself modernity. It is a tradition which denies its historical past, and valorizes present rationality, but there is no escaping the historical past which has led to notions of modernity and the valorization of present rationality. Most other people of the world do not think this way, and it took many millennia for western people to come to think this way, so we are essentially dealing with highly developed bodies of normative information, of long standing, which tell us how to live and how to solve our disputes.

Tradition, including legal tradition, is thus best thought of as a body of 'highly self-conscious' information,[14] necessarily normative in character because of its long duration, which would constitute the essential subject matter of today's 'information society'. The 'new orality' of the electronic world, for example, would thus be providing new vitality to oral traditions of previously limited geographical reach. It is true that much of the information which the world generates is simply noise, but the operation of the techniques of tradition, in effecting the necessary capture and transmission of the information of the tradition, eventually eliminates the noise and makes the past readable, and understandable, for those in the present.

As a long-standing body of normative information, tradition has also been castigated in western thought as inherently conservative in character. It is that which must be struggled against, in the name of many desirable reforms. This is a very particularized and inaccurate view of the real force of tradition. It is particularized because it derives from the European struggle against the *ancien régime*, a tradition well-worthy of being overthrown in many of its characteristics (social classes, privilege, corruption, etc.). It is inaccurate because the tradition was overthrown not on the basis simply of present rationality, whatever that might be, but because the reformers of the enlightenment justified their conduct by appealing to sources of rationality recognized to have originated with the Greeks. Hence we have the word 'revolution,' which involves a return, or revolving to an original, earlier position. In astronomy, this meant, for Copernicus,[15] the return of a planet or moon to the point of origin of its orbit. In revolutionary politics, it meant resort to an alternative tradition of rationality as a means of reform. The word 'revolution' thus acknowledges the *ancienneté* of the rationalist tradition, as well as the disruptive and legitimizing force of alternate traditions. In arguing for reform of western legal education, I find the notion of tradition essential in overcoming the grip of the idea of a legal system.

From within a legal system, the view is limited, since the system is exclusive, irreconcilable with other laws and conflictual in character. To critique the system, and make it respond to claims of alternative normativity, it is necessary to stand outside it and make it justify itself. The large, dumb animal must be made to speak. The social sciences attempt to do this in some measure, but lawyers of legal systems have been remarkably resistant to critiques coming from the social sciences, for reasons which will have to be returned to. Standing outside the system, an effective critique of it must nevertheless come from a recognizably legal position, or one at least potentially recognizable as legal. The notion of a legal tradition thus stands in an intermediate position between that of a legal system and that of tradition or culture in general. The legal tradition would be both cognitively and normatively open to what is known as culture, and would provide the legal underpinning of the system. Three avenues open up in this regard. They all have the effect of surrounding legal systems and requiring them to justify themselves.

The first avenue of critique is through the history, and even pre-history, of legal systems themselves. Positive legal thought grounds legal systems on contemporary social facts of obedience (Hart) or efficiency in operation (Kelsen). But, one may well ask, where did these ideas come from? In philosophy, the idea of a 'fact' is now questioned, as it is in legal traditions other than western, so it can be demonstrated that the standard definitions of a legal system are historically grounded.[16] Legal systems would not be grounded on what positivists say they are, since that is a definition internal to the systemic, positive, manner of thought. Legal systems would rather be grounded on the thought, or tradition, which enabled positive legal theorists to reach these conclusions. Legal systems are thus best conceptualized as instantiations of a particular legal tradition. As such, they are conceptually equal to, and on a par with, other legal traditions, which all exist as self-conscious bodies of legal information, sustained over considerable periods of time. So one can stand outside western legal systems, as a western lawyer, but still stand within law, by placing oneself within a western legal tradition, and even a western tradition of positive law and legal systems (now cognizant of its traditional character). There would thus be an underlying common law, or ius publicum, justifying the range of distinct states which emerged in Europe and the world.[17] This tradition is not dumb; it speaks to the need and justification for legal systems, and is capable both of recognizing their weaknesses, their need for reinforcement, and degrees of effectiveness in their implementation. Western legal tradition is normative; it speaks to questions which legal systems, as purported facts, are unable to speak to. This is why Article 6 of the Treaty of Amsterdam of the European Union speaks of Europe's 'common constitutional traditions', since it is necessary to resort to such underlying common tradition as a means of critiquing, and going beyond, the national systems of Europe.

The second avenue of legal critique is through the juxtaposition of the national legal system with other legal traditions within the national territory.

This cannot be done by legal theorists posing abstract questions. There is a large and important empirical requirement, which is that of a population which adheres to non-state normativity, and an equally important procedural requirement of accessibility to formal institutions of adjudication on the part of this population. These requirements are now met in many of the jurisdictions where the idea of a legal system has been well-received, such that the concept of an exclusive system is now challenged from within. Once this happens, once it is recognized that there is a challenge by lawyers, raising justiciable issues, to the exclusivity of the system, the system can be made to respond, to argue back and even to yield to other forms of normativity which thus come to be recognized as law. In Canada, until the 1970s, the Canadian government rejected the negotiation of claims of aboriginal or chthonic peoples as too 'vague' for legal recognition. This position changed once the Supreme Court recognized the justiciability of these claims.[18] A tradition of unwritten law was thus recognized as a *legal* tradition; as a legal tradition, it required a response from the state legal system, now more clearly recognizable as an alternative tradition and no longer a large, dumb animal. In Australia as well, the lex non scripta of the Australian aborigines is now explicitly designated as 'traditional law'.[19] Parties may also adopt non-state law by contract, and it transpires that state law will yield to such law in most instances, since its own law of contract turns out not to be of mandatory application. Islamic financing is thus of increasing importance in many non-Islamic jurisdictions, since state law provides no obstacle to its choice. The concept of tradition is thus an accommodative one. It encompasses many different types of law, including that of the state. And since tradition is defined in terms of information, the information of each tradition is accessible to the others, so the possibilities of dialogue and conciliation are enhanced.

The third avenue of legal critique has today become the most evident, and it is through the development of law which surpasses and influences the law of the national legal system. Transnational law is not international law. It regulates not the relations of states, but the relations of non-state actors, and in a substantive manner. There would thus today be a transnational *lex mercatoria*, a transnational law of human rights, a transnational Islamic law, a transnational Hindu law (both of which reappear as justification for normative claims made by minorities within western states), a transnational criminal law (applied in tribunals created by treaties of international law) and the ongoing transnational common laws which have survived the period of nationalization of law and now contribute greatly to transnational judicial collaboration.[20] These are all laws which lack the systemic and formal characteristics of state law, so the best and perhaps only general description of them is as law rooted in tradition. As normative traditions, they argue for themselves and their content. They are not simply facts and they require response from the lawyers of the state. Possibilities of reconciliation are thus generated.

These three means of critique of the national legal system all rely on other concepts of law as a means of challenge to state law. As laws often of long standing, they are necessarily powerful instruments. What of the social sciences and humanities? Can they make the dumb animal of the national system speak and justify itself, or will the dumb animal continue its mute hegemony? This depends at least in part on the other disciplines themselves. It is said by many that the social sciences today are in crisis, even that they have failed entirely, notably through emulation of the physical sciences in attempting to impose general laws of behaviour on a fractious humanity.[21] To the extent that other disciplines use legal examples as simple artefacts, in pursuit of general laws of behaviour, it is likely that they will not have a great effect on those working within the systems.[22] Legal education will continue to ignore them, or acknowledge them as entirely peripheral phenomena. One can, however, envision the social sciences and humanities playing a more constructive role, in working within categories and concepts recognized as legal, providing explanatory, critical and even legitimating information which the bare texts of the law cannot provide.

There remains the question of how such different legal traditions, and different perspectives on law, can be integrated into a law school curriculum.

Teaching Legal Traditions

It is difficult to reform a law school curriculum. The manner and content of legal education is a tradition of long standing. As a tradition it is not binding law (though in some states it is set out in legislation), but Roscoe Pound wisely spoke of 'the power of the taught tradition'. Reform must overcome a millennium of teaching an *us unum*, though it may come about, in much the same manner as state law is challenged in application. It is thus necessary to teach other traditions which challenge those of state law, in terms of historical legitimacy and historical importance. There are two main problems.

The first is to obtain recognition from those presently engaged in teaching state law that other forms of legal normativity deserve instruction, and in a way which is non-peripheral. In current language, courses in non-state law must be 'mainstreamed' so that they no longer occupy a peripheral place in the curriculum (assuming they have any present place whatsoever). In the Canadian law school recently established in the Inuit territory of Nunavut, Inuit law was not originally taught, but, after student protest it came to be taught, and in an obligatory manner for all students. In my law school, McGill, the civil and common laws have long been mainstreamed,[23] since both degrees are awarded, but we are now embarking on an enquiry as to how best to mainstream aboriginal law in Canada. This would involve bringing aboriginal law into standard courses, such that the standard course on contract would include discussion of aboriginal concepts of a collective contract. The University of Michigan in the United States has recently amended the classic, first-year, private-law curriculum to include an obligatory course in transnational law, in its many dimensions. There are many other examples.

The second problem relates to the manner of instruction of non-state law. The traditional means of instruction of western law are generally unsuitable. This is obviously the case for instruction in oral legal traditions, such as adat law in Southeast Asia, but it is a question of the most appropriate and effective means of instruction in all forms of law which do not conform to western theories of legal sources. Here there is much room for legal and pedagogical imagination, and reason for optimism, since the last quarter century has seen great progress in expansion of the field and legal instruction. The ability of lawyers to deal effectively with the many laws of the world is thereby enhanced.

Notes

[1] Glenn (2004: 11).

[2] For fear of 'contamination' through active comparison of laws, see Thunis (2004: 6).

[3] Regarding the view that obedience on part of the 'bulk of the population' is 'all the evidence we need', see Hart (1994: 114) and the need for obedience by the general population and acceptance by officials of the system, see Hart (1994: 116).

[4] For the notion of obligation being 'fundamentally' connected with that of sanction, see Kelsen (1967: 115–16).

[5] Raz (1979: 233).

[6] Hart (1994: 24).

[7] Kelsen (1967: 330, 332).

[8] Raz (1979: 119).

[9] Luhmann (2004: 80).

[10] On the tendency of legal philosophers to cling dogmatically to classificatory ideas, rejecting analysis of legal systems as matters of degree, see Füsser (1996: 124, 155).

[11] Glenn (1990: 9).

[12] Shils (1981: 6).

[13] On the changing ways of talking about tradition, see Waldman (1985) who writes about an enlightenment concept prevailing until 1960s, first disturbed by disenchantment with the pace and results of development work founded on a dichotomy between traditional and modern societies, now surviving in a 'criticized form'. Also, Eisenstadt (1973) who mentions the 'widespread dissatisfaction' with the dichotomy between traditional and modern societies which dominated development studies through 1960s; and Phillips and Schochet (2004) who discuss how 'tradition' became lost as a term though not as problem in the social sciences and is currently underused, 'certainly undertheorized'. For the role of Max Weber in this 'ideological polarization', due largely to his 'inadequate education' in medieval thought, Stock (1990: 117–22).

[14] Philips and Schochet (2004: ix).

[15] *De Revolutionibus* (1543).

[16] Putnam (2002: 63) writes that the terms one uses even in description in history and sociology and the other social sciences are invariably ethically coloured. For the history or tradition of the concept of 'fact,' see Shapiro (1994). Shapiro (2000: 3, 9, 11, 60, 107, 110) discusses the notion of fact in medieval common law procedure drawn from the Romano–canonical tradition and then adopted by other disciplines.

[17] Glenn (2005: 52–53).

[18] *Calder v. British Columbia* (1973) S.C.R. 313, 34 D.L.R.(3d) 145.

[19] S.223(1), *Native Titles Act*, as cited in *Yorta Yorta Aboriginal Community v. Victoria* (2002) 194 ALR 538.

[20] For the latter, see Glenn (2003: 839; 2005).

[21] Flyvbjerg (2001). For the persistence of the efforts to use physics as an explanation for economics ('econophysics'), Mantega and Stanley (1999) and Ball (2004).

[22] For such 'nonembedded' scholarship where 'legal artefacts [are] mentioned, at most, as illustrations of problems or solutions', Rakoff (2002).

[23] For the McGill programme, Kasirer (2002), Morissette (2002) and Blackett (1998).

References

Ball, P. (2004), *Critical Mass: How One Thing Leads to Another* (New York: Farrar, Straus and Giroux).

Blackett, A. (1998), 'Globalization and its Ambiguities: Implications for Law School Curricular Reform', 37 *Col. J. Trans. L. 57*.

Eisenstadt, S.N. (1973), 'Post-Traditional Societies and the Continuity and Reconstruction of Tradition', *Daedalus*, No. 1.

Flyvbjerg, B. (2001), *Making Social Science Matter: Why Social Inquiry Fails and How It Can Succeed Again* (Cambridge: Cambridge University Press).

Füsser, K. (1996), 'A Farewell to "Legal Positivism": The Separation Thesis Unravelling', in R. George, ed., *The Autonomy of Law: Essays on Legal Positivism* (Oxford: Clarendon).

Glenn, H.P. (1990), 'Law, Revolution and Rights', Archives for Philosophy of Law and Social Philosophy, Beiheft No. 41, *Revolution and Human Rights*.

——— (2003), 'A Transnational Concept of Law', in P. Cane and M. Tushnet, eds, *The Oxford Handbook of Legal Studies* (Oxford: Oxford University Press).

——— (2004), 'Legal Education and Legal Hegemony', in *Imperialism and Chauvinism in the Law*, Swiss Institute of Comparative Law (Geneva: Schulthess).

——— (2005), *On Common Laws* (Oxford: Oxford University Press).

Hart, H.L.A. (1994), *The Concept of Law*, second ed., (Oxford: Clarendon Press).

Kasirer, N. (2002), 'Bijuralism in Law's Empire and in Law's Cosmos', 52 *Journal of Legal Education* 29.

Kelsen, H. (1967), *Pure Theory of law*, translated by M. Knight (Berkeley/Los Angeles: University of California Press).

Luhmann, N. (2004), *Law as a Social System* (Oxford: Oxford University Press).

Mantega, R. and H. Stanley (1999), *An Introduction to Econophysics* (Cambridge: Cambridge University Press).

Morissette, Y.–M. (2002), 'McGill's Integrated Civil and Common Law Programme', 52 *Journal of Legal Education* 2.

Phillips, M.S. and G. Schochet (2004), 'Preface', in M.S. Philips and G. Schochet, *Questions of Tradition* (Toronto/Buffalo/London: University of Toronto Press).

Putnam, H. (2002), *The Collapse of the Fact/Value Dichotomy* (Cambridge, MA: Harvard University Press).

Rakoff, T. (2002), 'Introduction' to symposium 'Law, Knowledge and the Academy', 115 *Harvard Law Review* 1278.

Raz, J. (1979), 'The Obligation to Obey the Law', in *The Authority of Law: Essays on Law and Morality* (Oxford: Clarendon Press).

Shapiro, B. (1994), 'The Concept "Fact": Legal Origins and Cultural Diffusion', *Albion*, No. 1; reprinted in D. Sugarman, ed. (1996), *Law in History: Histories of Law and Society*, Vol. II (New York: New York University Press).

——— (2000), *A Culture of Fact: England, 1550–1720* (Ithaca/London: Cornell University Press).

Shils, E. (1981), *Tradition* (Chicago: University of Chicago Press).

Stock, B. (1990), *Listening for the Text: On the Uses of the Past* (Baltimore: Johns Hopkins University Press).

Thunis, X. (2004), 'L'empire de la comparaison', in F.R. van der Mensbrugghe, ed., *L'utilisation de la méthode comparative en droit européen* (Namur: Presses universitaires de Namur).

Waldman, M.R. (1985), 'Tradition as a Modality of Change: Islamic Examples', *History of Religions*, No. 25.

Teaching Legal Culture

Volkmar Gessner

Introduction[1]

The last two decades have been characterized by a strong movement toward legalization which may be discussed on a theoretical level, focusing on the assumptions underlying vast literatures, programmes and projects. One approach ('Law and Development'/'Modernization') claims that modernization processes lead naturally to legal structures similar to those that can be observed in western societies, and that global structures will also emerge on the same model. In the domestic sphere, some (such as the post-communist) countries are generally defined as lacking the rule of law while others (such as the Latin American countries) are considered as having a weak court system. In the international realm, legal rules are developed for public policy areas, such as trade, environment, labour, money laundering and copyright, as well as for contract enforcement.[2] Countless international conventions, uniform laws, codes and rules of conduct attempt to regulate the most varied aspects of global dealings by means of uniform rulings. In the area of commercial law, the first objective is predictability and stability in international commercial relations by the establishment of universal standards and the reduction of legal risks of global trade. Unification efforts, therefore, have concentrated on contract law and the resolution of contractual disputes. Development strategies emphasize legal certainty as a prerequisite for a market economy. Most law faculties in western countries have some members, or even entire departments, active in promoting the rule of law in developing countries, in countries in transition from state to market economies or in the global arena where cross-border exchanges lack calculability and certainty.

Another prominent theory often alluded to as justification for legalization is that of Institutional Economics, where rules and institutions are considered mechanisms for effective transaction at a low cost. Institutional economics recognizes non-legal institutions as important and – even in developed economies – ubiquitous limits to individual choices.

> Institutions define the structure of human interaction. By 'institutions', I mean three things: (1) the formal rules of the game that are defined in legal terms, (2)

the informal norms of behavior that supplement and complement and modify institutions, and (3) the effectiveness of enforcement mechanisms. It is the mixture of the three that determines the effectiveness of institutions in influencing transaction costs. And the effect of institutions on transaction costs is obviously important.[3]

Informal norms of behaviour are customs and conventions, standards, rules and values. They define and limit preferences of economic actors either generally or within specific groups (minorities, occupations, geographically bounded industries, age groups etc.). They complement formal rules, compete with them or negate them. Within the school of Institutional Economics, there are some who maintain that welfare maximizing actors use informal rather than formal rules.[4] But the realm of co-operation is limited to close-knit groups. Moving from personal to impersonal markets leads to formalization and institutionalization: when shifting from a world of personal exchange to a world of impersonal exchange (to use a game theory analogy), one moves from a world in which it pays the players to co-operate to a world in which it pays them to defect. Co-operative institutions are replaced by coercive institutions in order to cope with 'free-rider' behaviour. Other forms of coercion being absent, or limited to specific groups or specific situations, legal institutions prove more efficient in limiting choices and reducing uncertainty.

A third theory offered frequently as justification is Max Weber's process of legal rationalization running from traditional, irrational forms to formal, bureaucratic forms of legal domination. Whether legal rationalization is our 'fate' (Weber) and informal rules and institutions are necessarily outdated cannot be taken for granted. New social situations outside the realm of the western nation state might require a reassessment of established theoretical assumptions.

The centrality of law in Weber's theory has to be qualified not so much because of his 'England problem' but for empirical assumptions which hold true neither for developing or transformation countries nor for structures created by the globalizing economy. The observation that England, the birthplace of capitalism, seemed to lack the calculable, logically formal legal system that he identified as necessary for capitalist development, troubled Weber.[5] His discussion on that issue is often considered ambiguous and contradictory.[6] England is certainly a deviant case for a theory of formal legal rationality, but not necessarily for a theory of the centrality of law in modern society. Weber criticized the English common law for its lack of formal rationality and its class bias, but he recognized its importance for the English economy. Due to strong links between the capitalist class and English lawyers, and the lawyers' crucial role in generating precedents, the English legal system was predictable for social and economic elites.[7]

Weber's empirical assumptions leading to his thesis regarding the centrality of law read as follows:

From a purely theoretical point of view, legal guaranty *by the state* is not indispensable to any basic economic phenomenon. The protection of property, for example, can be provided by the mutual aid system of kinship groups. . . . But an economic system, especially of the modern type, could certainly not exist without a legal order with very special features which could not develop except in the frame of a public legal order. Present-day economic life rests on opportunities acquired through contracts. It is true, the private interests in the obligations of contract, and the common interest of all property holders in the mutual protection of property are still considerable, and individuals are still markedly influenced by convention and custom even today. Yet the influence of these factors has declined due to the disintegration of tradition, i.e., of the tradition-determined relationships as well as of the belief in their sacredness. . . Modern economic life by its very nature has destroyed those other associations which used to be the bearers of law and thus of legal guaranties. This has been the result of the development of the market. The universal predominance of the market consociation requires on the one hand a legal system the functioning of which is *calculable* in accordance with rational rules. On the other hand, the constant expansion of the market . . . has favored the monopolization and regulation of all 'legitimate' coercive power by *one* universalist coercive institution through the disintegration of all particularist status-determined and other coercive structures which have been resting mainly on economic monopolies.[8]

The assumption is that the 'modern economy' has destroyed conventions and customs in particularistic structures which previously had guaranteed contract enforcement and the protection of property. The enlargement of markets resulted in the replacement of small-scale regulation by universalistic coercion. Weber thus clearly recognizes informal norms and institutions as equivalent to legal coercion in providing calculability and legal certainty. He only believes that those non-legal norms and non-state institutions have ceased to be relevant in a modern economy.

It is already questionable whether this assumption is correct for modern western economies. Legal sociology and anthropology have produced numerous examples of particularistic regulatory structures, as well as informal universalistic rules, around us. But the absence and irrelevance of non-state regulation in general, and within the economy in particular, can definitely not be assumed for developing and transition countries or the global economy. Hence Weber's main thesis on the central role of law proves not to be universally applicable. If calculability is the only problem for economic actors – which is questionable – law in most societies is not the only remedy.

From Teaching Law to Teaching Legal Culture

The above insights lead to a change in law school curricula – and particularly so if the subject of the course deals with non-western or global law. Rather than law as state law and legal doctrine, it is legal culture which students should try to become familiar with.

Definitional Problems

Legal culture is sometimes taught as a normative discipline encompassing the value systems, concepts and doctrinal principles of a legal system. Hence,
while Roman law is praised as a legal culture, the barbarian societies surrounding the empire lacked a legal culture. Europe developed a legal culture following
the Enlightenment and the French Revolution; one achievement in particular was
the *Rechtsstaat* form of organization of modern western societies. Central and
eastern European countries lost their legal culture during the communist period
and are currently generating a replacement with the assistance of western scholars and institutions. Culture is understood as the product of a cultivation or
civilization process; therefore, this approach is legitimate (at least if the underlying value assumptions are made clear) and very much akin to the teaching of
law in general. It encourages students to engage in the development of a better
society.

A social science course on legal culture cannot adopt this normative
approach since culture is value-neutral. Within Germany, for example, the diverse Weimar, Nazi and Bonn societies developed distinctive autochthonous cultures. The mafia has a culture, as does the Catholic Church.

But this descriptive approach, uncontested in the social sciences, leads to
enormous definitional problems for cultural studies. The narrowest definition
deals only with mental processes (values, attitudes and consciousness), while a
broader definition includes behaviour and the broadest definition considers institutions – disregarding a conceptual difference between structure and culture. In
research, everything goes; but in teaching, one must make a choice from the very
beginning. This is particularly true for a legal cultural curriculum in law school,
which always attempts to add something that is not already taught in courses on
constitutional law, administrative law or procedural law. If law students are
familiar with government, courts, mediators and arbitrators as legal institutions,
they can be taught how actors within these institutions understand their tasks
(administrative cultures, court cultures and cultures of alternative dispute resolution), and how citizens interact with these institutions. The course then explains
the institution (as a dependent variable) through the behavioural patterns of those
who interact within these structures or who approach them or react to their
commands. An institutional, local, regional or national legal culture would then
be the sum of these behaviours, which for their part are dependent on prevailing
values, attitudes or situational constraints.

A crucial question is whether the law is defined as being part of a legal
culture or as a structure potentially modified, accepted or rejected by cultural
patterns. On one hand, one may argue that all rules, formal and informal, are
part of the culture of a society. The coercive power behind state law can hardly
make a difference because some non-legal norms show a similar or even higher
coerciveness than state law. On the other hand, what is the structure of a modern
society if not the law? From the birth certificate to compulsory school attendance
to labour law to pension rights, life, to a large degree, is legally shaped, pushing

other societal structures such as family, class and gender to the background. This Janus-face character of the law should not be hidden in a law school course but should rather be made a focus for discussion: law in its historical development, philosophical background and in its current construction in the minds of professionals and lay people, is a cultural phenomenon. But it is also external, limiting or extending our options – and is too firmly established to be influenced or 'constructed' by every single individual and in every single situation. This description is characteristic of a societal structure.

Coping with Complexity

The approach chosen above for a curriculum on legal culture is considerably more complex than current courses and textbooks, which take the judicial system or the civil courts or litigation rates as indicators of a legal culture. In our textbook, *European Legal Cultures*,[9] we have attempted to develop a manageable way of coping with as many aspects of a legal culture as seem necessary for understanding a particular problem. Understanding a whole legal culture (e.g. the Japanese or the American legal culture) is an option which is not excluded as a theoretical project but which is for the moment too complex to be achieved. This model tries to visualize our approach:

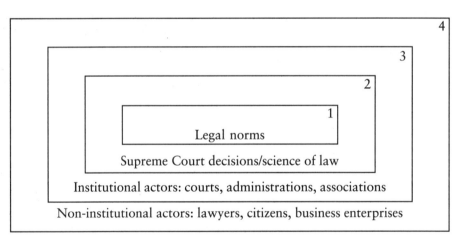

In class, the model helps show the level of complexity at which the instructor is arguing. If a statute, a precedent, a doctrinal position, a legal-philosophical principle or a legal theory is discussed, the legal-cultural complexity stays on its lowest level. But ideas that are abstract and remote from practice and common sense also may be part of a legal culture. Legal sciences contribute to legal culture by producing these abstract ideas, as do legislators when they intentionally generate laws and regulations that disregard implementation problems or that serve as purely symbolic policy. The class will appreciate these ideas in their own right and at the same time, will avoid confusing ideas with social reality.

In some scientific cultures, legal sciences may do more than develop abstract ideas and systematize legal knowledge. They may relate legal norms to social problems, propose practical solutions and generate legal innovations. Supreme courts often follow these propositions or take the initiative to reform existing law. This knowledge still may be largely irrelevant because it is produced without sufficient empirical experience, is politically naive or refers only to rare social constellations. Students will be taught to understand these limitations. But on the basis of the model, they also will understand the significant increase in legal-cultural complexity achieved by stepping into the second level which adds to the first. Precedents are a social reality in both common law and civil law countries, and the huge commentaries which exist in civil law countries – written mostly by law professors in order to promote their interpretation and facilitate decision-making – are part of the living law as a result of their reputation and their frequent use by lower courts and legal practitioners.

If the course extends its perspective to all institutional actors of a legal system which either help implement legal norms or, like most interest groups, do everything in their power to obstruct implementation, students are encouraged to go beyond the world of ideas and to learn the behavioural aspects of law. Lower courts and governmental agencies may have their own informal rules and sometimes even pursue goals different from what the legislators had in mind. The bulk of legal sociological knowledge offers this kind of information and the instructor's task is to add it to the previous levels of the model. This last aspect accounts for the fundamental difference of a course in sociology of law and a course on legal cultures. The former may be confined to behavioural aspects, whereas the latter also has to cover the normative aspects of law which – as we have seen – are part of the conception of legal culture.

The fourth level, then, also encompasses the behaviours, attitudes, political goals and values of individual actors – the legal subjects which law students know from the fictitious cases of doctrinal exercises. But now these individuals do not automatically sue if they are told they have a legal claim. Instead, they settle, bribe or give up. Business cultures are intervening factors and the legal profession has its own attitudes and interests. No doubt this level, which again is not a separate course but complements all previous levels of the course, arrives at the threshold of manageability. The picture which should have become transparent gets cloudy and fuzzy. The course will have to make a choice between depth and width, either remaining on previous levels of complexity or limiting its perspective to one legal phenomenon or one (or few) regulatory devices, which then can be dealt with at all levels of legal cultural activity.

Historical and Comparative Aspects

It would run against the logic of the course to simply add – as do many legal textbooks – a historical and/or comparative chapter in the beginning. These aspects are not just another level (a first or a fifth level in the model), but are to be considered part of each level. The phenomena on level 1 have a history quite different from those on level 3, and a comparison of legal doctrines is a fundamentally different approach than a comparison of citizen or business behaviour. This gives the instructor an option at every single step to include historical and comparative aspects. Since time is always short and the readings for the students have to be limited, the course will have to cut down on one or the other of our dimensions.

Our textbook *European Legal Cultures* demonstrates what a comparative dimension could look like. We cannot claim that our selection of readings covers the comparative dimension at all four levels equally well: at some levels there was simply too much, at other levels too little, comparative literature available. The historical dimension was chosen mainly for the Nazi and the Soviet totalitarian legal cultures. This is not the place to spell out the dilemmas of the (always objectionable) selection of the material. By using the book in an US undergraduate class, it became clear that both the comparative and the historical dimensions require considerably more basic information than we were able to render in the collection of readings. In order to improve their understanding, students can be required to produce this basic knowledge by themselves. If every student in a class of 50 students prepares and distributes a copy of a paper on a keyword like 'Inns of Courts', 'Constitutional Court' or 'European Court of Justice' in the comparative dimension, or 'Corpus Juris Civilis', 'National Socialism' or 'Supreme Soviet' in the historical dimension, the texts may be complemented considerably and students are encouraged to use the library (rather than the more and more popular Internet).

Examples of a Course in Legal Culture
Teaching the Concept of Legal Certainty

The distinction between the two functions of law as regulating or enabling which is common in domestic discourses also makes sense in areas affected by the globalization of law. Many global actors are producing norms and rules not to implement a policy goal (like the protection of the environment or the prevention of war) but to facilitate exchange processes. They develop contract norms or procedural norms for conflict resolution which are not compulsory but are meant as an offer in order to better secure exchanges against opportunistic behaviour. Unlike in the area of regulation, where coercion prevails, one would assume this to be mainly or exclusively a matter of private organization. But beginning with Roman law, states have established enabling infrastructures which include civil law, civil judges, registers, notaries and lawyers. In western legal cultures, civil cases are by far the most important part of the caseload of the state court system. In the Weberian tradition, the production of enabling law is seen as a state obligation and recently international organizations like UNCITRAL, the World Bank, IMF or the European Union also feel responsible for establishing structures for facilitating and securing economic exchange.

Max Weber was, of course, wrong in assuming such a central role of the state in market exchanges. He writes: 'The modern capitalist enterprize rests primarily on *calculation* and presupposes a legal and administrative system, whose functioning can be rationally predicted, at least in principle, by virtue of its fixed general norms, just like the expected performance of a machine.'[10]

From a sociological as well as from a socio-legal perspective, economic behaviour is embedded in social structures and social relations. In the following, mainly two variables will be taken into account: power and trust. They are located at the third and the fourth levels of our model for a legal culture.

Power

State as well as private legal systems are largely irrelevant for securing economic exchange as soon as one party assumes a dominant position in the contractual relationship. The weaker party simply complies in order to stay in business. This is already the typical situation in most manufacturer-supplier relations. But the best example is the multinational enterprise where goods and services are moving without any legal risks between legally and economically dependent subsidiaries. The very reason to create these big enterprises is their command structure which not only reduces the transaction costs (as emphasized by Ronald Coase) of drafting and enforcing contracts but also minimizes the effects of legal and cultural diversity.[11] In general terms, economic transactions are, wherever they are vulnerable, internalized within hierarchically organized firms rather than performed by market processes across firms.

Personal trust

Personal trust is emphasized as an alternative to institutional and legal support by anthropologists,[12] economists,[13] legal sociologists[14] and sociologists.[15] This well-established knowledge has led to practical consequences in relational management training of business people and in attempts at adopting relational elements in contracts and even in contract law.[16] Granovetter's term 'embeddedness' is widely used in approaches which study the importance of personal relations as an overlay in economic transactions and which criticize the dominant framework of 'atomized' profit-seeking actors. The trade of Chinese business people is 'embedded' in family solidarity and ethnic networks;[17] the Sicilian mafia operates in relationships that evoke blood imagery like agnatic kinship (consanguinity), affinal kinship, ritual kinship, ritual friendship (blood brotherhood);[18] the diamond trade is socially secured by the Jewish religion.[19] Granovetter's 'personal embeddedness' is based on inter-firm mobility, interlocking directorates and other contacts among business elites, long-term associations between contractors and subcontractors and between purchasing agents and suppliers, and generally on past dealings with the trusted person. These past dealings, according to him, offer better information than 'reputation' as frequently used in institutional economics: '(1) it is cheap; (2) one trusts one's own information best – it is richer, more detailed, and known to be accurate; (3) individuals with whom one has a continuing relationship have an economic motivation to be trustworthy, so as not to discourage future transactions; and (4) departing from pure economic motives, continuing relations often become overlaid with social content that carries strong expectations of trust and abstention from opportunism'.[20]

Impersonal trust

The above summarized insights that power and personal trust substitute for legal support are by now fairly obvious and, after two decades of research and debate, almost commonplace. It is also obvious that power and personal trust penetrate economic life irregularly and in different degrees.[21] Wherever their influence is less relevant, we seem to finally have to deal with the classical model, the rational actor in anonymous market exchange. But, as Susan Shapiro (1985) has shown in her article on impersonal trust, social control is effective in economic action even beyond hierarchy and social relations. When multiple norms and organizational forms of social control of risk and distrust become relevant, rational choice again is pushed to the background.

Social differentiation means that all actors ('principals') in society let others ('agents') fulfil most of their tasks on their behalf. Responsibilities are divided between the members of a family, parents entrust their children to professionals such as teachers and housekeepers and employers transfer custody of their property to employees. One's money is deposited in a bank account, assets and properties are turned to experts like stockbrokers, one's health to doctors, future uncertainties to insurance companies and pension funds. Newspapers as well as scientists are agents entrusted with the production of knowledge; the mechanic is an agent who takes care of the security of one's car. This social differentiation requires a complex organization of risk protection and markets of trust production *beyond* personal trust created in close social relationships. Governments are next to private organizations and professions among the guardians of trust substituting for kinship and friendship when dealing with strangers. Contracts are the usual strategy by which principals can assume some control over the behaviour of those who act on their behalf. But they provide only limited control over the agency relationship, over future contingencies and over non-compliance. Agents rather than principals set the normative agenda: typically, the principals are 'one-shotters' whereas agents are 'repeat players' with experience and power.

Some aspects of Shapiro's 'social organization of distrust' are discussed in legal sciences as ways to provide 'legal certainty', and in economics – in particular New Institutional Economics – as institutions which reduce transaction costs. Recently, political scientists have discussed institutional trust as a prerequisite for stable democracies.[22] But an approach which – as in Susan Shapiro and others[23] – conceives trust as a social construction is more general and much more complex. Social control of impersonal trust is neither mainly legal nor is it based only on rational choices by profit-seeking actors. Still, in explaining in particular economic behaviour, legal as well as economic approaches contribute to the understanding of structures and markets of trust production. In addition, cultural variations of the social organization of distrust have to be taken into account. According to Hollingsworth and Boyer, support structures and social regulation of trust control is achieved in some cultures predominantly by horizontal modes whereas in others by vertical modes of economic coordination. Horizontal modes of coordination are markets and communities, vertical modes of coordination are firms and the state. In addition, placed between the horizontal and the vertical modes, networks and associations contribute to the regulatory system.[24] Both horizontal and vertical modes make use of two different incentives (called 'action motives'); economic actions are guided either by self-interest (both at the level of the market and of individual firms) or by obligations (to communities and the state).

Teaching the Emerging Global Merchant Law

A whole set of rules forms part of the emerging global merchant law: Incoterms, Uniform International Rules developed by the International Chamber of Commerce, Hague Rules, Hamburg Rules, CMR and CIM Conventions on the international carriage of goods by road or by rail, etc. If the instructor chooses to remain at the first level of complexity, he or she will, in order to distinguish the course from a legal course, emphasize the autonomous character of these rules and their role in the globalization of law. A historical perspective would either remain in the twentieth century when these rules were elaborated, or go back to their origins in medieval northern Italy. A comparative aspect would be that the rules are worked out only by, and in the interest of, a few industrialized countries, and that only recently their scope has been broadened with the assistance of various United Nations organizations.

On the next level of legal cultural complexity, the emerging global merchant law becomes a lively battlefield between supreme courts (which do or do not recognize the emerging global merchant law rules as law), arbitration courts (which either have wide discretion in applying and creating emerging global merchant law rules or abide by private international law restrictions) and legal doctrine (which generally fiercely attacks attempts of non-state institutions to create law). A comparative approach that looks at the legal scientific cultures of various countries will provide interesting insights into legal methods and into varying degrees of state-centredness in legal thinking. Historically, the old global merchant law of medieval and early modern merchants in Europe will be described, and also its breakdown in the course of nation-building and codification.

More legal cultural information will be introduced into the course if, at the third level of our model, daily legal practice with lower state courts, arbitration courts and business associations will be discussed. There exist quantitative judgments analyses, court file research and interviews with arbitrators, judges and trade institutions regarding the use of emerging global merchant law rules which show the social background and biases as well as the creativity of autonomous law creation in the area of international trade. Historical research has provided numerous documents of early traders such as the Hanse, or of merchants like the Fuggers or of cities like Genova or Aix en Provence. A comparison of legal cultures reveals the increase of autonomy in some business areas and of increased state-orientation in other areas. A unique institution worthy of detailed discussion in this context is the London Commercial Court, where judges decide business cases on the basis of their previous practice as barristers or solicitors in the same field of commercial activity.

If the fourth level is included in the course, the students will learn about contract drafting, the practice of international law firms in creatively developing liability, hardship, price or currency clauses and the selective use of state law, international conventions like the UN Convention on the International Sale of Goods, or standard contracts offered by their business clients or trade associations. They will learn the role of cultural differences in contract negotiation and the use of courts. They may even be encouraged to carry out interviews in small or large export firms or to enquire how experienced and inexperienced lawyers cope with the problems of cross-border lawyering.

There is no doubt that the interest and even excitement of the students will increase with every additional level of complexity reached in the course.

Teaching Global Legal Cultures

Rule scepticism seems to be even more justified for the global economy.[25] Enabling law, as far as it is effective, is mainly domestic and in conflict with other states' enabling law. The globalization of enabling law through unification of contract law, insolvency law, property law, tort law, company law or civil procedure is in its infancy despite current efforts. Differences prevail and prevent calculability. Law, rather than producing legal certainty, creates insecurity and risk for cross-border economic exchanges. Economic actors do their utmost to escape from state law, although not always successfully. Some research points to inefficiencies, transaction costs and costs of regulation, frequently leading, instead of public regulation, to the existence of autonomous, private legal systems.

What we have learnt from the above briefly (and incompletely) summarized research is that impersonal trust is a complex social achievement, highly developed in some but absent in most parts of the world. It is constructed at the level of societies and is exceptional in close-knit communities like the famous diamond traders. Law is a frequent but not a necessary part of its structural devices.

We also know that global business is predominantly based either on power or on personal trust. But what are the sources of security and confidence in the remaining (small?) part of the global economy, the world of anonymous business transactions? There is scattered research on, for example, ebay transactions,[26] on the globally active reinsurance industry,[27] on the strategies of debt collection agencies in enforcing cross-border claims,[28] on civil courts in international cases[29] and on the consular services.[30] Law (mostly domestic law) and state courts (all domestic) provide some support, but, in the main, the structures offered are private. Great expectations are directed toward the norms and institutions of the famous *lex mercatoria*[31] and toward the support provided by international law firms. A more radical approach assumes global business to function with little or without any support structures[32] due to flexible organizational devices and adaptive business strategies. These three approaches of private government and their tensions with state law and domestic and international legal institutions will have to be discussed in class. The possible emergence of an autonomous global *legal* support structure (parallel to the emerging global or regional regulatory structure) does not have to stay in the background. Legal activities toward the creation of unified or harmonized support structures abound and their relevance for global business will have to be studied empirically.

Notes

[1] This introductory part draws on my article 'Legalization and the Varieties of Capitalism' in Antons and Gessner (forthcoming).

[2] Wiener (1999).

[3] North (1990: 7).

[4] Ellickson (1991).

[5] Weber (1964: 719, 724, 1036).

[6] Trubek (1972: 747); Treiber (1989: 376).

[7] Weber (1964: 1049); Treiber (1989: 374); Francis (1983).

[8] Weber (1968: 336–37).

[9] Gessner, Hoeland and Varga (1996).

[10] Weber (1968: 1394).

[11] Coase (1960)

[12] E.g., Yang (1994); Wiessner (2002).

[13] E.g., Landa (1981); Gulati (1995).

[14] Macaulay (1963).

[15] Granovetter (1985); Appelbaum (1998).

[16] Macneil (1980); Gottlieb (1983).

[17] Landa (1981).

[18] Blok (2002).

[19] Richman (2005); Bernstein (1992).

[20] Granovetter (1985: 490).

[21] Ibid.: 491.

[22] Hartmann and Offe (2001).

[23] E.g., Zucker (1986); Luhmann (1979).

[24] Hollingsworth and Boyer (1997: 9, 12).

[25] Gessner *et al.* (2001).

[26] Pitta (2002).

[27] Stammel (1998).

[28] Budak (1998).

[29] Gessner (1996).

[30] Petzold (1998).

[31] Teubner (1997).

[32] Luhmann (1982).

References

Antons, Christoph and Volkmar Gessner, eds (forthcoming), *Globalization and Resistance* (Oxford: Hart).

Appelbaum, Richard P. (1998), 'The Future of Law in a Global Economy', 7 *Social & Legal Studies*, 171.

Bernstein, Lisa (1992), 'Opting Out of the Legal System: Extralegal Contractual Relations in the Diamond Trade', 21 *Journal of Legal Studies*, 115.

Blok, Anton (2002), 'Mafia and Blood Symbolism', in Frank K. Salter, ed., *Risky Transactions: Trust, Kinship, and Ethnicity* (New York: Berghahn Books): 109–28.

Budak, Ali Cem (1998), 'Cross-Border Debt Collection: Examples of Germany and Turkey', in Volkmar Gessner and Ali Cem Budak, eds, *Emerging Legal Certainty: Empirical Studies on the Globalization of Law* (Aldershot: Ashgate): 17–53.

Coase, Ronald H. (1960), 'The Problem of Social Cost', *Journal of Law & Economics* 3(1): 15.

Ellickson, Robert C. (1991), *Order without Law: How Neighbors Settle Disputes* (Cambridge, MA: Harvard University Press).

Francis, Clinton W. (1983), 'The Structure of Judicial Administration and the Development of Contract Law in Seventeenth-Century England', 83 *Columbia Law Review* 35.

Gessner, Volkmar, ed., (1996), *Foreign Courts: Civil Litigation in Foreign Legal Cultures* (Aldershot: Dartmouth).

Gessner, Volkmar, Armin Hoeland and Gaba Varga (1996), *European Legal Cultures* (Aldershot: Dartmouth).

Gessner, Volkmar, Richard P. Appelbaum and William L.F. Felstiner (2001), 'The Legal Culture of Global Business Transactions', in Richard P. Appelbaum, William L.F. Felstiner and Volkmar Gessner, eds, *Rules and Networks: The Legal Culture of Global Business Transactions* (Oxford: Hart).

Gottlieb, Gidon (1983), 'Relationism: Legal Theory for a Relational Society', 50 *University of Chicago Law Review* 567.

Granovetter, Marc (1985), 'Economic Action and Social Structure: The Problem of Embeddedness', 91 *American Journal of Sociology* 481.

Gulati, Ranjay (1995), 'Does Familiarity Breed Trust?: The Implications of Repeated Ties for Contractual Choice in Alliances', 38 *Academy of Management Journal* 85.

Hartmann, Martin and Claus Offe, eds, (2001), *Vertrauen. Die Grundlage des sozialen Zusammenhalts* (Frankfurt/Main: Campus).

Hollingsworth, J. Rogers and Robert Boyer (1997), 'Coordination of Economic Actors and Social Systems of Production', in J. Rogers Hollingsworth and Robert Boyer, eds, *Contemporary Capitalism: The Embeddedness of Institutions* (Cambridge: Cambridge University Press).

Landa, Janelle (1981), 'A Theory of the Ethnically Homogeneous Middleman Group: An Institutional Alternative to Contract Law', 10 *Journal of Legal Studies* 349.

Luhmann, Niklas (1979), *Trust and Power* (Chichester: Wiley).

——— (1982), 'The World Society as a Social System', *International Journal of General Systems*, No. 8: 131–38.

Macaulay, Stewart (1963), 'Non-Contractual Relations in Business: A Preliminary Study', 28 *Am.Soc.Rev.* 55.

Macneil, John (1980), *The New Social Contract* (New Haven).

North, Douglass C. (1990), *Institutions, Institutional Change and Economic Performance* (Cambridge: Cambridge University Press).

Petzold, Andreas (1998), 'Obtaining Information on Foreign Legal Systems', in Volkmar Gessner and Ali Cem Budak, eds, *Emerging Legal Certainty: Empirical Studies on the Globalization of Law* (Aldershot: Ashgate): 283–312.

Pitta, Julie (2002), 'Banking on Reputations', *Relationship Journal*, No. 1: 10.

Richman, Barak D. (2005), 'How Community Institutions Create Economic Advantage: Jewish Diamond Merchants in New York', *Law & Social Inquiry*, No. 31: 283–420.

Shapiro, Susan P. (1985) 'The Social Control of Impersonal Trust', 93 *American Journal of Sociology* 623.

Stammel, Christine (1998), 'Back to the Courtroom?: Developments in the London Reinsurance Market', in Volkmar Gessner and Ali Cem Budak, eds, *Emerging Legal Certainty: Empirical Studies on the Globalization of Law* (Aldershot: Ashgate): 61–91.

Teubner, Gunther (1997), '"Global Bukowina": Legal Pluralism in World Society', in Gunther Teubner, ed., *Global Law without a State* (Aldershot: Dartmouth): 3–28.

Treiber, Hubert (1989), 'Zur Rechtssoziologie Max Webers', in H. Treiber, ed., *Vollzugskosten des Rechtsstaats* (Baden-Baden: Nomos).

Trubek, David M. (1972), 'Max Weber on Law and the Rise of Capitalism', *Wisconsin Law Review* 720.

Weber, Max (1964), *Wirtschaft und Gesellschaft* (Koeln: Kiepenheuer & Witsch).

—— (1968), *Economy and Society: An Outline of Interpretive Sociology*, edited by Guenther Roth and Claus Wittich (New York: Bedminster Press; Berkeley: University of California Press).

Wiener, Jarrod (1999), *Globalization and the Harmonization of Law* (London: Pinter).

Wiessner, Polly (2002), 'Taking the Risk out of Risky Transactions: A Forager's Dilemma', in Frank K. Salter, ed., *Risky Transactions: Trust, Kinship, and Ethnicity* (New York: Berghahn Books).

Yang, Mayfair Mei-hui (1994), *Gifts, Favors, and Banquets: The Art of Social Relationship in China* (Ithaca, NY: Cornell University Press).

Zucker, Lynne G. (1986), 'Production of Trust: Institutional Sources of Economic Structure, 1840–1920', *Research in Organizational Behavior*, No. 8: 53–111.

Of Pedagogy and Suffering

Civil Rights Movements and Teaching of Human Rights in India

Sitharamam Kakarala

> . . . statist human rights discourse does not relate to languages of pain and suffering in its enunciations of human rights. In contrast, peoples' struggles against regimes practicing the politics of cruelty are rooted in the direct experience of pain and suffering. (Baxi 1998: 5)

Nearly two decades ago, Upendra Baxi, in a widely circulated article, forcefully argued a case in favour of linking suffering as strategically significant and nuanced qualification to provide meaning and content to the idea of human rights. In a way, it was a sharp response to the somewhat straightforward appeal of liberal humanist constitutionalism advocating 'taking rights seriously' (Dworkin: 1977). In his responses,[1] Baxi tried to communicate two important points. First, that all languages of human rights, especially those of the state and of social movements, cannot be equated and seen as similar; second, without strategically significant qualifications to provide the substantive meaning of human rights in non-statist languages, they are likely to be vulnerable to the appropriations of the state and other dominant agencies. This specific insight is very significant in the Indian (or even newly independent or erstwhile colonial countries) context, for, first, it acknowledges, reaffirms and provides a theoretical justification to a longstanding insight which has emerged from the practice of the civil rights and civil liberties movement in India; second, it was an exhortation to the Indian academia, especially legal academia, which was attempting to bring human rights as a core theme into teaching law, that direct and simple importations of curriculum practices and methodologies would not be appropriate for our conditions.

In this paper I want to look critically at the trajectories of human rights teaching and curriculum practices as they have evolved in the Indian case in the light of this exhortation of Baxi and the contributions of the civil rights and civil liberties movement, which has a reasonably long history in India. I intend to suggest that the human rights education scenario tends to share the same concerns as the legal education debates presented in this volume elsewhere, viz., should the objective of human rights pedagogy be to produce professionally competent lawyers or to create sensible and knowledgeable citizens? The problem further accentuates when 'human rights' becomes an increasingly visible and important measure of governance processes,[2] for the challenge then is how to create and sustain diverse institutional spaces within the state which are sensitive and responsive to the concerns of 'suffering'. While the spaces and opportunities of professional training and education have grown significantly over the last decade, the curricular and pedagogic practices stand far away from the experiences of the civil rights and civil liberties movements, and hence need a closer scrutiny. The translation of constitutional norms into citizenship performance and movement praxis into pedagogic practice in the human rights curricular process still await a major intervention.

Civil Rights Movements

India has a long history of civil rights and civil liberties activism.[3] However, the movements acquired a new momentum and significance in the wake of violent mass movements like the naxalite movement of the early 1970s and the experience of the internal emergency of 1975.[4] Until about the early 1990s, the civil rights and civil liberties movements were primarily represented by voluntary action groups, completely self-funded and informally organized. The primary focus of these groups was police excesses and gross violations such as custodial violence and extra-judicial killings.[5] Since the beginning of the 1990s, there has been a gradual and growing NGO-ization of the movement's space.[6] This naturally led to changes in focus resulting in more specialized campaigns and actions.[7] Today, the rights movements – civil rights, civil liberties, human rights – consist of diverse actors ranging from classical 'voluntary' movement groups, NGOs that are primarily driven by a social action motive and agenda, NGOs that are primarily intended to do service delivery, NGOs that are primarily intended to be diplomacy and advocacy organizations, and so on.

Some of the widely acknowledged contributions of these diverse actors have been the popularization of civil and human rights languages, the keeping alive of the debates on crucial issues in the public sphere through media and court litigation processes, and the attempts to create a more 'professional' approach to human rights protection and monitoring. What, however, is not yet a seriously recognized contribution, though very crucial from the pedagogic point of view, is that these actors have provided an opportunity to think of an alternate history of the post-independent Indian state through a series of resources that engage with the normative concerns of modern constitutionalism negotiated through a complex process of 'radical' movements' agendas and their translation (or lack of it) in the day-to-day politics of popular democracy.

Human Rights Lawyering

Human rights lawyering,[8] which is also referred to by some as social justice lawyering or 'cause lawyering', has been an important contribution of the rights movement in India. Beginning as a process of professional lawyers providing pro bono legal services, which was later transformed by politically active lawyers in the civil liberties movement, it remained so for a long time.

Human rights lawyering has now, however, acquired predominantly the form of an action group or NGO.[9] What is perhaps striking in these developments is the trajectories of the life of an idea that has left a significant impact on the legal profession and contributed to unique and creative transformations in the way the legal profession evolved and yet, when it comes to the pedagogic process of rights, hardly finds any place in the classroom or curricular practices. This disjuncture between movement praxis and pedagogic practice is somewhat surprising, for unless the unique ways by which human rights lawyering happen (or tends to happen) in India is understood and presented in the classroom space, it would be out of context. This is a serious concern which needs to be explored in the context of the profession and its ability to respond and be sensitive to the needs of social justice in India. The often loosely made remark about lawyers being insensitive to the social cause, or 'elitism' in the new law schools of the NLSIU kind, I would submit, is to be attributed partly to such a disjuncture. Questions such as 'what makes lawyers interested in human rights issues?', 'how do human rights norms acquire their meaning in the context of a court or general life?' etc., so far only tend to have speculative answers. Above all, unless there is a narrativization of personal and organizational commitment to negotiating normativity in the face of political opposition, the techniques of alternative strategies and argumentation, social defaming and such other hardships that the human rights lawyering process has to face in India, generating even the necessary enthusiasm, leave alone legitimacy, in human rights lawyering becomes a difficult task. This partly explains why there are not many, despite the widespread presence of rights movements, human rights law courses successfully run in India.[10]

Sources of Alternative Histories

Another important contribution of the rights movements in India is the generation and documentation of a huge body of material that unfolds stories of violation, abuse, disrespect, both of sporadic as well as systematic varieties, by the state machinery.[11] Written with a firm conviction in constitutional principles and a commitment to reconstructing the truth about the event concerned, these reports provide a vantage point to understand the nature and functioning, or lack of it, of state institutions, especially related to criminal justice administration, and constantly highlighting the yawning gap between the letter of the law and its hermeneutic incarnations as (re)presented in the day-to-day bureaucratic interpretations. Drawing inspiration from a long 'tradition' of fact-finding,[12] many rights groups significantly invest and painstakingly pursue the investigations ranging from a very localized incident of a 'dowry death' or a custodial violence case, to gross violations such as 'communal riots' or prolonged police repression.

This, however, is not to indicate that these 'fact-finding' enquiries are without their share of controversies. It is but natural that a highly politically contested 'alternative' truth claim vis-à-vis that of the state would invariably generate controversy. What could, however, be said about the process is that the rights movements have not evolved any 'standards'[13] in the process of the appointment of committees and the methods of enquiry, and thus the quality of the data and findings tend to vary highly from one inquiry to another. Thus, while some of the reports had become milestones of post-independent India,[14] some of the others tend to be localized reports.[15] This inequality notwithstanding, the fact-finding reports and the thematic reports (which are often based on the fact-finding reports) form an important source of understanding and critiquing the modern Indian state and society. However, as mentioned, there is hardly any mainstream textbook that engages with this extensive and rich source of state critique.

Rights and the 'Cultural Questions'

A third set of questions that the rights movements could throw light on are the 'culture questions' in human rights discourse: How is 'culture' related to 'rights'? How does it influence the making or the unmaking of, or modifying the meaning of rights? What are the sites and trajectories through which meaning making and meaning forming take place? While it is possible that on the surface that all 'rights talk' appears to be alike and perhaps referring to similar concerns, it is always mediated by the socio-cultural context and that presents an opportunity to understand the way the 'universal norms' acquire their contextualized expression and meaning. In other words, to borrow Upendra Baxi's distinction, the 'modern' and the 'contemporary' are not one and the same in rights talk – while the former represents the ideas of European origins and the universalizing claims of Eurocentrism, the latter suggests a process of appropriation of rights talk by the local social action processes through infusing the expression of suffering and thus providing a meaning that need not be the same as the one claimed by the 'modern' rights talk.[16]

I would further supplement the above argument with another dimension of the culture question: the radical trajectories through which 'liberal' rights talk percolated into the Indian context. The origins of the modern rights talk in India dates back to the national movement. Many leaders of the national movement attempted to articulate a perspective on rights.[17] However, many of them tried to articulate conceptions of 'liberal' rights, while holding some form of 'radical' ideologies – often left, but at times even rightist philosophies.[18] I would thus suggest that both the conceptual debates as well as the praxis of the rights movements in India have had an inherently ambiguous approach to the concept of rights, for many believed that they were concerned about 'liberal' rights, while constantly articulating their meaning from a non-liberal ideological location.[19] The praxis of the rights movements therefore would be of a crucial resource for understanding the nature and character of what is being referred to as 'Indian liberalism,' and characterizing Indian constitutionalism. Here, the potential of the praxis of rights movements in India is beyond the pedagogic realm, for it could help theorize the processes of articulation, representation, percolation and appropriation of the idea of rights in its complex and multi-layered journey from Europe to India.

To sum up this point, I have tried to suggest that the experience of the rights movements in India could potentially help us rethink three important areas of knowledge, viz., human rights lawyering, an alternative history of the post-independent Indian state and society, and theorizing Indian constitutionalism. In this manner, we may arrive at a perspective on the circulation of ideas. I will provide a sketch of the human rights teaching experience in India over the last two decades.

Human Rights Teaching

The curricularization of human rights began primarily from an international perspective, especially the international law perspectives. This trajectory in a way contributed to popularizing human rights primarily in the legal departments, which in turn influenced the way the curricular and pedagogic practices emerged over time (Meron 1984). The curricularization of human rights in India which began in the mid-1980s took a similar trajectory by focusing on the site of law departments and colleges. While the final official formulation of a curriculum took nearly a decade and a half more,[20] three important individual figures – Upendra Baxi, Nandita Haksar and G. Haragopal – must be mentioned who still remain important contributors to the curricularization process.

Upendra Baxi's contribution to human rights teaching consists of various forms. First, he is one of the earliest teachers to attempt at generating syllabi and materials to teach human rights in India; second, he is one of the foremost and prolific contributors on the subject; third, he has been one of the most prominent activist-scholars who has demonstrated by personal example the possibilities of linking social action processes and justice systems and legal norms; and last but not least, he was the Chair of the law panel of the UGC Curriculum Development Committee (CDC) during the mid-1980s, which evolved perhaps for the first time a systematic syllabi for human rights law at the LLM level.

It would naturally be impossible to summarize a multi-faceted and extensive contribution of this kind in a meaningful way. For the present purpose, however, it is important to take note of some of the key contributions. The foremost contribution of Baxi could be presented as evolving a third or developing world perspective on human rights outside the vision of a state-centric paradigm. The extensive body of writing[21] he has contributed over the last three decades makes him one of the very few non-western scholars attempting at taking rights theorization beyond the liberal constitutional paradigm that could help us to understand the contextualized and local forms which the universal norms acquire. Another important contribution is his inspiring teaching, both in Delhi University as well as at the University of Warwick, which generated a number of enthusiastic younger generations of teachers and activists in the field of human rights.

An important inadequacy, however, is that notwithstanding the impressive body of literature he has contributed, neither could he place a lasting imprint on the (formal) curricular or pedagogic practices nor did he attempt at a 'textbook' or a reader that could be directly useful for classroom teaching of the younger teachers. However, his contribution in the CDC report on human rights curriculum is still highly relevant in the evolution of human rights teaching in India.

Nandita Haksar, an advocate and a member of the PUDR for a long time, has always been an inspiring activist, and has contributed to the curricularization through three important interventions. The first was her attempt at teaching human rights law at the National Law School of India University (NLSIU) during the early 1990s; the second was her efforts in teaching human rights at the Cochin University of Science and Technology during the late 1990s; and third, as a member of the Curriculum Development Committee on Human Rights Education (CDCHRE) established by the UGC during 2000–2001.

The most significant of all these is Haksar's mammoth effort in creating a unique syllabi and an outstanding set of materials to teach the course on Human Rights Law and Practice at NLSIU. It was perhaps the first attempt in India at providing a comprehensive and systematic syllabus for teaching human rights to law students. The materials contained themes that were both uncommon, if viewed from a western context, and a significant investment in contextualizing rights issues. It was also an important attempt at bringing the experiences of social movements/rights movements into classroom teaching.

G. Haragopal,[22] an inspiring teacher and a longstanding civil rights activist from Andhra Pradesh, has probably provided the most sustained and systematic curricular intervention. He has been instrumental in creating the popular Post-Graduate Diploma Course in human rights at the Hyderabad Central University. The uniqueness of the course is its materials which are lessons written by a large number of activists and activist-academics and is an attempt to translate social movement praxis into curricular practice. Another important contribution is his committed teaching which has inspired many young students. He was also a member of the CDCHRE appointed by the UGC during 2000–2001.

While there are many other curricular interventions in human rights teaching,[23] I confine myself here only to the above three as these are the only efforts from within the academic world to have attempted to translate social movement praxis into pedagogic practice. While these attempts have inspired a number of individuals and have had their own share of success, they have nevertheless remained largely isolated and symbolic.

Ironically, the subsequent curricularization efforts of the UGC during 2000–2001,[24] though it had both Nandita Haksar and G. Haragopal as members, did very little to bring the human rights movement contributions into classroom teaching and curricular practices. The UGC curriculum for the post-graduate course on human rights consists of 5 'core papers'[25] and 14 'optional papers'.[26] Although the overall focus of the papers is largely interdisciplinary, except the optional paper 14 and occasional references in a few other papers to the human rights movement, the curricular focus has no significant translation of rights movement contributions into pedagogic practice.

In terms of the classroom practice in the law schools such as the NLSIU, which has began to incorporate human rights law as a compulsory subject for the bachelors degree course, the emphasis continues to be on the 'professionalizing' of human rights law and hence a focus on the black letter. While the professional focus is inevitable to an extent in the law school context, ignoring or underplaying the sites on which the real experience of human rights practice takes place makes the Indian university experience significantly inadequate. Besides, the higher education institutions, by not taking into cognisance the need to contextualize law, tend to miss out important opportunities of elevating their ability to engage with social reality and provide newer perspectives.

On the teaching of human rights in the non-law departments and colleges, there is not much documented data. But from the available evidence,[27] it is clear that many of them suffer from the known problems such as lack of quality materials, competent teachers, etc. There is also a growing tendency of caution, especially since the recent overwhelming terrorism discourse among the departments and colleges teaching human rights, in incorporating critical materials on the state. Thus, for various reasons, the teaching practice of human rights, for political (in the case of the social sciences) and professional (in the case of law) reasons, the classroom practice is tending to view rights from a statist perspective as opposed to taking suffering seriously.

Conclusion

Thus it is clear that the gap between rights movements praxis and pedagogic practice is significant, and with the exception a few valuable individual efforts there is more disappointment than cause for hope, including the major effort of the UGC's CDCHRE. However, I would like to suggest that the failure of the Committee should not be viewed as a problem in framing syllabi. Rather, it is a larger problem of the lack of independent research traditions, with a few exceptions to which some references were already made above, and of critical reflections on the larger intellectual questions on the concept of rights, the trajectories through which it has percolated, transformed itself, and become part of the popular imagination, as well as of theorizing the praxis of the rights movements.

As such, interest in theorizing social movements and citizenship performance has been of relatively recent interest to the social sciences scholarship in India and it is especially so in the case of the rights movements. The problem acquires a new dimension with the recent erosion of the legitimacy of nineteenth-century social theory, for it is now imperative to narrativise the histories of the movements and help construct the trajectories of the concept within its performative locations. It is only then that we could perhaps have a really contextualized historical account of rights, unfolding the stories of translation, subversion, and transformation of its liberal content.

Notes

[1] 'Suffering' has been a central theme in Upendra Baxi's rights-related writings over the last two decades. Especially, see Baxi (1988; 1998; 2006). Although the 'response' was in no way intended to address Dworkin or liberal humanism, I take the liberty to interpret it as such, for the spirit of Baxi's analysis of social action before the Supreme Court is indeed a critique of conventional constitutional wisdom.

[2] Since the mid-1990s there are a number of measures that make human rights both visible and important in assessing the governing processes. The establishment of the National Human Rights Commission followed by a number of State-level Human Rights Commissions, Human Rights Committees, Human Rights Courts, and more recently the entire institutional setup under the Right to Information Act, form the core framework of this visibility. Besides these, human rights has emerged as an important component in the institutionalized training programmes for police officers and security personnel.

[3] For an overview of the history of the pre-independence movement, see Kakarala (1994).

[4] The majority of the active civil rights and civil liberties organizations emerged in the background of these two events in post-independent India's history. Examples include Peoples' Union for Civil Liberties; Peoples' Union for Democratic Rights; Andhra Pradesh Civil Liberties Committee; Association for Democratic Rights; Organization for Democratic Rights; Naga Peoples' Movement for Human Rights and numerous such other groups.

[5] For an overview of these groups see Shah (2004); Haksar (1991); Rubin (1987); Ray (1986); Haragopal and Balagopal (1998); Kakarala (1993).

[6] The NGO-ization of the movement space has provided newer opportunities of bringing new issues into the movement's fold, greater professionalization, institutionalization and documentation practices. However, all these did not happen without any baggage. There is a greater tendency among the NGO groups to borrow the agendas that have currency in the international human rights context, or to borrow Upendra Baxi's phrase, in the 'human rights markets', and feed into the legitimizing state-agendas on rights issues. For a critique of the NGO-ization process, see Baxi (2006). Some of the most prominent NGOs working in the area of civil and human rights include the Human Rights Law Network (Mumbai, Delhi), Lawyers' Collective (Delhi), Majlis (Mumbai), Centre for Social Justice (Ahmedabad), People's Watch Tamil Nadu (Madurai), National Centre for Advocacy Studies (Pune), Rural Litigation and Entitlement Kendra (Dehradun).

[7] For instance, National Campaign for Dalit Human Rights, National Campaign for Elimination of Child Labour, National Campaign for Right to Information, etc.

[8] I draw the spirit of the argument from Nandita Haksar's introduction to the teaching materials compiled for the NLSIU students in 1993, especially the chapter on 'What is human rights lawyering'. While there are many accounts of rights lawyering practices in the west, Austin Sarat and Stuart Scheingold's recent work (1997), *Cause Lawyering* provides an account of the experience in the United States, especially in the globalizing context.

[9] The practice of professional lawyers associating with civil liberties organizations continues to exist, but the expanding nature of human rights activities and the growing demands on human rights law related services have led to the emergence of newer forms of associations. There are primarily three types of organizations that have emerged in the last decade or so. The first is an organization that perceives itself as an activist organization. Useful examples are Majlis in Mumbai which primarily works in the area of women's rights and the Alternative Law Forum in Bangalore. The second type is a professional lawyer who is networked into a group which advocates human rights lawyering. The illustrative case here is the work of the Human Rights Law Network, Delhi. Finally, there are attempts at creating law as a situated social justice actor by the Centre for Social Justice in Ahmedabad.

[10] Even in the NLSIU, where technically the human rights law programme began as

early as 1992, the LLM programme in Human Rights began only in 2002–2003 and is still limping for a variety of reasons. The same is the story of the Cochin University of Science and Technology programme of LLM in Human Rights, which began before the NLSIU LLM.

[11] 'Truth'-finding has been central to the rights movements' activities across various jurisdictions. It has often been deployed as a measure of creating counter-factual situations to that of the official versions of 'truth' and an effective source of opinion mobilization. While the method as such has been deployed by rights movements over the last century or so, it has acquired further significance with the United Nations embarking upon the periodic establishment of 'Truth Commissions', especially to investigate gross violations. In India, this activity is generally referred to as 'fact-finding'. By now, there are thousands of such reports, telling stories that the main-stream public sphere often tends to gloss over. However, these reports do not enjoy the stature of the mainstream literature and hence their shelf-life tends to be short and only survives within small circles of concerned activists of different rights groups. The only major exceptions in this regard are the important contribution of A.R. Desai (1986; 1990; 1991), who compiled and presented some of the key reports of the rights groups under a thematic classification and within a broad perspective of the crisis of the Indian constitution, and a set of fact-finding reports of the Andhra Pradesh Civil Liberties Committee (APCLC) published as *Life, Liberty and Livelihood* (1989).

[12] It is generally a belief among many rights activists that the practice of 'fact-finding' evolved as an integral part of the national movement. Well before the formation of the major civil liberties organizations in the west, such as the American Civil Liberties Union (ACLU) in 1920 and the National Council for Civil Liberties (NCCL) in 1933, the Indian National Congress enquired into the mass violations caused by the Jalianwalla Bagh incident and the report is said to have written by none other than M.K. Gandhi (1920). There is evidence of many subsequent fact-finding enquiries by regional Congress organizations. This 'tradition' of fact-finding has ever since been an important form of activity that is viewed as central to the legitimacy and opinion-building processes in rights movements.

[13] For example, the broad fact-finding guidelines provided by the United Nations for its Truth Commissions, or such similar operations. Generally such standard procedures are followed in major country-level fact-finding operations by international human rights groups such as Amnesty International and the International Commission of Jurists.

[14] The most prominent examples could be the Civil Rights Committee (CRC) appointed by Jayaprakash Narayan soon after the end of the internal emergency in 1977 to inquire into three incidents of alleged encounter deaths in Andhra Pradesh during 1975–1977. The committee, consisting of prominent jurists and public personalities such as Justice Tarkunde, Kuldip Nayar, Arun Shourie, K.G. Kannabiran and ten others concluded that many encounter deaths are actually 'coldblooded murders' for they occur not in exchanges of fire but often under captivity (CRC 1978). Since then the term 'encounters' (or extra-judicial executions in the United Nations parlance) never ceases to be uncontested in the public sphere and it may not be far from the truth to suggest that in fact the term has been identified with 'murder'. A number of popular films, both in Hindi and the vernacular languages, made on the theme of 'encounters' further highlighted this hidden meaning in the cultural publics. Another major illustration could be the fact-finding report of the Peoples' Union for Civil Liberties (PUCL) and the Peoples' Union for Democratic Rights (PUDR), *Who are the Guilty?* (1984), on the anti-Sikh riots in Delhi in the aftermath of Prime Minister Indira Gandhi's assassination in 1984. While substantive justice to the victims has long been delayed, the report highlighted the close nexus of the Congress organization in taking part or even leading the 'riots'. Mention must also be made of the numerous inquiries conducted by the Indian Peoples' Human Rights Tribunal during the mid-1980s to the mid-1990s.

[15] These fact-finding reports are often found only in the monthly bulletins or magazines of various rights groups, such as the *PUCL Bulletin*.

[16] There are a few interesting treatises on rights written by the leaders of the national

movement. It would be interesting to apply Baxi's conceptualization of modern versus contemporary rights to scrutinise these writings such as, for example, of Srinivasa Sastri (1926) and Satyamurthy (1919).

[17] Prominent personalities include Jawaharlal Nehru, Jayaprakash Narayan, Ram Manohar Lohia and K.B. Menon.

[18] For example, all those who were associated with rights conceptualization within the national movement had a socialist or social democratic ideology. Soon after independence, rights became a concern for the Jan Sangh and other such right-wing actors. From the mid-1960s, the left, especially the Communist Party of India (Marxist) for a while, and then the Naxalite parties/groups have significantly invested in articulating rights in an unequal and unjust society. Reference must be made at the least to the debate within the rights movements after the emergency in 1977 on what should be the appropriate focus for the rights movements in India – democratic rights or civil liberties. It was argued that the former takes issues of structural (class) inequalities into account in the conceptualization of rights, while the latter tends to emulate the liberal conception.

[19] It is worth recollecting here the work of K. Balagopal, who played a significant role in shaping the rights movement in Andhra Pradesh during the 1980s and the 1990s, in constantly clarifying what ought to be the approach and boundaries within which a civil liberties group should function. Reference must be made to his contribution titled 'What is Socialist Freedom' (1992), which was an attempt to clarify the distinctions between 'bourgeois freedom' and socialist freedom.

[20] The University Grants Commission appointed a panel of experts, the Curriculum Development Committee, to evolve a human rights curriculum at various levels ranging from short-term certificate courses to higher education degrees in 2000. The CDC finally submitted a non-binding curriculum, comprising a detailed set of papers and resource list for teaching human rights in the Indian universities in 2002. (See UGC 2002). In the area of legal studies, the Bar Council of India declared human rights as a compulsory subject in the Bachelor of Law degree in 2003.

[21] It would not be possible to provide a comprehensive bibliography of his writings here. But I would like to indicate some of the major writings (1982; 1986; 1994; 2006 and Baxi and Mendelsohn 1989).

[22] Professor at the University of Hyderabad.

[23] For instance, N.R. Madhava Menon's contribution in the making of the Post-Graduate Diploma in Human Rights Law during 1996–1997 at the NLSIU. There are some efforts outside mainstream academic interventions which tried to produce movement-based resource materials for teaching human rights. In this regard, the efforts of the Karnataka Women's Resource Centre, Bangalore deserve special mentioning.

[24] Responding to the letter written by the National Human Rights Commission (NHRC) dated 18 October 1999, the UGC appointed a Curriculum Development Committee for Human Rights Education (CDCHRE), which comprised of 17 members drawn from various walks of life related to human rights theory and practice. The committee met between June 2000 and December 2001 and finally prepared its report in early 2002.

[25] They are: 1. Historical and Philosophical Perspectives of Human Rights and Duties; 2. Human Rights and Duties in International and Regional Perspectives; 3. Societal Issues of Human Rights and Duties in India; 4. Human Rights and Duties in India: Law, Politics and Society, and Importance of Internalizing Human Rights and Duties; and, 5. Research Methodology and Dissertation/Field-Based Project Work.

[26] They are: 1. Science & Technology and Human Rights and Duties; 2. International Obligation to Protect Human Rights and Duties 3. Development, Trade and Human Rights; 4. International Humanitarian and Refugee Laws; 5. Peoples' Right to Self Determination; 6. Women and Human Rights and Duties; 7. Children and Human Rights and Duties; 8. The Aged and Disabled and Human Rights and Duties; 9. Socially/Economically Disadvantaged People and Human Rights and Duties; 10. Working Class and Human Rights and Duties; 11. Minorities and Human Rights; 12. Human Rights and Criminal Justice System; 13. Environment and Human Rights and Duties; and, 14. Social Movements and Human Rights in India.

[27] As per the UGC's data, there are over a hundred university departments and colleges that offer human rights either at the masters level or as a post-graduate diploma. CSCS is currently conducting a small study to understand the human rights teaching practices in different higher education institutions. The draft report is in file with the author.

References

Andhra Pradesh Civil Liberties Committee (1989), *Life, Liberty and Livelihood* (Hyderabad: APCLC).

Balagopal, K. (1992), 'What is Socialist Freedom?', *Economic and Political Weekly*, April 16.

Baxi, Upendra (1982), *The Crisis of Indian Legal System* (Delhi: Vikas Publishing).

—— (1986), *Towards a Sociology of India Law* (Delhi: Satavahan).

—— (1988), 'Taking Suffering Seriously: Social Action Litigation Before the Supreme Court of India', in *Law and Poverty* (Bombay: Tripathi).

—— (1994), *Inhuman Wrong and Human Rights* (Delhi: Har-Anand).

—— (1998), 'Voices of Suffering and the Future of Human Rights', *Transnational Law and Contemporary Problems*: 126–38.

—— (2006), *Future of Human Rights* (New Delhi: OUP).

Baxi, Upendra and Oliver Mendelsohn, eds (1989), *Rights of the Subordinated People* (Delhi: OUP).

Civil Rights Committee (1978), '"Encounters" are Murders, reproduced in Arun Shourie (1980), *Institutions in Janata Phase* (Bombay: Popular Prakashan).

Desai, A.R. (1986), *Violation of Democratic Rights in India* (Bombay: Popular Prakashan).

—— (1990), *Repression and Resistance in India* (Bombay: Popular Prakashan).

—— (1991), *Expanding Governmental Lawlessness* (Bombay: Popular Prakashan).

Dworkin, Ronald (1977), *Taking Rights Seriously* (Cambridge, MA: Harvard University Press).

Gandhi, M.K. (1920), 'Congress Report on the Punjab Disorders', in *Collected Works of Mahatma Gandhi*, Vol. 20 (Ahmedabad: Navjeevan Trust).

Haksar, Nandita (1991), 'Civil liberties movement in India', *The Lawyers' Collective*, June: 4–8.

Haragopal, G. and K. Balagopal (1998), 'Civil Liberties Movement and the State in India', in Manoranjan Mohanty, Partha Nath Mukherji and Olle Tornquist, eds, *People's Rights, Social Movements and the State in the Third World* (New Delhi: Sage Publications).

Kakarala, Sitharamam (1993), *Civil Rights Movement in India*, Surat: Centre for Social Studies (Unpublished Ph.D. thesis).

—— (1994), 'Human rights movement in Colonial India', *National Law School Journal*, 6(1).

Lillich, Richard B. and Frank C. Newman (1979), *International Human Rights: Problems of Law and Policy* (Boston and Toronto: Little, Brown and Company).

Meron, Theodor (1984), *Human Rights in International Law: Legal and Policy Issues*, 2 vols (Oxford: Clarendon Press).

PUCL and PUDR (1984), *Who are the Guilty?* (Delhi: PUCL and PUDR).

Ray, Aswini K. (1986), 'Civil Rights Movement and Social Struggle in India', *Economic and Political Weekly*, 21(28).

Rubin, Barnett R. (1987), 'The Civil Liberties Movement in India', *Asian Survey*, 27(3): 371–92.

Sarat, Austin and Stuart Scheingold, eds (1997), *Cause Lawyering: Political Commitments and Professional Responsibilities* (New York: Oxford University Press).

Sastri, V.S. Srinivasa (1926), 'Kamala Lectures: "Citizen" and "Subject" and The Rights of Person', reproduced in *Speeches and Writings of the Right Honourable V.S. Srinivasa Sastri,* (1969), Vol. 1 (Madras: Srinivasa Sastri Endowment Fund).

Satyamurthy, S. (1919), *Rights of Citizens* (Madras: Ganesh and Co).

Shah, Ghanshyam (2004) *Social Movements in India: A Review of Literature* (New Delhi: Sage).

Sohn, Louis B. and Thomas Buergenthal (1973), *International Protection of Human Rights: Cases and Materials* (Indianapolis: The Bobbs-Merrill Company).

UGC (2002), *Syllabus on Human Rights and Duties*, 2 vols (New Delhi: UGC).

Retrieving Indian Law

Colonial Erasures, Postcolonial Pedagogies

Dattathreya Subbanarasimha

What is the framework necessary for a comprehension of, and engagement with, the complex issues that the historical evolution of the contemporary Indian legal system has bequeathed us? This is a very urgent matter especially for those like us engaged in legal pedagogy, as it has a profound bearing on what we teach in our classes and how we go about teaching it.

I reflect here first on the career/fate of the notions of tradition and modernity in western social theory. I then digress and recapitulate the major characteristics of the British Indian (colonial and postcolonial) legal system in India and how this appears when viewed through the kaleidoscope of modern Indian democratic history and contemporary Indian democracy. Finally, I tie up the discussion of the foundational categories of western social theory with an account of what effects British colonial history and the dominant social–theoretical vocabulary of modern western social theory have produced in the domain of Indian – more specifically, Hindu – legal traditions over the last two hundred years.

Tradition and Modernity in the Dominant Strands of Western Social Theory

I will consider here three major western social theorists of the last two hundred years in whose work the notions of tradition and modernity have featured in varying degrees of prominence and significance. It is my general argument that over the last two hundred years the notion of tradition has, in a majority of the cases considered, become the unwilling sparring partner of modernity in the theories propounded by the various western purveyors of scientific, social and evolutionary progress of a universalized mankind. The theorists I have chosen for this purpose are, perhaps predictably, Max Weber, Émile Durkheim and Karl Marx.

One of the conceptual oppositions that undergirds Max Weber's work is one taken to obtain – naturally – between tradition and modernity. Starting with *The Protestant Ethic and the Spirit of Capitalism*, Weber's major corpus of work has at least two major theses: (a) that capitalism has successfully emerged only in the west and that (b) capitalism did not emerge in other civilizations of the world, such as China, India, Egypt, etc. The great corpus of work that he generated concentrated on trying to provide explanations for precisely how and why capitalism came to be in the west and why it purportedly did not emerge in China or India. Readers familiar with the general narrative of *Protestant Ethic* would be able to recognize straightaway that Weber's narrative is ambivalent about the historical transformations that the west is undergoing while he is writing his books. On the one hand, when he writes of the achievements of western capitalism and western legal organization, his tone is a triumphant one, proclaiming proudly – almost vainly, some might say – to the world that these are achievements that no other society on earth has been able to match. On the other hand, when he is in a more reflective mood, that triumphant tone is replaced by a more circumspect – some would say gloomy – one.

This ambivalence is inherent in Weber's imagination of the perceived movement of western societies from tradition to modernity. This experience of a movement from one to the other is the quintessence of the narrative of modernity that Weber's story is structured around. For Weber, western society is clearly, irretrievably, moving from tradition to modernity. In this, Weber only partook of the general tendencies that were an inescapable part of nineteenth century Europe, and which were virtually affirmed by entire sections of the western European middle classes. Just as the west was 'discovering' other lands and colonizing them, it also supposed that what it was experiencing was something totally unprecedented. It was inevitable then that the whiff of liberty that generally characterizes the experience of all things new should also have infected the spirit of the western middle classes. This sense of the new and unprecedented infected at least two major domains of western cultural experience: (a) the west's experience of nature through the now-dominant discourses of modern science, and (b) the west's experience of other peoples around the globe through violent colonialisms. Weber's sense of the movement of the west from tradition to modernity was inextricably linked to these two major domains of the western cultural experience just recounted.

But sadly, neither Weber nor most of his contemporaries were aware of the extent to which these threads were interwoven. While, in reality, these other societies were never sought to be understood on their own terms, people such as Weber – and the western middle classes of the nineteenth century more generally – used these other societies of the world merely as enormous canvases upon which to project their own experiences of triumph (on the arrival of modernity) and, sometimes, as in Weber, also of loss (at the loss of tradition). Thus, while Weber seems to have a vague awareness of the experience of the loss of tradition in late nineteenth century Europe – recall here the now very famous theory about 'disenchantment' and about modernity/modern capitalism trapping the modern west in 'an iron cage' – nonetheless this experience of loss does not ever go on to determine Weber's intellectual agenda. Instead, a great part of Weber's corpus of writings takes the sense of western civilizational triumph with capitalist modernity for granted, and goes in search of explanations for why capitalism purportedly 'failed' to emerge in other civilizations/societies.

All in all, Weber's intellectual agenda, then, participates in the opposition that nineteenth century European social theory set up between modernity and tradition, and modernity, as usual, is proclaimed as the historical winner in this alleged race.[1]

Durkheim's perspective offered a contrast to that of Weber and those of most other western social theorists of nineteenth century Europe. Most intellectual historians would perhaps agree that Emile Durkheim looked at his self-image as a scientist far more critically than Weber did. However, despite his critique of rationalism and the 'scientific progress' narrative of western society, Durkheim ultimately relied upon an implicit privileging of modernity (West) over tradition (East), especially clear in his work on mythology and primitive religion. He follows nineteenth-century hegemonic understandings of non-western peoples being locked in tradition and, therefore, lover on the evolutionary ladder than the west.

Where Durkheim was inclined towards being non-judgmental about the cultural experiences/transformations that the western world was experiencing in the nineteenth century, Marx was nothing less than celebratory about the putative achievements of 'bourgeois' capitalism of the nineteenth century west. Indeed, as Marx insisted, capitalism (of the western kind) constituted nothing less than a condition of possibility for socialism, communism, revolution or any kind of human attempt at emancipation. Marx insisted for most of his life that his critique/criticism of capitalism was not a moralistic one (based only on its alienating consequences), but a 'scientific' one, that sought to debunk the philosophical assumptions of the discipline of political economy.[3] His theory of ideology sought to demonstrate the hidden truth behind what Foucault might have called discourses of the discipline of political economy.

But perhaps the most important Marxian text from the point of view of our analysis would have to be *The Communist Manifesto*. Co-written with Friedrich Engels in 1848, this was a manifesto that sought to rouse the working peoples of the world to a revolution to overthrow bourgeois capitalism and liberalism (and other assorted 'reactionary' political formations). But strangely enough, before Marx could embark on his critique of bourgeois capitalism and liberalism, he felt it necessary to declaim the achievements and virtues of the very same bourgeois capitalism. Revolution, Marx insisted, would be impossible without the achievements of bourgeois capitalism. It was only where bourgeois capitalism had managed to establish itself that revolution could be attempted. This was because of Marx's theory about how 'contradictions' would develop within the structures of bourgeois capitalism and it was only when these contradictions had arisen and worked themselves out that the moment for revolution would arrive. To quote Marx on this:

> The bourgeoisie, wherever it has got the upper hand, has put an end to all
> feudal, patriarchal and idyllic relations. It has pitilessly torn asunder the motley
> feudal ties that bound man to his 'natural superiors', and has left remaining no

other nexus between man and man than naked self-interest, than callous 'cash payment'. It has drowned the most heavenly ecstasies of religious fervour, of chivalrous enthusiasm, of philistine sentimentalism, in the icy water of egotistical calculation. It has resolved personal worth into exchange value, and in place of the numberless indefeasible chartered freedoms, has set up that single, unconscionable freedom – Free Trade. In one word, for exploitation, veiled by religious and political illusions, it has substituted naked, shameless, direct, brutal exploitation.

The bourgeoisie has stripped of its halo every occupation hitherto honoured and looked upto with reverent awe. It has converted the physician, the lawyer, the priest, the poet, the man of science into its paid wage labourers.

The bourgeoisie has torn away from the family its sentimental veil, and has reduced the family relation to a mere money relation.

The bourgeoisie has disclosed how it came to pass that the brutal display of vigour in the Middle Ages, which reactionaries so much admire, found its fitting complement in the most slothful indolence. It has been the first to show what man's activity can bring about. It has accomplished wonders far surpassing Egyptian pyramids, Roman aqueducts, and Gothic cathedrals; it has conducted expeditions that put in the shade all former Exoduses of nations and crusades.

The bourgeoisie cannot exist without constantly revolutionizing the instruments of production, and thereby the relations of production, and with them the whole relations of society. Conservation of the old modes of production in unaltered form, was, on the contrary, the first condition of existence for all earlier industrial classes. Constant revolutionizing of production, uninterrupted disturbance of all social conditions, everlasting uncertainty and agitation distinguish the bourgeois epoch from all earlier ones. All fixed, fast-frozen relations, with their train of ancient and venerable prejudices and opinions, are swept away, all new-formed ones become antiquated before they can ossify. All that is solid melts into air, all that is holy is profaned, and man is at last compelled to face with sober senses his real conditions of life, and his relations with his kind.[4]

These famous lines from Marx and Engels' *Communist Manifesto* make it clear that for Marx, the changes that were ushered in by bourgeois capitalism were in fact necessary before any emancipatory project could be undertaken. And for Marx, too, all the transformations that he took bourgeois capitalism to have ushered in, including those of the development of the productive forces, the breaking-up of 'feudal' and 'patriarchal' relations, and the tearing asunder of older assumptions and prejudices, are transformations that only modernity has the capability to bring in and not anything else. Indeed, the contrasts that Marx writes of in the last couple of sentences of the excerpted paragraph are a telling statement on the extent to which Marx was convinced of modernity liberating the west from the purported tyrannies of tradition.

One may see from the above that Durkheim the three western social thinkers we've considered so far, i.e., Max Weber and Karl Marx, formulated in very explicit terms the sense of what was claimed to characterize modernity. And modernity itself was proclaimed to have rescued the west from the purported tyrannies of tradition. One may also extend the applicability of this generalization to virtually the whole of western social theory of the last hundred and fifty years. Indeed, even third generation Marxists such as the German thinker Jürgen Habermas have pretty much continued to be 'progressivist' thinkers, arguing that modernity does indeed mean emancipation from the ways of life of a different era (i.e., tradition).[5] That rhetoric about modernity, especially in terms of the achievements of the rational–legal order over the conception of tradition as outdated and backward, has, however, continued to be a primary and defining shibboleth for virtually all of western social theory of the last two hundred years, much to the detriment of a more nuanced and complicated understanding of processes of colonial and historical exchange, growth and change which challenges such a static dichotomy and shows how tradition and modernity are both part of a dynamic continuum.

Excursus: The British Indian Legal System and the Aporetics of Democracy

British colonialism in India has had a variety of very important consequences. One of the most recognizable domains in which many of these consequences are evident is that of law. A few scholars have looked at the historical aspects of our contemporary legal system and have commented insightfully on them. Clearly the most basic issue, an issue that was exposed and exploited to the fullest degree by the popular movement of the Indian National Congress of the first half of the twentieth century, was that of the democratic deficit in the institutions and processes concerned with law-making, law-enforcement and law-adjudication under the British Indian colonial state. The sources of most of the laws made by the British Indian colonial state were clearly institutions and processes (under the British Parliament through the Governor General/Viceroy in India) that completely lacked any democratic legitimacy within India. A really tiny political elite of British generals and civil servants made the laws for nearly half a billion people.[6] The processes the British Indian state had set up did not involve any Indians in any of their processes. Mohandas Gandhi, more than anyone else, showed up these facts and used them as the fundamental plank of his campaign against the British Indian colonial state in India.

Since those days, there have been few attempts to examine systematically the nature of the Indian legal system and the presence of the features of the British Indian colonial state in it. It is only in recent times that any such systematic attempt has been made. One of the first to do so in recent times was Upendra Baxi. In an essay that Baxi published nearly 25 years ago, he sought to outline the nature of issues that the history of colonialism raises for any scholar studying post-independent India's legal system.[7] Evidently inspired by the then radical theories of 'dependency' in the context of the economies of different regions of the world, especially Latin America, Baxi sought to draw an analogy with the historical heritage/baggage of the Indian legal system:

> The phenomenon of juristic *depedentia* manifests itself most strikingly in planning or initiating through legislative or judicial processes, evident in copycat drafting of laws or reliance on obsolescent Anglo–American decisional law (or legislative models) *which have undergone drastic changes even in the countries of their origin*.[8] In 90 per cent of the cases, the legislative draftsmen follow the model and language of English laws: judicial interpretation continues to rely heavily on Anglo–American decisional materials. The point is that through these processes legislative and judicial development remain conditioned by development and expansion of 'overseas' models (mainly Anglo–American) and the Indian legal system became a subordinate, almost a *vassal* legal system, thereby only *occasionally* serving the needs of Indian society.[9]

There is much truth in this allegation, and anyone familiar with the Anglophile predilections of much of our judiciary and bureaucracy would no doubt be able to recognize these features straightaway. However, the more fundamental points that Baxi makes relate to the democratic deficit in the practice of law-making and law-enforcement that was the norm under the British Indian colonial state and that, to a large extent, continued to mark the legal processes in post-independent India. As Baxi puts it bluntly:

> The British Indian model of law-making was a top-down model: it was a paradigm of Austinian type. There was a group of determinate human superiors which issued commands; the political inferiors had the option either to comply or to risk the application of sanction.[10]

Such is the context in which the contemporary Indian legal system operates. Little wonder then that this system presents us, contemporary Indians, with more problems than it resolves. In particular, professionals that work in the field of legal pedagogy face a unique set of issues in the domain of legal pedagogy that perhaps no other professional class in India does. It is but a platitude to note that British colonial discourse is all over the Indian legal education curriculum, from Latin maxims, through Dicey on the Rule of Law, Salmond on Jurisprudence, and to (the purported civilities of) 'the conventions of British parliamentary democracy'. Not to mention, of course, the fact that many of the most significant legislations in modern Indian legal history – Indian Penal Code 1872, the Indian Contract Act 1882, the Indian Evidence Act 1872, etc. – were all drafted by committed British colonizers in the high noon of British colonialism in India.

All of this puts us – native Indian teachers of law in contemporary India – in a rather peculiar situation. We are forced to present to our students in their original form all the principles and rules that lie in these legislations and laws inherited from British times, and yet at the same time we have also to remind our students that this was the same British colonial empire that had as its singular explicit mission the task – or 'burden', if you will, – of 'civilizing' our forebears. And in all the law that I learnt at Law School, that paradox, of the *law-giving-and-yet-violent* colonialism, was left unexplained and unaccounted for.

Today, when I think seriously of conceptualizing and teaching law courses for my students, I feel that that paradox needs to be addressed in rather explicit ways. What forms would such measures need to take? And what kinds of implications would they have for the various specific domains of the law that one engages with as a teacher?

Let us take one instantiation of this phenomenon. It was one of the great dogmas of British colonial knowledge that India was characterized by such as thing as 'the caste system'. Even after multiple tomes were authored on the subject through scores of years not only by missionaries and colonial administrators,[11] but also by expert Indologists and anthropologists,[12] the nature and form of the 'the caste system' is today no clearer to the western mind than it was to the first Europeans that arrived on Indian soil in the sixteenth and seventeenth centuries.[13] Thus it is that at the beginning of the twenty-first century, it has become clear to many western minds that 'the caste system' was as much an invention of the lazy and fearful colonial British mind as it apparently was *the essence* of India and Hinduism. (The caveat here of course is that there are empirically real *jatis* that do operate as endogamous communities throughout most of India. However, the characteristics attributed to them do not necessarily allow us to speak of 'the caste *system*' that could be taken to operate throughout India).

Now when I go look up a book on 'legal traditions' of the world to teach my first year law students, the proclamations I find there on Hindu law are rather extraordinary. H. Patrick Glenn writes in the year 2000, in *Legal Traditions of the World*:

> Castes exist because they are dictated by accumulated karma, in previous lives. If castes didn't exist, there would be no demonstrable evidence of the effect of bad karma, so castes must exist. They are a kind of necessary grouping or classing of the consequences of different kinds of previous lives, a consequence of the ongoing soul, and no historical work has been able to show them as a product of particular social circumstances in India at a particular time. So far as is known, they have existed since the Vedas became known, prior to the Smriti....[14]

A western legal scholar continues to write as if nothing new on caste has 'come to light' to the western mind since the time that this scholar read his earliest Indological treatises, probably during his undergraduate days. Is this colonial excuse for a knowledge of Indian social realities good enough for us law teachers in India today? On the other hand, we must be aware of the particular processes involved in historical account of Indian law. Werner Menski writes:

> The widespread assumption that Indian law today is merely a distorted form of English law, or that the British simply gave the Indians their law, as though there

had been a legal void before, are strange myths that refuse to die and are being fed by inadequate education systems both in Europe and India. Legal textbook authors tend to perpetuate such myths. For example, Desai writes: '. . . the spontaneous growth of Hindu law was retarded if not wholly stopped with the reduction of [*sic*] India under British rule. . . .'[15]

Opening any of the leading Hindu law textbooks today, unwary readers are seriously befuddled as to the nature of Hindu law and its later manifestations. Since . . . confusing and irreconcilable statements are found in textbooks classed as leading practitioners' handbooks, selling thousands of copies and probably influencing what the next generation of Indian lawyers knows and reads, it is important to highlight those outdated and confused perceptions of Hindu law. . . . Unless modern editions of the leading textbooks on Hindu law are assiduously rewritten, future generations of Indian lawyers will continue to be forever confused.[16]

So what happened to the traditional law and traditions of the more than three hundred million Hindus that lived through the late eighteenth and nineteenth centuries under the British Indian colonial state? Strange as it may seem, the argument of textbook writers such as Desai seems to be that there was no traditional law. Surely it had to be some form of law that held Hindu social life together before the coming of the British to India.[17]

This whole subject of the legal system under British rule and what happens to Hindu law and traditions under it is very complex, but nonetheless extraordinarily important. Let us try to get a basic grip on the most salient of the features of this history that we are thus far familiar with. From the time that the *Diwani* rights (to administer justice) in Bengal was transferred to the East India Company in 1765, the British in India began to conceptualize ways of adjudicating disputes amongst Indian litigants. Generally speaking, for a hundred years after the transfer of the *Diwani* rights, the British focused on two or three major moves: (a) they appointed Hindu pandits in the local court jurisdictions as experts that would interpret the Hindu texts and scriptures (*shastras*) and convey to English judges what they took to be the Hindu position on that particular question of law was; (b) they commissioned translations of Hindu texts and scriptures that English judges would themselves use in order to determine what the position on that question in Hindu law was; and (c) they gradually introduced the principle of *stare decisis* (precedents) and this was made an acceptable source of Hindu law. The first two methods chosen did not necessarily succeed too well. Although during the early period of these new methods – i.e. during the time of William Jones – there was some earnestness and enthusiasm for these jobs, this was not to last too long. The sheer enormity of the challenge ultimately put paid to these methods. They became edifices and testaments to distorted and failed communication, rather than to a successful bi-cultural or hybrid set of products. As Werner Menski puts it: 'Despite . . . initial sympathies . . . the attempted cross-cultural communication over legal concepts during this crucial early period contains precisely the evidence of malfunction and distortion that we are looking for . . . .'[18]

Thus things did not stay this way for very long. 1864, by which time the British had started to feel confident that they had accumulated a sufficient amount of case-law/precedents in Anglo–Hindu law, proved to be a momentous year for the nature of this legal system. In this year, the British Indian colonial state (power had now – in 1858 – been transferred from the East India Company to the British Crown and Parliament) declared that henceforth the British Indian judiciary would assume knowledge of Hindu law.[19] British judges were now relying on this body of case-law in order to make determinations on all legal disputes between Indians. The previously flexible and context-sensitive Hindu law was gradually turned into something far more rigid. As Duncan Derrett has put it:

> In 1864 judicial knowledge of Hindu law was assumed. If this had been refused, and the system had been treated as a foreign law (to be proved in evidence), the growth (of Hindu law) would have been continuous. But the apparent unreliability of the pandits indirectly obviated this possibility. Even otherwise, pandits' powers of 'text-torturing' were not boundless. To introduce western-type grounds for divorce, and inheritance of shares by daughters along with sons, was impossible for them – yet this, it is evident, was the sort of growth the (modernist and modernizing) reformers wanted.[20]

However, even this was not to last. There were loud voices among influential sections of the Indian population that called for codification, modernization and the like. Thus over the next eighty years, i.e. till the time the British left India in 1947, although the British Indian state continued with the hotch-potch system of Hindu law that they had summarily cobbled together, the modernizers – even among Indians – continued to perceive Hindu law and traditions as 'backward' and consequently in need of 'reform'. Clearly, one of the fundamental reasons why Hindu law and traditions were perceived to be 'backward' was the belief amongst this class of people that somehow British law was inherently superior to that of Indian law, and that Hindu law was somehow so beset with superstition and backwardness that only state-led legislations and codification could probably retrieve it from its state of decay. Indeed, this was the case with the most prominent Indians of the nineteenth and early twentieth centuries. Thus, today names such as those of Raja Rammohun Roy are recalled primarily as those of 'social reformers'.

That state of embarrassment and self-hatred continues to be the norm amongst most Indian textbook writers and commentators on Hindu law even today. On the other hand, scholars such as Menski have argued that traditional Hindu law sought to achieve a harmony of life and law, which rendered formal/positivist law, as we understand it today in jurisprudence and philosophy, superfluous.[21] Menski repeatedly emphasizes the enormous gulf that exists between the specific legal propositions of Anglo–Hindu law and the actual social reality of Hindu law. In Menski's laconic, but sharp, phrasing, the consequence is summed up thus: 'Like an ice-berg, most of Hindu law became (under British colonialism) submerged and virtually invisible to lawyers and modernist analysts.'[22] The simile of the ice-berg introduces the conception – equally problematic – that 'Hindu Law' can simply be disinterred from beneath British history in India. Textbook writers and commentators, who tend not to have so much as a conceptual apparatus to even recognize or to describe either the whole or even the discrete elements of Hindu law, need to historicize Hindu law. There is an inviting challenge that awaits us here on how each concept in the our legal traditions may be remedied and replaced by a rigorous historical account and more intimate, first-hand ('local') knowledge of Indian social realities that is already readily available to all Indian law teachers.

Ultimately, the challenge for Indian teachers of law – and the profession of Indian legal pedagogy in general – is to ensure that, at the minimum, everyone in the Indian legal classroom, teacher and student alike, share the same horizon of meaning.

Notes

1. For a general survey of the important books relating to the current discussion, see Weber (1905/1930), especially the introduction here; Weber, *The Religion of India*; Weber (1951; 1958).
2. See on this the introduction entitled 'Subject of Our Study: Religious Sociology the Theory of Knowledge' in Durkheim (1967).
3. One would do well to recall here that Marx's most famous work was actually subtitled 'A Critique of Political Economy'. See Marx (1976).
4. Marx and Engels (1848/1977: 223–24).
5. Even if the 'progress' that these thinkers talk about tends to focus more on the deepening of the democratic processes in their own societies rather than on any social-evolutionist programmes reminiscent of late nineteenth-century Europe.
6. Even on the eve of the British leaving India, the total number of British people in India was only 100,000. And what is more, out of these 100,000, it was only a few hundred who were actually involved in the government; virtually the whole of the rest was made up of British soldiers and army officers. This tiny elite of a few hundred people ruled over, and made laws in the name of, four hundred and fifty million people.
7. Baxi (1982: 41–83), also excerpted in Deva (2005: 45–59).
8. Italics in the original.
9. Baxi in Deva (2005: 47).
10. Ibid.: 48.
11. See the works by Abbé Dubois (who talks of caste incidentally) and Herbert Risley.
12. E.g., the late anthropologist Louis Dumont (1970) relies on Indological (scriptural) knowledge for his most important claims about Hindu society.
13. See, for instance, Dirks (2000).
14. Glenn (2000: 264).
15. Menski (2003: 158).
16. Ibid.: 186.
17. The word 'law' is being used here in its more expansive sense, as something that includes, but also transcends, sublates, mere positive law.
18. Menski (2003: 166–167).
19. Ibid.: 167.
20. Derrett (1968).
21. Menski (2003: 183).
22. Ibid.: 181.

References

Baxi, Upendra (1982), 'The Colonial Nature of the Indian Legal System', in *The Crisis of the Indian Legal System* (New Delhi: Vikas).

Derrett, J. and M. Duncan (1968), 'Administration of Hindu Law by the British', in Deva (2005).

Deva, Indra, ed. (2005), *Sociology of Law* (Delhi: Oxford University Press).

Dirks, Nicholas (2000), *Castes of Mind: Colonialism and the Making of Modern India* (Princeton: Princeton University Press).

Dumont, Louis (1970), *Homo Hierarchicus* (Chicago: University of Chicago Press).

Durkheim, Émile (1967), *The Elementary Forms of the Religious Life* (Boston: The Free Press).

Glenn, H. Patrick (2000), *Legal Traditions of the World: Sustainable Diversity in Law* (Oxford: Oxford University Press).

Marx, Karl (1976), *Capital: A Critique of Political Economy*, 3 vols (Harmondsworth: Penguin).

Marx, Karl and Friedrich Engels (1848/1977), *The Communist Manifesto* in David McLellan, ed., *Karl Marx: Selected Writings* (Oxford: Oxford University Press).

Menski, Werner (2003), *Hindu Law: Beyond Tradition and Modernity* (New Delhi: Oxford University Press).

Weber, Marx (1905/1930), *The Protestant Ethic and the Spirit of Capitalism*, translated by T. Parsons (London: Allen & Unwin).

―――― (1951), *The Religion of China*, translated and edited by H.H. Gerth (Glencoe: Free Press).

―――― (1958), *The Religion of India: The Sociology of Hinduism and Buddhism*, translated and edited by H.H. Gerth and D. Martindale (Glencoe: Free Press).

The Performance of Law

The Unspeakable Violence of Isoor, 1942

Janaki Nair

Introduction

Comparisons between the judge and the historian have been made at least since the nineteenth century. Lord Acton is supposed to have said of historiography that 'when it is based on documents it can rise above disagreements and become an established court of law', reflecting widely prevailing optimism about positivist evidentiary protocols. He was also recalling a long-standing link between the judge and the historian which Carlo Ginzburg suggests has existed in the western tradition for at least 2500 years with the Greek invention of the literary genre called 'historia'. Though the term itself, Ginzburg reminds us, is derived from medical parlance, its reasoning skills are derived from the law. 'History as a specific intellectual activity was founded at the intersection of medicine and rhetoric' since 'history examines cases and situations, seeking out their natural causes, in emulation of medicine, then sets them forth in accordance with the rules of rhetoric, an art of persuasion that developed in the courtroom'.[1]

The methods of the lawyer and the historian have thus been compared for their extraordinary similarities: collecting and evaluating evidence (the evidentiary method), bearing the burden of proof and using the persuasive argument. But it would be dangerous for the delivery of justice and equally impoverishing for the practice of history if, as Ginzburg so well demonstrates, the paths of the historian and the judge intersect for too long. A historian, he says, has the right to 'detect a problem' where a judge might find an 'absence of grounds for proceedings', though the two may be linked on the crucial question of proof. Historians have the privilege of using a degree of conjecture, of venturing speculatively into areas where there might be little or no evidence, without running the risk of judicial error.

Shahid Amin has shown that the historian is under no compulsion to read judicial evidence in order to indict wrongdoers or deliver justice. Nevertheless, in his discussion of Chauri Chaura, the event that brought the Non-Cooperation movement to a halt in 1922, 'in order not to write like the Judge, I have tried to find out how the judge wrote'.[2] Historians thus have a freer space of enquiry though by no means one that is free of responsibility. The historian's skepticism about the judicial record, and her questions regarding the modes by which often illiterate plaintiffs, witnesses or defendants are incited to speak, is enabled by the freedom to establish truth within parameters of dissonance. The freedom to read the copious judicial record for purposes *other than those which were intended*, that is, against the grain, allows the recovery of a truth other than the pre-history of an intention to commit a 'crime'.

In India, the field of the law has intersected with history at a slightly different point, especially since both fields were radically recast following the advent of colonial rule. History thus became both a resource and a contentious subject in the making of law. At the same time, it produced new historical subjects in the process of transforming a real historical experience into a 'matrix of abstract legality'.[3] Law, meanwhile, served history with an archive of unparalleled richness. Law's 'incitement to discourse' produced a vast web of relations, dependencies and antagonisms, as well as occasional solidarities, within and between communities, in the course of affixing guilt 'beyond reasonable doubt'.

It is thus transgression of the law, particularly in moments of political rebellion, that provides the historian some glimpses of subaltern consciousness, even when the 'truth' of such events is always already classified as crime. The appearance of colonial law in the lives of the subaltern classes, Ranajit Guha says in his analysis of Chandra's death, heralds 'an abstract legality so that the will of the state could be made to penetrate, reorganize part by part and eventually control the will of the subject population in much the same way as Providence is brought to impose itself on mere human destiny'.[4] Upendra Baxi has pointed out that Guha's work on peasant insurgency is a celebration of the productive *violence of the law* as well as the *law of violence*, where the latter inverts the will of the state, through the 'subversion of the insignia of subalternity' or the valorization of crime as a pathway to justice'.[5] This article attempts to trace these two processes in a series of events during the Quit India movement of 1942 in Mysore.

I

In 1970, when the then Chief Minister of Mysore, Veerendra Patil, sanctioned Rs 1 lakh for a memorial to the martyrs at 'Esur' (*sic*) in Shikaripur Taluk, baffled journalists had to 'dig into the past' to find out which event was being commemorated.[6] Clearly, an important nationalist 'event' had not become a 'metaphor' for the people of Mysore/Karnataka in the same way as Chauri Chaura had become part of the nation's historical 'common sense'.[7] This, despite several contemporary accounts of Mysore nationalists who used the swift and brutal reprisal of the state apparatus – in particular the death sentence to five men, the life sentence to seven including three women, and varying terms of imprisonment to a further fourteen – as a way of raising the volume of nationalist opposition to colonial rule after 1943.[8]

There were several other attempts at writing Isoor as an important event in the making of modern Mysore: semi-fictionalized accounts of the struggles of the people of Isoor,[9] the recorded memories of those who participated in the struggle,[10] an account of Quit India in Mysore,[11] and of the Isoor struggle [12] by professional historians and, most recently, a touching personal memoir by C. Lingappa.[13]

All these accounts insist on the broad consensus that was achieved during the Quit India movement, and stick close to the script of R.R. Diwakar's first report of the tragedy that struck the 'highly Congress-minded' village of Isoor. They leave largely unquestioned the nationalist narrative which sees it as the last great Gandhian struggle against British imperialism.[14] As a result, the treatment of the moment of popular violence leading to the death of an Amaldar and a Sub-Inspector which in turn triggered the brutality of the state apparatuses, is striking in its brevity. What is unspeakable about this act of violence, apart from its shocking departure from anything that Gandhi might have stood for? Indeed, if it was nationalist condemnation of the peasant violence at Chauri Chaura that led a historian like Shahid Amin to work towards a recovery of alternative, subaltern memories of the struggle of 1922, it is the unquestioned celebration of the heroism of the people of Isoor that gives me pause, and leads me to ask a different set of questions about this event and its meanings for the making of modern Mysore.

The event must be seen as an illuminating flash which brought a relatively little-known village to renown, and, in the process, highlighted many of the disjunctions in a seamless narrative of Gandhian mobilization. To recount the bare bones of the event: the village of Isoor, in Shimoga district of northern Mysore state, had been drawn into the Quit India struggle from the early days of August 1942, though daily processions through the village (*prabhat pheris*) were the principal mode of local involvement. Between September 25 and 28, 1942, more than a month after the Quit India movement had been muffled by mass arrests of the leadership and thousands of participants, Isoor declared its independence from British rule. A large number of students, and young men and women of the village, were the main supporters of nationalist activity that had preceded the declaration of independence, while the leadership was provided by the three most influential Sahukars of Isoor, the brothers Rachavalli Rudrappa and Basavanappa, and the former's son Shantaveerappa. On September 28, 1942, a party of visiting revenue officials and police was violently attacked by the crowd at Isoor, after police firing in which two protestors were grazed. The crowd's response resulted in the deaths of Amaldar Chennakrishnappa and the Sub-Inspector Kenche Gowda. Retaliation was swift and brutal, and five peasant rebels were hanged for their role in the Isoor deaths, while 21 others were sentenced to varying lengths of imprisonment.

Shahid Amin has pioneered the modes by which one may rescue the subaltern from both judicial and nationalist discourse by using the judicial archive itself. My task here too is to ask of an event that was 'depoliticized' by judicial discourse: how was it silenced and displaced in the nationalist narrative, deserving not even the condemnation of the upper caste/class leadership of the national movement? What was *unspeakable* about the violence of the crowd that resulted in the deaths of the state's emissaries? Does the judgment offer the possibility of retrieving elementary aspects of a contradictory peasant consciousness in order to deny both the colonial judicature and the nationalist 'court' of history their moments of triumph? And finally, what can such retrieval tell us about the modes of power that were emerging at a time of political and economic transition?

II

Let us recall Gandhi's words on the eve of his arrest at 5 am on August 9, 1942:

> Everyone is free to go to the fullest extent under ahimsa. Complete deadlock by strikes and other non-violent means. Satyragrahis must go out and die, not to live. They must seek and face death. It is only when individuals go out to die that the nation will survive. *Karenge ya marenge* (We shall 'do or die').

How did this call to 'Do or Die' get fatefully interpreted as killing on behalf of the nation in Isoor? The walls of the Veerabhadraswamy temple, the centre of the Isoor struggle, included the slogan 'Let there be unity! Let the Government servants be cut to pieces! Ryot brethren be united; give up communal differences!'[15] Gyanendra Pandey has pointed out that in northern India, the Hindi *'Karo ya Maro'* was all too easily corrupted into *'Karo ya Maaro* (Achieve or Kill)' to produce the series of violent incidents and guerilla actions that formed the staple of the Quit India movement.[16] In addition to pointing to the more complicated relationship between official leadership and the popular radical movement within the nationalist struggle than has been admitted, an interrogation of the people's violence and the nature of peasant participation will disrupt the narrative of unquestioning 'unity' attributed to the Isoor struggle of 1942.[17] How, in the light of detailed studies of the parallel governments of Satara Parti Sarkar in western India,[18] Tamluk Jatiya Sarkar in Bengal[19] and Talcher state,[20] the messianic quality of Laxman Naiko's revolt in Orissa and his tragic execution,[21] may we understand the short-lived, three-day parallel government in Isoor, ostensibly 'run' by two young boys? For it was Jayappa, the 10-year-old grandson of Rudrappa who was named the new 'Amaldar' of the village and another family member, 12-year-old Mallappa, the 'Sub-Inspector' of Isoor's 'parallel government'.

For the most part, these unusual features of Isoor's parallel government have not been allowed to disturb the singular focus on the village's tragic heroes. Since 1970, the event has been memorialized in a number of interesting ways which increasingly appear as the modern nation-state's *way of forgetting*. The thoroughly neglected and run-down official memorial at Isoor is only the most visible sign of a strategic forgetfulness. By becoming a lasting reminder of the brutalities of colonial rule, it deliberately silences *the law of violence* in order to foreground the *violence of the law*.

To begin the process of an alternative recovery, one must recount two contemporary memories of the days of 1942 at Isoor. The memory of

Kotrabasappa, the priest who still resides near the Veerabhadraswamy temple, which was the seat of the Isoor 'parallel government', is less than celebratory. He was a young boy in 1942 and speaks in a voice tinged with bitterness about the unkept promises of the independent Indian state. Pointing out that 'people come and write the history claiming it as their own,' he adds, 'They said that they would make this into a "Dattograma" where everything would work. This was Yediyurappa's [BJP MLA of Shikaripur for 18 years] promise but nothing has happened'. The nationalist narratives of heroism have not even secured a minimum recognition for many in Isoor, he claimed, since 'there are about 35 people who do not get pension even though they struggled'.[22] The memory of collective political action, whatever its failures or achievements, when refracted through the paltry economic compensations of the state, however unjust, robs nationalism of its ideological shine. A similar sense of dismay is expressed by C. Lingappa in his memoirs, when he claims that neither the formal gestures of the state government nor the informal memorials to the 'heroes' of Isoor adequately acknowledge and honour the real heroes in his village.[23]

A far more complex recuperation of the event is in the memorial tablets which were installed in 1995 at the considerably extended Shri Veerabhadraswamy temple, the fulcrum of the 1942 struggle itself. C. Lingappa records with loving detail the renovation of the temple and the additions made by members of the committee set up in 1984 which included himself. It is a way of compensating for the lapses, neglect and indifference of the nation-state for the 'heroes' of Isoor.[24] Equally disappointing were 'the people of [Isoor who] did not devote much attention to the matter,' writes Lingappa, taking on himself the task of reconstructing memory. A black polished granite slab lists the names of all the men who went to the gallows, and those people who were awarded life imprisonment or rigorous imprisonment of various terms. The most interesting inclusions in this list are two other sets of people: 'Praanaarpisida Adhikaragalu', namely, Chennakrishnappa (Tahsildar) and Kenchegowda (SI), the murdered state officials, and 'Bhugathakaryakartharu', namely, Sahukar Basavanappa and Angadi Halappa, who absconded after the event and evaded arrest, the former dying in relative obscurity and the latter emerging from the jungles only after August 1947. Here is an act of recovery that wishes to bestow a new unity on the citizenry of Isoor. It is one which would find the virulent hostility of the peasant to the state apparatuses too dangerous to foster even as a memory. The hallowed precincts of the temple confer a post-independence 'citizenship' as it were, on all its Indian heroes even when they were the emissaries of the colonial state.[25] By placing the tragic heroes from among the peasantry, the state officials and the absconding leaders, on the same plane, Isoor is made to serve as a reminder of the many victims of colonialism.

If the nationalist accounts have largely reconstructed the scale and brutality of the state's emissaries, it is, as always, the 'prose of counter insurgency' that richly recounts the act of popular violence. In revisiting this archive, my intention is not to perform, once more, the role of the judge in condemning this act as 'crime'. Nor is it to glorify the response of the peasant community to Gandhi's call. Rather, one might recover from the folds of this voluminous document some of the paradoxical elements of peasant mobilization in northern Mysore on the eve of independence. By this, it is hoped, some elements of the *law of violence* will be made visible.

III

Commenting on the seriousness of the offences committed by the people of Isoor and emphasizing the need for exemplary state violence, Chief Justice of the Mysore Chief Court D'Arcy Reilly, who undertook the review in 1943 of the Special Court's judgement, expressed his inability to fathom the arrival of nationalism in Mysore in ways that could explain the violent act:

> [I]t is extraordinary that such offences should have been committed against public servants of this state in the circumstances. What it appears had caused a disturbed feeling in the village of Isoor was something which had been done under the orders of the Government of India or the Government of some part of British India to persons who are not connected with Mysore in any way. It was quite open to the villages of Isoor as to anyone else in the world to have their own opinion about what was done in British India in that way. But only by the most perverted reasoning could any one be brought to think that the Government of Mysore or any officer of Mysore was in any imaginable way responsible for what was so done. . . . This case has disclosed not only disloyalty and rebellion [against His Highness the Maharaja of Mysore] but savagery, which no one would have imagined could be found in any village in Mysore.[26]

Isoor was thus made 'the byword throughout the country for savagery'. Indeed, so localized was this 'savagery' that 'only when people more human came from another village' were those who were still alive on that fateful day rescued. But in admitting the rebellious nature of the events at Isoor, Reilly was acknowledging the challenges posed to the existing political order.

Reilly's words were echoed by Abdul Aziz Khan, IGP of Mysore, when he remarked that the Quit India activities were everywhere, but took an unexpected turn only in Isoor. 'In fact, the Issur tragedy stands as the one solitary incident of organized defiance to constitutional authority, of a most brutal type that has no comparison, at any rate as far as Mysore is concerned'.[27]

Special Judge A. Sundararaja Rao's earlier judgement at Sagar in December 1942 was less puzzled by the reasons for the extraordinarily 'unMysorean' violence: Isoor was a 'rich and prosperous village' that was seven miles from Shikaripur by road and four miles by country track. Its geographical remove from the reach of administrative power made its inhabitants defiant. Due to its inaccessibility, 'the villagers seem to be of a lawless type little recognizing the Government of His Highness the Maharaja'. Unlike Reilly, Rao acknowledged that 'the Congress movement had its effect in the villages in Mysore as well as in British India'.

How did this prosperous multicaste village in Shikaripur Taluk, with about 400–500 houses, and a population of about 2000 come to the forefront of the Quit India agitation?[28] Shikaripur taluk was studded with *kattes* (tanks) and long earthen bunds separating lush fields of paddy and sugarcane. The establishment of the Anjanapur project, constructed between 1935 and 1939 allowed for the spread of the cash crop sugarcane.[29] Although dominated by Lingayats, Isoor was also an important weaving centre, at least until the devastating fire of March 1928, when there were nearly '200 houses belonging to the weaver community of which 30 lived by their profession'.[30] At that time, there were at least 35 very wealthy Lingayat landowning families who engaged in money-lending as well, but, in the 1940s, it is clear that several Lingayat families were also working as agricultural labourers, a sign that the new cash crop economy had realigned economic destinies in the village.

Apart from the wealthy Lingayat households and the Devanga families were a host of small landholders, though the majority of Isoor residents were landless.[31] At the bottom end of the social scale were 50 odd Adi Karnataka and Woddar families. Other intermediary castes who made up the village were the Kumbaras, Darjis, and Vishwakarmas, most of whom combined work on small plots of land with their professions. There were finally a small number of Muslim families in the village. Some of them, Sattar Mohamed Dastagir for instance, combined service with agricultural work. Dastagir doubled as the school master and, along with his sons, leased in and cultivated the lands of a wealthy Lingayat leader Gurushantappa.[32] Others, including Pore Sab and Peerkhan, worked as labourers under Gurushantappa for wages.[33] Police witness Imam Sab and defence witness Budan Sab were intermediary cultivators, leasing in land from one Phakeera and in turn subletting to other persons for rent of one third of the total yield.

The Lingayats, and the wealthy, land-owning Lingayats in particular, enjoyed social and political dominance in the region. The Sahukars of the village were identified before the court as those who paid between Rs 1500 and 2000 per annum as assessment, in addition to income tax. Although Sahukar Rachavalli Rudrappa lost the most during the 1928 fire – jewels and cash amounting to Rs 1,20,000 – he donated 40 acres for the rebuilding of the village in a new extension which came to be known as New Isoor.

The leading Lingayats patronized poorer members of the caste and supported activities of the Mutts and temples in the area: this generosity was also extended to the Congress.[34] There were at least two identifiable factions at Isoor, one led by Basavanappa and his brother Rachavalli Rudrappa, while the Sadar Lingayats were led by Dodda Sivappa (the Patel faction). Lingayat factions in Isoor, it was claimed in court, were spatialized in specific ways: there was thus a 'Patel Street' and 'Sowcar Street' to signify the two power centres.

The courtroom of the Special Judge became another theatre for staging the factional struggles between the village elites. Police and defense witnesses alike were called on to testify to 'faction' wars. The disjointed answers to a prosecution seeking to anchor the Isoor violence in local ill will thus testify to the animosity between the various branches of Lingayat families. This animosity could be summoned to serve the colonial judicature at will. Dodda Sivappa showed no hesitation in testifying against Basavanappa and his brother, since the latter had testified against him in the murder case some years earlier.[35] Sowcar Rudrappa appeared as a prosecution witness in that case, in which Mahadevappiah and Patel Gurushantappa, both sons of Dodda Sivappa, were accused, leading to the conviction of the former.[36] Similarly, many witnesses referred to the tensions between the Balehalli Mutt and the Sirigere Mutt, among whose adherents interdining was prohibited.[37]

Past grievances were thus made to flower in the court.[38] Testimonies referred to the fierce contests over the post of Patel.[39] The Isoor Patel Channabasaviah declared in court that although the *barawad* of Isoor Patel was in the name of Patel Gurushantappa, also one of the Isoor accused, 'I am acting as the Gumastha Patel of Isoor for the part 11 years.' Following a contest for the office of Patel between him on one side, and Gurushantappa and his brother on the other, the Deputy Commissioner had decided in Channabasavaiah's favour in 1940.[40]

Each faction also retained adherents through forging links with those in need from the opposite faction: Dodda Sivappa's son Mahadevappiah testified on behalf of Siddamma that she had been fined by the Sadar Lingayat party for going to cook for Basavanappa. Her inability to pay the fine resulted in the Sadar faction refusing to bury her mother. Siddamma was forced to turn to Basavannappa in her time of need.[41]

Despite this dense patchwork of alliances and animosities that was etched in the court, there were still the inexplicable solidarities that were forged at the time of the Quit India movement in Isoor. Despite the effort of the court to establish the *crime* of 1942, with the spotlight turned on local grievances, the *political* was impossible to repress in the staccato utterances of the Isoor peasantry in the court.

IV

The Congress had a presence in nearby Shikaripur, and Shimoga town was swept up in the nationalist currents of the Bombay Karnataka region, but Isoor was relatively inaccessible and somewhat slower to receive and respond to the nationalist call. In the 1930–31 Civil Disobedience movement, the people of Shikaripur taluk were among those who defied the revenue authorities, with some villages meeting less than ten per cent of the revenue demand. Revenue officials noted that the ryots of the area were encouraged to use the 'same tactic by a set of agitators in this tract [as in Bombay Karnataka, which it bordered] against the payment of land revenue enforced by *social boycott and excommunication*'. There was, then, active deployment of existing forms of social power in the new political movement. This called, in turn, for the adoption of 'necessary and effective coercive measures' by the state until such revenue arrears were recovered.[42] When revenue officials admitted that the fall in the price of agricultural commodities and the failure of the rains had led to distress, economic explanations were being seen as the reason for the political demand for revenue remission. Yet revenue collections in the period immediately before 1942 were more than satisfactory, and close to the state average of 85 per cent.[43]

The students from Isoor in the nearby Shimoga High School, such as C. Lingappa, were among the important bearers of nationalist ideologies to the village of Isoor, and were more attracted to guerilla tactics during the Quit India movement. Mariswamy Hiremath who had been active in the Civil Disobedience movement and Vasappa Gogi of Shikaripur were among those who conducted a Congress camp in Isoor 1938.[44] Ramalli Holebasappa, one of those convicted for his role in the events, recalls that the arrival of H.C. Dasappa in a nearby village in 1937 led to the conversion of Isoor satyagrahis such as Thyavanigi Malleshappa, Sahukar Basavanappa, Holeyappa, Nageshachar, Phaniappachar and Suryanarayanachar to the 'khadi' path.[45] After Gandhi's arrest on August 9, 1942, the actions at Isoor were confined to *prabhat pheris*, though reports from nearby regions spoke of intermittent acts of violence on government property.

Although they were late in joining such actions as the cutting of telegraph wires, damaging bridges and culverts, the people of Isoor did participate in actions nearby. Vasappa Gogi was implicated in the cutting of Baloor bridge, and on September 25, the culvert at Haragoppa was damaged by 'the leaders of Gama and Isoor', namely, Annadana Siddalingappa, Kugali Mahadevappa, Gurubasaviah of Gama and Sahukar Basavanappa, Nirvana Halappa, Devangada Shankarappa of Isoor. Nagavandada Bharamanna became a volunteer in Isoor in 1942 and converted others such as Angadi Halappa, urging them to stop revenue payments. It was he who urged Sahukar Basavanappa in September 1942 to organize a parallel government.

Basavanappa, the acknowledged leader of the movement in Isoor, himself wavered between the attractions of Gandhi's non-violent tactics and the lure of Subhas Chandra Bose's defiant style. Reports of Bose's Berlin speech, says Lingappa, had a powerful impact on Basavanappa who was an active organizer of the meetings at Isoor and even accepted the presidentship of the local Congress. Yet the parallel government was run by a young surrogate for Sahukar Basavanappa, the ten year old Jayappa, assisted by another twelve year old member of the Sahukar family, K.G. Mallappa, who took on the role of 'Sub-Inspector'. The parallel government ran for three days, in which time it continued with *prabhat pheris*, exhorted the villagers to engage in an assortment of violations of the law (withholding payment of *kandaya;* cutting sandal and toddy trees, telephone wires; damaging culverts and bridges; setting fire to the post office, etc.). Above all, the parallel government punished with fateful consequences the state's emissaries who entered the village.

The government's actions on the three days of its existence were, as Chief Justice Reilly noted, 'much more serious than childish pranks'. On 25 September, the visiting Patel Chennabasavaiah and Shanbhogue Ranganatha

Rao were humiliated by Jayappa, Mallappa and other young members of the 'government'. The officials, who had reached the village for (revenue) collection, were asked to adopt the Gandhian sartorial code and resign their official posts. Their account books were seized and not returned. On September 27, punishments were inflicted on the two for entering a 'liberated area' despite the dangling threat which said 'Irresponsible Sirkar people must not come to the village. If they come . . .' (*bejavabdari adhikaaragalu barakuudadu, bandare* . . .).

What was the nature of the alternative power centre, this 'play acting' by the 'Amaldar' and the 'Sub-Inspector'? The surrogacy of the government, with young boys 'taking power' in the name of their landlord/moneylender elites of the village was a striking feature of the Isoor movement. While it is true that students were among the most active constituents of the Quit India movement throughout India, none of the parallel governments appears to have handed over power to surrogates in this manner. Jayappa's 'appointment' to the post of Amaldar signified no diminution in the local dominance of the Lingayats, only a generational transfer of power, as if in anticipation of arrangements of power in the new Indian nation. For there was no disguising the source of the directions received by the boy officials. Shanbogue Ranganatha Rao testified that there were about 100 adults 'including Sowcar Basavanappa, Shantaveerappa, Angadi Halappa' with about 100 boys on September 27, and 'Sowcar Basavanappa said that we must undergo the punishment inflicted by the [boy] Amaldar'.[46] The Patel recalled the 'Amaldar' Jayappa saying: 'It is our salt that you eat. You are our servants. It is not right that you should do thus. Send up your resignations. Else we will burn your papers. Don't you know that Isoor is a Congress village?'

It was to Sowcar Basavanappa's house that the Police Constable Ramanna went on September 26, to tender the resignation that was demanded of him. When Vithoba refused to ink the slogans in the temple that Lingoji (Lingappa) had chalked up, 'Sowcar Basavanappa beat him and compelled him to ink that writing'.[47] In the course of the trial, witness after police witness acknowledged the Sahukar's role in inciting the crowd to beat the officials with sticks, using nothing but the choicest abuse for those pleading for water or pity.

Most of the demands that were put up on the walls of the temple and actions against the officials of the state were anti-colonial, but of a kind that would have only limited appeal to a multi-class village. There was the usual exhortation to promote communal amity and wear *khadi,* although Sahukar Basavanappa himself appears to have retained his hat and tie, as did many of his cohorts: criticism of some Lingayat leader's westernized dress code at the Shikaripur meeting was quickly swept out of the public eye.[48]

But the 'don't pay *kandaya*' demand could not have held the same meaning to the tenants of the big landlords (for whom a no-rent demand would have been more appropriate) as it would to the landlords themselves, for, as we have seen, they were substantial payers of revenue. From as early as the Civil Disobedience movement, it was clear that they were the quickest to seize the opportunities of resisting state power. S.J.P. Epstein, speaking of the areas of Bombay–Karnataka that bordered Shimoga, suggests that 'a Lingayat conference in Haveri, Dharwar, [in August 1930] formally swung the most influential of the market-oriented rural castes of the division behind the nationalist campaign'.[49] By the second Civil Disobedience campaign, Karnataka had overtaken Gujarat as the locus of nationalist activity.[50] The Karnataka region maintained its lead and became the 'main focus of underground activity in western India' after the first round of arrests in August 1942, a lead it maintained throughout the Quit India period.[51] The richer landlords then had the most to lose by abstaining from the Quit India movement.

To be sure, the purely economic reasons for rich Lingayats being drawn to the national movement were of interest to the revenue officials, and even the court which was trying to establish the private motivations for the crime of 1942. Revenue Inspector M. Muniappa testified in court that Gurushantappa's paddy crop was attached and sold for the lower price of Rs 4–12–0 instead of the prevailing Rs 5 or 5–8–10 per palla to meet revenue arrears in 1941. Yet the Isoor campaign conformed to the Bombay–Karnataka 'model' only to some extent. Some smaller artisanal castes, the Vishwakarma, Devangas and Darjis, were drawn into the struggle, and for most people the call to cut trees and stop paying tolls would have held a certain appeal. Yet, unlike the other parallel governments, anti-landlord/anti-caste slogans and actions were non-existent. Neither a single demand nor action attempted to alter the local power structure: the Quit India movement in Isoor was fully in the control of the local elites. Gyan Pandey suggests that the colonial state's swift arrests thwarted a second wave of pitched struggle against local power structures in other regions of the country. In Mysore too, by the time of the release of most of the Congress members in 1943, the spirit of nationalism had been seriously dampened and, by 1945, such gains had not even been translated into Representative Assembly seats (with the Congress winning only 130 of 310 seats).[52]

The significant absence of the Muslims, who had been totally alienated from the Congress-led movement at this time, is thus better explained. As tenants, and as intermediaries, they would have no stakes in a no-revenue demand. We know of certain tensions between Patel Gurushantappa and his Muslim tenant who was only able to pay half his rent in 1942. An element of coercion may have prompted one of Gurushantappa's Muslim labourers to appear as his defence witness.[53] These tensions had a great deal to do with the structure of the local economy: both police and defence witnesses testified that there were no animosities between Hindus and Muslims in this area. In the words of Dastagir Sab, 'there is no ill will between Hindus and Muslims in Isoor'. But Muslims en bloc remained impervious to appeals to join the movement, signifying political resistance that cannot be explained by the economies of the village alone. The historian need not follow the reasoning of either the revenue official or the judge in establishing purely economic motives for the actions of the peasantry at Isoor.

The alienation of the lower castes and Muslims are not easily explained in a village where they were sizeable numbers of them and where ethnic tensions were relatively minimal. Only one of the 50 accused, Thejanna, an Adi Karnataka, was discharged for want of evidence in the Isoor case. In the fire of 1928, only the tiled roof houses of the upper castes were burned to the ground: the thatched and flimsy homes of the Adi Karnatakas and the Woddars miraculously escaped the fire. The second 'fire' of nationalism seems to have given the lower castes a go-by as well. They are not mentioned by the Congress narratives, defence witnesses, or the police witnesses as having participated in this cataclysmic event.

There is, on the other hand, more than a hint of coercion by the upper caste Shikaripur Congressites on the Kurubas of the area, and by the Lingayats on the Muslims of Isoor.[54] Gandhian nationalism's call to reconstitute the self found some faint echoes in the pious stretching out of the hand to lower castes in such instructions as: 'the conditions of the depressed communities is lowered by praising the people of the forward communities. What steps to be taken to avoid this, etc.'[55] By and large however, the signs and symbols of nationalism came to reinforce, rather than challenge or overturn, the local structures of power. Although a pandal set up at the main entrance of the village on September 25, with its table and chairs, became the site of the new parallel government, the centrality of the Veerabhadraswamy temple as the organizing locus could not but communicate the continuance of the earlier modes of power. What new community could be fashioned from these symbols of upper caste Hindu religiosity?

V

The Veerabhadraswamy temple was not merely a place of worship for the upper castes of the village but a regular meeting place for both the people of Isoor (Muslims and other lower castes included) and the revenue officials who periodically visited the village. There were at least two other older temples, the Thontadarya and the Kote Rameswara temples, and a Ganeshwara temple, in addition to three smaller and relatively newer ones to Banashankari, Ajjayya and Mariamma.[56]

C. Lingappa's description of the village religiosity does not include the mosque which was at a short distance from the Veerabhadraswamy temple. The invisibility of the mosque was not accidental to accounts which attempted to map the Kadamba era (c. 500 AD) temple onto a historical geography of revolt – the legacy of the twelfth century anti-caste Veerashaiva movement, a veritable breeding ground of heroes. The gong of the Veerabhadraswamy temple was sounded daily to summon people to participate in the rituals of the Quit India days.

At least from the early days of the Quit India movement, the temple walls were used to communicate messages to the people of Isoor. Justice Reilly was convinced that the incendiary inscriptions of 1942 'could not have been on the village temple unless a large number of the grown up people of the village approved of that and connived at them being put up there'.[57] To the right of the temple were inscribed messages in chalk:

Brother ryots, learn Hindi. May God grant independence and victory to India. The suffering of the ryots is the suffering of India and their happiness is the happiness of India. All contempt to traitors. 'Vande Mataram'. Let English schools be closed and let Britishers be imprisoned. Don't drink toddy which make [*sic*] one unsteady. Every one wants independence. Don't smoke cigarettes and bidis. The Government servants are unfit to sit here. Don't offer mats and chairs for the Government servants to sit on. We are free. Do not pay respect to the government servants, the houses of those who respect them will be set fire to by us . . . take care! Government servants are the slaves of ryots. India is independent.

This jumbled mass of exhortations, demands, warnings and disjointed slogans (further disjointed by the work of the police transcriber), were ordered into greater coherence in the middle of the temple which declared it to be 'Gandhi's Abode: Those who cause pain to the poor cannot escape hell'. A four point 'Mahatma's message' followed: '1. Don't pay kandaya 2. Cut teak wood trees 3. Don't pay toll etc 4. Cut the wires'. Similar slogans were also inscribed on the left of the garbhankana, but above all 'Let there be unity. Let government servants be cut to pieces, ryot brethren be united, give up communal differences.'

Some witnesses testified to the slogans being written under the direction of Sahukar Basavanappa, the student Lingoji (Lingappa of the memoir) being among the principal slogan writers, admitting this even in court. The group of 'boys' clearly had the approval and encouragement of the elders in their actions. By this time, Basavanappa's control of the Isoor Congress was more or less complete. Lingappa describes the path taken by the daily *prabhat pheri* thus: after wending its way through the Harijan and the other *keris*, the procession reached the porch of the Sahukar mansion, where the Sahukar's first wife, Chandramma, performed *aarthi*, and blessed the crowd, which then proceeded towards the main 'headquarters' of the movement, the Veerabhadraswamy Temple.[58] A new sacred geography was thus traced by the procession, weaving the disparate elements of the village into a single fabric in the name of the nation, though there were no signs that the older social and political order had relinquished its hold on the village. If anything, older elites anticipated the arrival of renewed political power in new and interesting ways.

VI

Towards the end of his judgement, Reilly noted that the abject surrender of the police officers to the actions of the crowd, between September 25 and 28 1942, was a form of 'cringing' not appropriate to their designated task: 'I must point out that the [Police Inspector Zameeruddin Sheriff's] evidence discloses something very serious. It discloses that when this disturbance began, instead of standing up to the villagers, he cringed before them, and there is some evidence that some of the others concerned did that too'.[59] A Police Inspector who pleaded with a crowd of people he was familiar with, and one in which there were many children, was not fit for the role that he was expected to perform.

'Manliness' appeared as a desirable ideal among the nationalists as well. The frequent invocation of 'manliness' in the nationalist discourse at Isoor, once more at odds with the message of Gandhi, was heard in various parts of the country. Hitesranjan Sanyal talks of the men in the Tamluk Jatiya Sarkar who 'reddened their hands with blood' in order to avenge the rape of women. Thus said Gunadhar Mandal, a sharecropper and wage labourer who owned less than an acre, 'in this struggle every risk has to be run in order to cure ourselves of the biggest disease – a disease which has sapped our manhood and almost made us feel as if we must for ever be slaves'.[60] Such sentiments were expressed in a pamphlet that circulated in Isoor: 'They say that you are cowards, that you are not manly and that you are slaves. Are love of country and love of freedom empty words which mean nothing to you? They say we sell our souls for wages and food, that our men are moustachioed cowards and swine who die for pay and are frightened ghosts or shadows of men. Do you not flare up when you hear all this.'[61] This was followed by a rallying call to both men and women. Witnesses repeatedly spoke of the aggressively masculine incitements to beat and kill given by Sahukars Basavanappa and Rudrappa as well as several others who 'beat their thighs' to emphasize their capacity to stand up to their opponents.[62]

Other witnesses and the judges similarly noted a lack of femininity among the women. The disturbing lack of femininity among the female attackers led the judges to consider exemplary punishment, and not just for their 'crime'. Indeed, there was a very significant participation in the events of Isoor by women, and especially the young women, of the village: the group of 50–60 children, for instance, had a large proportion of girls. Other young women were also active.[63] 'A peculiar feature of the attack,' said Minister for Finance and Revenue in his report to the Dewan Madhava Rao, 'was that even women and children belonging to the well-to-do families in the village took an active part in the assault'.[64] The women showed an unusual ferocity in their attack on the Amaldar, the Sub-Inspector and other members of the party. Mohamed Zameerduddin Sheriff, the Police Inspector who fled the scene when the violence began, said: 'Ten to fifteen women were in the crowd. *None of them was crying.*'[65] This caused the judge to remark about Halamma:

> She has taken up a prominent part in attacking these people and there is evidence to show that when the injured and the dying people wanted water she refused to give water to them and offered urine instead. She is a diabolical woman. She looks thin in build and dwarf in structure. But she is capable of all things attributed to her.

Despite this attribution of agency to the young woman, Sundaraja Rao finally found reason to save her from the gallows, but only by taking it away once more. Deliberating on the death sentence for the two women Halamma and Siddamma, and deciding instead on transportation for life, Rao began by noting that 'the more surprising thing is that women were forced to enter into this move-

ment by the influential men of the village'. Why were women any more susceptible to the application of force, when the evidence of police witnesses did not
hesitate to point out the many forms of coercion that the Sahukars brought to
bear on reluctant peasant supporters? 'There are absolutely no extenuating circumstances in favour of any of the accused whom I have convicted for murder
except in the case of A10 (Halamma) and A37 (Siddamma). They are women
and *by nature* they would not have taken part in such a ghastly and diabolical
crime, unless *they were obliged* to do so by the male members of their household
or of the unlawful assembly' (emphasis added). The judge who was earlier baffled
by the 'unnatural' behaviour of the women, now explained their actions in terms
that deprived them of their volition and agency. Women were naturally disin-
clined to violence, but were subordinated to the will of not just the family, but the
crowd itself![66]

Reilly restored a notion of agency, while retaining a conception of 'natural' femininity when he noted: 'But there was nothing less brutal in what the
women concerned did in this case. Except in their physical confirmation, there
appears to be *nothing womanly* in any of the accused concerned . . .'[67]

It is striking that two of the three women were related to the Sahukar,
one as his second wife (Halamma) and another, Siddamma, bound to Sahukar
Basavanappa for arranging her mother's burial since she was excommunicated
by the Sadar Lingayats. Parvathyamma was the only wage labourer, as it were,
and predictably did not have even a single defence witness. Halamma was related to the Sahukars by the accident of marriage, but received not even a defence witness from her marital home. Those who testified on her behalf were
from her natal village (Honnali): not surprisingly, after her release she went back
to that village, and lived the rest of her life there.

In order to deny the people of Isoor the capacity to act as political beings, the judges appealed to notions of human nature, and ideals of masculinity
and femininity, from which the people had clearly strayed. Indeed, the Isoor
peasantry even appeared to have been temporarily deranged, distanced from
their 'humanity', when they left the dying Amaldar and Sub-Inspector, with their
five colleagues, tied by their thumbs to a wood pile, without water or help for at
least 4 hours. Even if the act of murder were un-premeditated, as Reilly argued,
there was little remorse that was shown for the condition of those who were
injured. Thus 'inhumanity' came to stand in the place of the anger of the peasants against the police firing as a cause of the intemperate acts. Two Koramaru
peasants from the neighbouring Churchgundi village, Kencha and Fhakeera, untied
the injured policemen and brought the dead and wounded to the hospital at
Shikaripur with Kadappa and Jaffer Sab.[68] Reilly urged the government to re-
ward those who showed this humanity towards the dead and injured.[69]

VII

Let us now reflect on the meaning of this violence, which was unprecedented and certainly unpremeditated. Isoor gained the attention it did because

of the gap between the failure of the state apparatuses to swiftly quell the rebellion, and the severity of the delayed response. Isoor's place in the state's history, whether representing an aberration of the Mysorean disposition, or a theatre of brutal retribution for an impulsive act, was made possible only because of these temporal gaps and delays. The peasants of Sravanbelagola, Hassan District, who in the same period came into confrontation with the police when they refused to pay taxes and held their shandy at a different place, received the instant response that would have heartened Sundararaja Rao and Reilly. When a reserve constable was beaten to death by the rebellious peasants of Kantarajpura and other villages, the police opened fire, killing seven and leaving thirty-seven casualties. In the case that followed, fifty-three peasants were prosecuted, of which forty-six were convicted.[70] Although the Congress made the plea two years later for the release of both the Isoor and the Sravanbelagola prisoners, there is no doubt that Isoor retained its singularity as an event that rewrote the heroism of the Mysore people.

It was in the interest of the court to impose a single collective will on the members of this heterogenous group. It was in the interest of the nationalists to dwell on a village population 'frenzied by the scene' of those who were wounded by the police firing, and driven to action by rumours of children dying.[71] Where one account stressed the inexorable march to criminality, the latter stressed the momentary act of madness, of which the crowd was absolved following the massive scale of the state's response to the killings.

If the Quit India movement went against the grain of Gandhian nationalism while invoking his name, the people of Isoor appear to have diverged from even the so-called 'Karnataka Model' of guerilla action.[72] They were not, as the judgment would have it, people who were driven inexorably to commit crime: the judge's reference to the 'clubs' wielded by the crowd, women included, for instance, transformed the stack of firewood near the Veerabhadraswamy temple into an always threatening weapon. The enthusiastic participation of the people of Isoor in this act of violence and, one might add, torture, does indeed need explanation, though not by turning its prehistory into a chronicle of violence foretold.

Lingappa admits in his memoirs that there were at least two groups of Isoor participants who had 'no proper training in non-violence' as a way of accounting for the act of murder. One wonders whether the historian's accounts are necessarily truer than the discourse of the colonial state. Shri Krishan has suggested that the 'norms of mass activity were determined by the nationalist discourse';[73] even S.U. Kamath has suggested that 'The fury of the people against the foreign government was demonstrated in their attack on these people'.[74]

The truth of the crowd action lies somewhere in between the purely criminal and the purely political act. No narrowly functionalist explanation of the motives can fill the enigmatic space left by the violence. But the surrogacy of these acts, in which the young men and women, the wives and the tenants of the rich landlords were goaded and incited into action, cannot be understated. There was no vision of a world turned upside down, no promise of a more just social order guiding these actions. It is no surprise that the surrogates paid the heaviest price for their actions. The chief instigators survived to live fuller lives. Rachavalli Rudrappa and his son Shantaveerappa emerged from the jungles in March 1943 to surrender before the police after the death of Basavanappa in hiding. Acquitted by the higher court in June 1943, Rudrappa did not serve his life sentence, while his son's life sentence was reduced to four years.

Even the more recent, fictionalized history of Isoor which annexes the event to a glorious retelling of Hindu nationalism cannot resist commenting: 'The main point was that those who ate the skin were arrested; the ones who enjoyed the fruit were not arrested. If they wanted, many could have avoided going to jail'.[75] In fact, the tragedy of Isoor is that the larger moneylenders and landlords such as Sahukar Basavanappa, Sahukar Rudrappa, Patel Gurushantappa and Angadi Halappa remained outside the dragnet of the police either by staying underground or through well-furnished alibis. The five martyrs were the dispensable 'heroes', largely small or medium peasants.

Reilly's review of Sundararaja Rao's judgement saved six from the gallows, and reduced the sentences of the twenty-one others, while acquitting one. But this did little to reduce the violence of the law, which sent the ironsmith, K. Gurappa (a Vishwa Brahmin), the peasant K. Mallappa (a Lingayat), goldsmith and peasant Suryanarayanachar (a Vishwa Brahmin), the poor peasant B. Halappa, a Lingayat, who was no active participant in the movement (though it was believed that he paid with his life for the accidental resemblance that his name bore to the absconding Angadi Halappa) and the peasant G. Shankrappa (a Devanaga) to the gallows. 'If the people had satisfied themselves with following the Congress creed of non-violence, this unfortunate incident would not have happened,' said Sundararaja Rao while underlining the need for punishing severely enough 'to prevent the recurrence of such crimes'. His failure to make a detailed examination of the accused, his outright dismissal of the evidence of the defence witnesses, as of 'no value', were reasonings with which Reilly found little to disagree. The outcome of the case was already foretold.

What may have held little value for reversing the tragic fate of the accused has however been found by the historian of use in reconstructing the mode of power that mobilized students, householders and peasants alike to a cause that betrayed their hopes and aspirations both within the courtroom and outside. The task has been to 'disrupt the self-sufficiency of the judicial discourse,'[76] on the one hand, and the easy assimilation of Isoor into a glorious nationalist narrative on the other. September 28, 1942, in Medinipur, Bengal, according to Hiteshranjan Sanyal, was marked by the organized action of the peasant masses against police thanas that eventually led to the establishment of the Tamluk Jatiya Sarkar from December 1942. In Isoor, it signified a tragedy that stifled the transfer of power to a local elite, whose day had not yet come.

Notes

1 Ginzburg (1999: 12).

2 Amin (1996: 1).

3 Guha (1987: 141). One may cite the path-breaking contributions of feminist scholars in revealing these two operations of the law, i.e. the summoning of history into the courtroom and the simultaneous creation of new subjects of law. This branch of feminist research is large and growing: see, for instance, Mani (1998); Arunima (1996); Carroll (1989); Kannabiran (1995: 59–71); Nair (1994: 3157–68).

4 Guha (1987: 142).

5 Baxi (1992: 247–64).

6 *Deccan Herald,* 29 May 1970.

7 Amin (1996).

8 For instance, R.R. Diwakar, *Isur Razed to the Ground* (undated pamphlet), R.R. Diwakar Papers, Karnataka State Archives (KSA). Also Lakshmidevi Kadidal *Isurina Durantha* (30.10.1946), in *History of the Freedom Movement*, Khadri Shankarappa Papers, Karnataka State Archives. Kadidal's short pamphlet was written in commemoration of the release of Parvathamma, Halamma and Siddamma, on the occasion of the wedding of the Mysore Maharaja's daughter on 21 October 1946.

9 Basavaraj (1975).

10 Oral histories of H. Neelakantappa and Ramalli Hole Basappa in Kamath (1998: 641–49).

11 Kamath (1988).

12 Mahabaleswarappa (1998).

13 Lingappa (2000).

14 Halappa (1964: 330–31, 725–27).

15 Exhibit page 18, Collection no. 115-42, CB 160-42-2.

16 Pandey (1988: 136).

17 For instance, Mahabaleswarappa (1998: 70) dwells on the widespread involvement of non-Brahmin castes.

18 Omvedt (1988: 223–61).

19 Sanyal (1988: 19–76).

20 Sarkar (1982: 402).

21 Pati (1988: 185–205).

22 Personal communication, Kotrabasappa, 17 September 1999.

23 Lingappa (2000: 137).

24 Ibid.: 137–42.

25 Pandey (1988: 15) recalls the sharp words of Vallabhbhai Patel in January 1947, for whom the 'struggle for nation building' was over. Patel said that 'the caricature of official activities in the manner reported in the press at a time when we are in office is open to serious objection.'

26 Criminal Case no. 1 of 1942–43, Judgement of Sir D'Arcy Reilly, Chief Justice of the Mysore High Court, 9 January 1943, CB No. 1–42–43: 74.

27 Abdul Aziz Khan, IGP Mysore to Vedavyasacharya, Chief Secretary, 30 June 1943, Collection no. 115–42 CB 160-42-2.

28 File no. 3–27, Sl. No. 13, 14, 15, 15(a), 17(a), 18(a), 19(a), 23(a), 24(a), 37 and 50, Revenue Miscellaneous, KSA.

29 File no. 343–29, Sl. No. 4, 5, 6, 7, 8, 9, 10, February 1933, Revenue Miscellaneous, KSA. Lingappa *Swtantra sangramadalli Isooru.*

30 File no. 3–27, Sl. No. 13, 14, 15, 15(a), 17(a), 18(a), 19(a), 23(a), 24(a), 37 and 50, Revenue Miscellaneous, KSA.

31 Lingappa (2000: 1). Lingappa lists 'Chamars, Kammars, Kshourika, Chippige, Agasa, Achari, Valmiki' castes and some Muslims in addition to the Lingayats and Devangas.

32 Deposition of Sattar Mohamed Dastagir, 6/11/42, Collection no. 115–42, CB 160–42-2, KSA.

33 Deposition of Pore Sab , 6/11/42, Collection no. 115–42, CB 160–42-2, KSA.

34 Exhibit page 33 (b); S.B. Report dated 28–8–1942. Collection no. 115–42, CB 160–

42–2, KSA. This report contains information about those who contributed to the Congress funds.

[35] Dodda Sivappa was the father of Gurushantappa, (A28). Deposition of Dodda Sivappa 6/11/42 Collection no. 115–42, CB 160–42–2, KSA.

[36] Deposition of K.G. Pati Mahadevappaiah, 26/11/42; deposition of Rudrappa, (also a witness in the murder case), 4/11/1842. Collection no. 115–42, CB 160–42–2, KSA.

[37] Deposition of Holiyappa, 27/11/1942, Collection no. 115–42, CB 160–42–2, KSA.

[38] For instance, between PW 32 Jettappa and A6 Veerappa, deposition of Siddappa, 28/11/1942, Collection no. 115–42, CB 160–42–2, KSA.

[39] Deposition of Chennabasavaiah 4/11/42, Collection no. 115–42, CB 160–42–2, KSA.

[40] Ibid.

[41] Deposition of K.G. Pati Mahadevappaiah, 26/11/42, Collection no. 115–42, CB 160–42–2, KSA.

[42] File no. 191–31, Sl. no. 1–2, Land Revenue, KSA (emphasis added).

[43] File no. 217–40, Sl. no. 1–3, Land Revenue, KSA; File no. 406–41. Sl. no. 1 and 2, Land Revenue, KSA.

[44] Kamath (1988: 152).

[45] Kamath (1998: Vol. 2, 643).

[46] Deposition of Ranganatha Rao, 4/11/1942, CB 12–45–82, 1945–46, KSA.

[47] Deposition of G. Veerappa, 12/11/1942, CB 12–45–82, 1945–46, KSA.

[48] Exhibit 26(a) reports a meeting at Shikaripur town, where speakers were admonished for wearing hats and ties, which was followed by a heated argument with Halappa, and an agreement reached about not raising such unhealthy points.

[49] Epstein (1988: 66).

[50] Ibid.: 72.

[51] Ibid.: 91.

[52] Collection no. 86/45 CB 12–45–82, 1945–46, KSA.

[53] Deposition of Pore Sab, 26/11/1942, 26/11/1942, CB 12–45–82, 1945–46, KSA.

[54] SB reports of 27/8/42 and 25/9/42, 26/11/1942, CB 12–45–82, 1945–46, KSA.

[55] Exhibit page 19 (c), 26/11/1942, CB 12–45–82, 1945–46, KSA.

[56] Lingappa (2000: 4).

[57] Criminal Case no. 1 of 1942–43, Judgement of Sir D'Arcy Reilly, Chief Justice of the Mysore High Court, 9 January 1943, CB No. 1–42–43: 20.

[58] Lingappa (2000: 21–22).

[59] Criminal Case no. 1 of 1942–43, Judgement of Sir D'Arcy Reilly, Chief Justice of the Mysore High Court, 9 January 1943, CB No. 1–42–43: 74.

[60] Pandey (1988: 23).

[61] As Exhibit no. 19(e), CB 12–45–82, 1945–46, KSA.

[62] Deposition of S.M. Abdul Sattar, CB 12–45–82, 1945–46, KSA.

[63] Exhibit page 20, CB 12–45–82, 1945–46, KSA.

[64] Collection 62/42/43 Confidential, CB 160–42–1, KSA.

[65] Deposition of Mohamed Zameeruddin Sheriff, 6/11/1942, CB 12–45–82, 1945–46, KSA.

[66] Regarding the conceptualization of agency that underlies this reasoning, we may ask: if women were 'by nature' more inclined to non-violence, how would their participation in non-violent political action be understood? Would it be a realization of their 'natural' attributes, in which case their capacity for agential action is once more removed?

[67] Criminal Case no. 1 of 1942–43, Judgement of Sir D'Arcy Reilly, Chief Justice of the Mysore High Court, 9 January 1943, CB No. 1–42–43, p. 76.

[68] Deposition of Kencha, 5/11/1942; deposition of Fhakeera, 5/1/1942.

[69] Registrar HC of Mysore to Narayanswamy Naidu, Secretary Law Department, January 1943, Collection no. 115–42, 160–42–2, KSA.

[70] Administration report of the Police Department for year 1942–43; collection no. 86/45, CB 12–45–82, 1945–86, KSA.

[71] R.R. Diwakar *Isur razed to the ground* (undated pamphlet).

[72] The killing of a Reserve Policeman at Shravanabelgola in 1942 and the deaths of seven others are less often cited as an example of heroism.

[73] Krishan (1996: 474).

[74] Kamath (1988).

[75] Basavaraj (1975: 86).

[76] Amin (1996: 193).

References

Amin, Shahid (1996), *Event, Metaphor, Memory: Chauri Chaura, 1922–1992* (Delhi: Oxford University Press).

Arunima, G. (1996), 'Multiple Meanings: Changing Conceptions of Matrilineal Kinship in Nineteenth and Twentieth Century Malabar', *Indian Economic and Social History Review*, 33(3): 283–308.

Basavaraj, R. (1975), *Isurina Chiranjeevigalu* (Bangalore: Rashtrothana Parishat).

Baxi, Upendra (1992), 'The State's Emissary: The Place of Law in Subaltern Studies', in Partha Chatterjee and Gyanendra Pandey, eds, *Subaltern Studies VII: Writings in South Asian History and Society* (Delhi: Oxford University Press): 247–64.

Carroll, Lucy (1989), 'Law, Custom and Statutory Social Reform: The Hindu Women's Remarriage Act of 1856', in J. Krishnamurthy, ed., *Women in Colonial India: Essays on Survival, Work and the State* (Delhi: Oxford University Press).

Epstein, S.J.M. (1988), *The Earthy Soil: Bombay Peasants and the Indian Nationalist Movement, 1919–1947* (Delhi: Oxford University Press).

Ginzburg, Carlo (1999), *The Judge and the Historian: Marginal Notes on a Late Twentieth Century Miscarriage of Justice*, translated by Anthony Shuggar (London: Verso).

Guha, Ranajit (1987), 'Chandra's Death', in Ranajit Guha, ed., *Subaltern Studies V: Writings in South Asian History and Society* (Delhi: Oxford University Press).

Halappa, G.S. (1964), *History of the Freedom Movement in Karnataka* (Bangalore: Government of Mysore).

Kamath, Suryanath (1988), *Quit India Movement in Karnataka* (Bangalore: Lipi Prakashana).

——— (1998), *Swatantra Sangramada Smritigalu* (Bangalore: Directorate of Kannada and Culture).

Kannabiran, Kalpana (1995), 'Judiciary Social Reform and Debate on "Religious Prostitution" in Colonial India', *Economic and Political Weekly*, 32(43).

Krishan, Shri (1996), 'Crowd Vigour and Social Identity: The Quit India Movement in Western India', *Indian Eeconomic and Social History Review*, 33(4).

Lingappa, C. (2000), *Swatantra Sangramadalli Isooru* (Bangalore: Namdeva Prakasana).

Mahabaleswarappa, B.C. (1998), *Quit India Movement in Isoor* (Unpublished Research Project, Gulbarga University).

Mani, Lata (1988), *Contentious Traditions: The Debate on Sati in Colonial India* (Berkeley: University of California Press).

Nair, Janaki (1994), 'The Devadasi Dharma and the State', *Economic and Political Weekly*, 31 (50).

Omvedt, Gail (1988), 'The Satara Prati Sarkar, in Pandey (1988).

Pandey, Gyanendra, ed. (1988), *The Indian Nation in 1942* (Calcutta: K.P. Bagchi and Co.).

Pati, Biswamoy (1988), 'Storm over Malkangiri: A Note on Laxman Naiko's Revolt, 1942', in Pandey (1988).

Sanyal, Hitesranjan (1988), 'The Quit India Movement in Medinipur District', in Pandey (1988).

Sarkar, Sumit (1982), *Modern India* (Delhi: Macmillan).

Colonial Laws and Indian Debates

Suggestions for Revised Readings

Tanika Sarkar

I

Just before freedom came to India, and for some time beyond Independence, the first flush of self-congratulatory optimism produced a markedly positive teleology about nineteenth century social reforms, especially of the new gender laws. They seemed to confirm a historical potential for progress that later inevitably culminated in independence from colonial bondage. Historians described those times as an Indian Renaissance:[1] some would find it a deeper and more moral renaissance than the European one.[2]

By the 1970s, as Independence failed to usher in significant social change or justice, the early phase of modernity predictably lost its bright lustre. Its history was now instead mined for clues to what went wrong, why no path could be found towards an authentic and positive Indian modernity.[3] Gender reforms and laws of the nineteenth century now signified loss or failure, to be read under a suspicious optic, a negative teleology.[4] I will briefly review some of the major historiographical trends on the matter, and try to situate my observations at some distance from both teleologies. I will talk critically about more recent postcolonial readings of colonial modernity since those remain the accepted wisdom at the moment. At the same time, while I argue for a largely autonomous Indian self-fashioning under colonial constraints, I find quite different possibilities for 'progress' in these times than what earlier historians had asserted. Rather than taking the new laws as an inauguration of substantive and substantial changes in lives of Indian women, I acknowledge their limited scope: they worked upon lives of middle class, upper caste women at best, and, that, too, not entirely effectively or comprehensively. At the same time, in highly mediated, non-deliberate and contingent ways, some of the nineteenth century legal debates introduced new thinking about women's entitlements and immunities, about the justice or injustice of their domestic location. These, in turn, created – again, in highly contradictory, even muddled ways – some new words and descriptive modes that would eventuate in a fledgling understanding about rights of subalterns, starting with upper caste Hindu women. In the subsequent century, a women's politics grew out of these debates and some middle class women activists came to define new themes in gender reform.[5]

First, though, a few words on dominant frameworks for looking at the constitution of modern selves. Among Marxist theorists, there is a disagreement about the possibilities of self-making, especially for hegemonized subaltern people. Althusser, in fact, would dispute such an eventuality for all subjects, arguing, instead, that subject positions are an effect of the ideological interpellation of people into the structures of class.[6] Gramsci, followed by social historians like E.P. Thompson, on the other hand, held out different possibilities: arguing that all people, including plebian men and women, can understand and act on the basis of their social experiences in counter-hegemonic ways.[7] Postcolonial historiography has shifted the basis of the argument onto the terrain of race and colonialism, away from the Marxian accent on class. But, somewhere, the Althusserian notion of the interpellated subject with an illusory sense of the self, persists. Colonial power-knowledge, so the thinking goes, has constructed an inflexible iron cage of attributed selves for the colonized, from which an escape is possible only through covert, over-the-shoulder glances at pre-colonial and pre-modern habits. Some, like Ronald Inden, would contest even this possibility. In Inden's understanding, colonialism achieved an epistemic break of such proportions that afterwards no recuperation of past knowledge was possible.[8] Partha Chatterjee has similarly argued that entirely derivative and mimic knowledge forms were born in modern times. Even the politics of resistance to colonialism carried colonial meanings since nationalism itself is a western construct.

Other kinds of postcolonial readings – that of Paul Gilroy[9] or Frederick Cooper,[10] for instance – would have a far more vibrant sense of self-making in modern times. Among Indian scholars, in their different ways, nationalist, Leftist, and early Subaltern Studies theorists had shared a strong perspective on the contestatory agency of poor people, even in colonial situations. A recent crop of studies of Indian labour has recuperated the sense of agency and selfhood in more complex and nuanced ways.[11] On a different note, Sumit Sarkar shifts the gaze back to different categories of Indians, whose mutual addresses, he thinks, should be traced more attentively than an exclusive and exclusionary accent on the colonizer-colonized binary.[12] Dipesh Chakrabarty talks of 'provincializing Europe', or remaking the encounter and knowledge flow on Indian terms. Though the accent lingers on the colonial encounter rather than on internal conversations and arguments, the possibility of reconfiguring the encounter on autonomous terms disrupts the notion of fixity and closure that marks much of postcolonial studies.[13] Homi Bhabha delineates a situation where colonizer and colonized – both conceived of in the singular – look at each other. He, however, constructs the gazing in supple ways: not simply as an effect of power that flows from the colonizer, but as the power-laden look of the colonizer that the colonized absorbs and sends back. The return of the gaze is disconcerting and not fully controlled.[14]

An important strand within new wave feminism has the same sense of closure for modern women that characterizes much of postcolonial thinking about modernity. Carole Pateman conceptualizes a male sexual contract that underpins the social contract which, in turn, gave birth to modern citizenship. Women, then, are excluded from both social contract and citizenship. Nancy Fraser sees a hardening of private-public divides in modern times: overwriting the woman's subjection in the private sphere happens through an empty, formal equality in the public domain.[15] Among Indian scholars, Partha Chatterjee has very powerfully conceptualized the privatization of female selves into the realms of spiritual and affective work that male nationalists designated as the woman's exclusive domain even as they reserved the public world for themselves. [16]

A formidable slice of postcolonial feminist thinking has happened under the sign of this understanding. The paradigmatic collection of essays, *Recasting Women: Essays in Colonial History*, was the first feminist effort to configure a single conceptual framework for colonial history under which all significant developments in gender relations could be enfolded. The dominant assumption was that the installation of capitalism in India through a colonial agency resulted in the dissemination of notions of Victorian gentility and domesticity among the modern Indian middle classes who realigned their patriarchal norms to western bourgeois forms of gender relations. Indian women, according to this understanding, came under what I would designate a double-negative teleology: that is, while patriarchy was refurbished, it simultaneously became de-indigenized and alien. Since the conceptual framework of the collection claims to express all of colonial gender history, its impact among feminists has been impressive.

One of the problematic consequences of such a totalizing understanding of gender and modernity, however, was the belief in the pervasiveness of capitalist relations in India under colonial aegis, the belief that a western capitalist paradigm (itself an oversimplified and overgeneralized category) was smoothly transplanted to colonial India. This, of course, is a notion which is contentious and is problematized within theories of Indian political economy. It is quite clear that colonialism made a difference, both in the highly limited and attenuated nature of Indian capitalism which was more stifled than enabled by the colonial stranglehold on the commanding heights of the economy; and, also, in its relationship with the domestic and household relations which would hardly be affected sweepingly by a very sectoralized economic change. In fact, recent economic historians dispute the idea of such a wholesale collapse even in the wake of English industrialization. In the Indian situation of a weaker and limited modernization of production, domestic and gender changes would be more mediated, opaque, socio-cognitive processes. A theory of modernization that flows entirely from notions attached to a transition in the mode of production will not be significantly meaningful.

Another problem lay with the method: it belonged to the era of working with patriarchal texts to locate patriarchal images of women, a procedure which is curiously self-fulfilling. Obviously, patriarchy as a broad framework of relations was not overthrown. By restricting economic options for poor women like spinning, colonialism certainly worsened the state of female dependency. At the same time, patriarchy was named as a structure of oppression and injustice, and multiple sites of interrogation and resistance were evolved. In fact, if we need to explain Indian feminism as a modern Indian phenomenon which was not simply a foreign construct, then the relationship between gender and modernity requires a far more complex framework of understanding.

How would historians of law read changes in gender laws in colonial times? Some of them find a sharp dichotomy between codified, written laws that the alien state compiled to create zones of Hindu and Muslim personal laws which it could define and manage on its own terms: and unwritten custom, norms and practices that had actually governed lives of pre-colonial Indians. The firm and inflexible codification – it has been argued – unmoored social practices from their traditional anchoring, and hardened what used to be a domain of fluid, variegated and kinder custom which had previously carried far more potential for self-modification and change. A range of such open custom was overthrown to install a regime of definitive Hindu and Muslim laws, derived from written, brahmanical scriptural sources that were endorsed and applied according to co-lonial understandings.[17]

A few critics, in some ways, come close to a Thompsonian perspective. E.P. Thompson had focused on the moral norms and plebian custom – real or invented – with which displaced and marginalized popular crowds in eighteenth-century England had fought back against the brutal new laws of modern capital-ism. Outlawed social practices of colonized Indians, now denigrated as mere custom under colonial laws, seemed to carry a similar burden of stigmatization by a victorious cultural and political power: they also seemed to promise a similar potential for resistance. There is a difference, however. Thompson had elaborated the ways in which popular crowds fought the onslaught of modern capitalist property rights in the name of custom. In the Indian colonial situation, the struggle against modernity, especially in the field of gender, most often took the form of reasserting the power of traditional authorities against subalterns. In the process, both ancient legal texts as well as ancestral custom were invoked. Moreover, we need to know if, indeed, custom became a fugitive under colonial directives.

II

The colonial legal apparatus had made a sharp distinction within civil law from the early days of the Company's rule. Production relations and eco-nomic activities were governed by a new set of Anglo–Indian norms, neither fully derived from English law, nor following older Indian precedents substan-tially, but developed through responses to the changing drift of the Company's politico-financial requirements. It is important to recognize, though, how insis-tently even the new revenue laws claimed to follow past Indian imperial prece-dents. In the entire arena of other private matters – marriage, divorce, dower, inheritance, succession, caste, belief and custom – different religious communi-ties were to be governed by their scripture and custom. While the effects of Census operations and their role in transforming fuzzy communities into enumer-ated ones with hardened boundaries is now widely accepted, it is not recognized sufficiently just how important law was in classifying Indians into monolithic religious entities, sharply differentiated in their daily habits and practices. However, it is also important not to exaggerate its scope. Law would be invoked only during disputes and only when Indians themselves chose to take matters to the colonial courts: law did not reach out to monitor and supervise everyday relations and practices unless there was a breach of criminal regulations.[18]

Up to the mid-nineteenth century, religious authorities would interpret scripture or ancestral custom in the courts. Later, written codes, compiled from scripture, were used as the basis for judicial verdicts. Despite the compilation of written codes, an amazingly large area of decision-making remained ambiguous and fluid, thrusts of judicial notions shifting over time and space. It is important to bring the uncertainties and the multiphonalities that we see in our study of case laws to revise the scholarly common sense that colonial codification of personal laws resulted in total inflexibility and stasis and reflected English notions or intentions rather than Indian ways of resolving disputes. After widow remarriage was legalized in 1856 with the proviso that remarried widows would forfeit their claims to their first husband's property, numerous cases were brought to the various local and high courts which ruled in very different ways.

In Bengal, on the whole, ancient and written scripture – a sign of India's advanced civilizational status, according to early Orientalists – was considered as a reliable basis for judgments. It was valued above oral custom which varied from caste to caste, and whose provenance and authenticity were difficult to establish firmly. In the early nineteenth century, Rammohun Roy managed to persuade a nervous colonial state, markedly reluctant to abolish a religious practice, that widow immolation on the pyres of their deceased husbands, was a custom and not a scripturally sanctioned injunction. In other parts, however, as in Bombay Presidency or in Punjab, there was a marked ethnographic thrust. There were detailed compilations of caste-differentiated custom in western India, and the construction of a category of 'tribal custom' that would apply to all rural communities, irrespective of religious difference among Hindu, Muslim and Sikh landholders, in Punjab. In the 1930s, the Muslim League forced an entry into Punjab politics on the question of female shares in paternal property which Islamic law sanctioned but which tribal custom disallowed. The League insisted that Muslims should secede from shared tribal custom and abide by strict Quranic principles, thus knitting up women's interests with communal ones. In the South, there was an oscillation between vernacular sources and customary practices, on the one hand, and Sanskrit scripture on the other. So, there was no definitive or pervasive transition from custom to codes. Nor was custom necessarily kinder than written prescriptions. Moreover, even when there was a multifariousness of customs, that would not mean that groups and individuals would be able to choose and move around freely among them. Each was firmly anchored to the domain of ancestral group practices.

Wherever scriptural law was followed more closely, a tendency existed to brahmanise gender practices since scripture reflected upper caste norms: or to align practice to classical Islamic injunctions as found in the *Hedaya* or in the *Hanafi* school of law. The distinctive marriage and inheritance traditions of Khojas, Memons or Mapillas were considered non-Islamic. At the same time, it is important to recognize that neither were they disallowed. In fact, the uncertainty about the relative weight of text and custom, about the precise meaning of each, lingered throughout the colonial era. It allowed very interesting reformulations of traditional injunctions and practices. Courts were massively used by Hindu widows and by upper class Muslim women, and litigation was a mode of altering domestic practice. Case laws, built on decisions related to individual families, would eventually move towards a brief equilibrium of changed practice, until the accumulation of divergent case laws would be invoked in a different set of disputes. Even Muslim women in deep seclusion innovated methods of speaking in courts without violating the purdah. This shows how important they found the courts as a new resource with which they could try and re-negotiate their lifeworld.

An interesting bargain was struck by Muslim women in 1939, desirous of the right to initiate dissolution of marriages which was difficult under the *Hanafi* law. They persuaded leaders of politicized Islam who wanted to enlarge their support base, to concede an application of Maliki law in this instance. Similarly, in the 1880s, Rukmabai, an educated girl from the carpenter caste in Bombay, refused to live with her illiterate and dissolute husband who demanded his conjugal rights over her. She argued her case on the basis of her caste custom which, she said, allowed her the right to dissolve her marriage. Lower caste widows, similarly, would argue in court that their caste custom allowed them to inherit the first husband's share of property even on remarriage, which both brahmanical scripture and the new colonial law of 1856 denied them. Law was trapped in a dilemma here, since the law that had allowed widows to remarry was made to reform brahmanical norms which denied the legality of widow remarriage. Colonial rulers were not yet so familiar with lower caste norms which allowed different forms of remarriage along with inheritance rights. At the same time, it is important to be a little wary of references to custom in such cases, as ethnographic data showed a widespread acceptance of the brahmanical taboo on remarriage even among lower castes; particularly among upwardly mobile segments who emulated upper caste domestic practices or who 'sanskritized' their caste custom to claim ritual purity. Their widows, desirous of inheritance rights, probably activated defunct custom through court interventions, claiming that they had always enjoyed the conjoint rights of remarriage and inheritance. Some of the provincial High Courts ruled in such cases that the entire community be governed by a single set of laws and follow the letter of the 1856 law which denied them inheritance rights while allowing remarriage. The Allahabad Court, however, decided that law should be 'most enabling': it would grant entitlements that did not exist before, such as the right to remarriage for upper caste widows. But it should not take away any existing entitlements, such as inheritance claims of lower caste widows whose custom had already allowed remarriage and hence who stood to gain nothing and to only lose from the new law. Here, the insertion of a new function into the prescribed role of law – it should be more 'enabling', restoring entitlements to those who lacked them – is a departure.

What muddled the legal waters most of all were not so much the several inconsistencies or mutual incompatibilities in the recognized codes themselves, or the multiple and contested readings and the vagaries of the judicial domain where law, in its application, could become substantially transmuted, reflecting the social norms and cultural preferences of judges, lawyers and juries. These are but the expected outcome of any legal regime. In colonial times, however, the attempts to devise new laws coincided with critical changes in material forms and modes of transmission of information, in the kinds of dissemination of legal and scriptural knowledge, in popular and public reception of laws. Between the state and the subjects fell the shadow of the emergent public sphere. Print culture, a rapidly developing vernacular prose, newspapers, cheap translations of laws and of classical scripture with accessible explanations, substantially enlarged the range of people who would come to know and discuss the new laws: especially as they touched on their everyday lives. For the first time in our history, such developments in communications produced an informed 'public' of interested people who read, wrote and argued about the norms and the laws that regulated their domestic practices. Around the new gender laws, then, we see the growth of a new history: that of public debates. As conversations accumulated, discussions vaulted across the letter of proposed laws. Discussants began to think critically or defensively about the faith, the texts and the cultural traditions that had engendered regulatory norms so far, some of which the laws now imperilled. The state, too, needed to argue strenuously to persuade the public about the ethical superiority of its laws. Neither conservatives nor reformers, neither the state nor the pandits could command without explaining themselves before this informal tribunal.

Despite the timid and highly circumscribed interventionist possibilities of legal reformism, law, thus, often stimulated new and daring social imaginaries that broadened the interrogation of brahmanical prescription: commands that effectively governed social practice, even among large swathes of lower castes. Over the widow remarriage debates, for instance, arguments over the specific issue refused to stay in place: they irresistibly rolled onto very wide and radical reviews of gender norms and invoked an ethic of equality as natural or divine law that should replace the brahmanical principle of hierarchically staggered privilege and dispossession. They also challenged profound social convictions about the absolute chastity and monogamy of the good woman who can have only one sexual relationship in her lifetime and who cannot move into a new relationship even if her first husband had been prodigiously polygamous, or was impotent, ill or dead. When reformers drafted the remarriage bill and presented it to a colonial legislature from which they, themselves, were excluded, large sections of the orthodoxy had said that they would accept the measure only if it applied to virgin and infant widows. The reformers, however, chose to stay with a highly limited support base in order to extend remarriage to mature widows, already exposed to a sexual relationship. Our discussion of legal change remains attenuated if we look only at the nature of the proposed legislation and its specific application. The collateral consequences were unruly and productive of new cognitive possibilities.

III

From the beginning of the nineteenth century, debates on the legal remoulding of gender, consent of women came to be acknowledged as a legitimate basis for law-making. Both reformers and conservatives appealed to it, wooed it and claimed it. The idea of consent usually contains an element of helplessness: I consent to what I have not made happen. However, the historical situation in which the consent of the subaltern has to be claimed and displayed by the dominant power is qualitatively different from one where it can be taken for granted: one where the lines of power are so settled that no reference need be made to such consent. When the former context obtains – one where the subaltern is wooed and is persuaded to proclaim her loyalty to a regime of power and discipline – a crucial shift has occurred in the practice of hegemony and important instabilities have been opened up within the field. Early nineteenth century debates around widow immolation occurred in one such historical moment.

Usually, the initiative for abolition is attributed to the colonial state, and is explained as a stratagem for cultural imperialism. What is important to remember, however, is that immolation was legal for more than half a century of colonial rule: or, to put it differently, for a third of the life of the colonial state in Bengal. What accounts for its longevity, if its abolition was so central to the strategy of imperialism?

From 1789, local level judicial and administrative officials would, on occasion, prevent an occurrence of immolation and then approach the state for instructions. Missionaries campaigned vigorously, as well, from the first years of the century, compiling horrific statistics – no doubt, somewhat inflated – about its scope and even citing Hindu scripture to prove that it was non-scriptural. So did a senior police official Walter Ewer. The higher powers, however, remained staunch about the legality of the practice. In 1812, the Fifth Report of the Select Committee on Indian Matters reported to Parliament: 'The government has deemed it expedient to take measures to put a stop to the barbarous practices of certain Hindoos not sanctioned by their Shaster [sic]. But in regard to immolation, no further interference is permitted to take place.'[19]

Sati was sanctioned – according to the great Orientalist, H.T. Colebrooke, as early as the late eighteenth century – by all holy scripture.[20] It thus comfortably lived on in the domain of textual prescription until Rammohun Roy sought to displace it from that protected zone and banish it to the domain of mere custom. Even though some pandits had previously tried to restrict its scope by disallowing a growing category of women from the practice – pregnant, below sixteen, menstruating, mother of suckling babies, and so on – none before

Rammohun had challenged its scriptural status. Previous to Rammohun's intervention, the limit of state control lay with a close monitoring of sati events to ensure that the scriptural conditions were being properly met. One such condition was that the widow would decide on the act out of her free will and should not be coerced, drugged or intoxicated. Police officers and district magistrates were told to ascertain their consent in their own words before they ascended the pyre.

Unintended and even unnoticed by colonial rulers and by later historians of sati, this last provision wrought a significant transformation in the meaning of the ritual. Earlier, the performance of the rite would save her matrimonial and natal families from all manner of sins in this and in past births. She, along with husband, were assured of a place in heaven for millions of years. She already enjoyed, then, crucial ritual agency. Under the new regulations, however, the scope of the agency expanded. It was made demonstratively obvious by the public official interrogation of the widow and her public affirmation of her decision, that the ritual lay in her hands, that it could only live with her consent. She had to declare her intention in public, often in the face of dissuation. Administrators had to record it. Her consent now became a public matter, a matter of state, a public articulation and display. Later, both reformers and the orthodoxy would claim that they alone possessed it. Unintended again, a discourse emerged where both sides seemed to assume that apart from her stated consent, the rite had no real basis.

Colonial authorities, on the whole, were happy to continue with this state of affairs. Lord Moira regretfully said in the 1820s that only if he had been a 'Brahman prince' he could have abolished the rite: a strange statement, as if colonial rule was not a matter of external power and domination.[21] As if colonial laws, at any time, were based on the consent of the governed. There was a further cause for inhibition. Early colonial criminal law followed Islamic codes which had not interfered with immolation. Sati, however, was banned before the overhauling of the early criminal codes which happened in the 1830s. The abolition thus violated past imperial precepts. Lord Bentinck, in his Minute on immolation which proclaimed the abolition, therefore, needed to do some special pleading. He laboured the point that he had acted as a legislator for Hindus – implying that the verdict on abolition was one that had come from inside the community.[22] The fact remains, nonetheless, that a ritual that the state had so far thought was scripturally underpinned, and deserving of protection on that ground, was rendered into a crime. What authorized that change?

We obviously need to move away from colonial imperatives which had so far ensured a stasis, into the field of Indian initiatives, now articulated in the new public sphere of print culture, vernacular prose, compilations of religious texts and their translations, debates and discussions in newspapers and printed tracts. In 1818, a group of orthodox Hindus petitioned the government to remove all restrictions that it had placed on the practice of immolation under the guidance of Brahman pandits; about the widow's age and condition. In reply, a group of reformers brought in a counter-petition, demanding that restrictions should be strengthened. This was the first public intervention of Indians on the matter of sati. Previous to this, pandits had responded when they were solicited by the state to explain the proper procedure for the rite. This was also the beginning of pamphlet wars, petitions and counter-petitions, tracts and newspaper campaigns around which, gradually, a public sphere came to adhere. Both sides included men from the embryonic modern intelligentsia, as yet self taught in western languages and texts, and deeply familiar with Sanskrit sacred literature. Both included traditional pandits. Rammohun Roy, the outstanding liberal reformer, was proficient in many traditions, both western and Indian, modern and classical. He wrote about Hinduism, Islam, Christianity and Judaism with comfort and fluency, citing scripture, criticizing them all, and also drawing many things of value from each. He spoke for each of them and he belonged to none of them. As the maker of Bengali prose and journalism, he advocated anti-idolatrous monotheism, he denounced brahmanical priesthood and he advised access of low castes and women to Sanskrit sacred texts which had, so far, been forbidden them.[23]

Our general postcolonial understanding of Indian modernity is something that is authoritative, claiming secure foundations and a stable world view. Rammohun, the first of the moderns, escapes from this descriptive straitjacket. There was a chimeric, chameleon-like quality about his self-proclamation and his self-presentation in public. Rather than an established proper name, he would often write under borrowed names or anonymously. He would write to himself under a new name and would answer his own queries under yet a third name.[24] Print and its anonymity thus allowed him many simultaneous identities, displayed through a play on fleeting and tantalizing half disclosures: a now-you-see-me, now-you-don't kind of tease.

Lata Mani thinks that for him, gender in general and the sati in particular, were merely a site for an argument for different issues: religion, tradition, modernity. Her thinking is based on the fact that Roy used scriptural citations extensively, almost exclusively, rather·than matters of gender practices.[25] To make her point, she relies on a book that Roy wrote in English and addressed specifically a British audience.[26] It is interesting that Roy would have used exclusively scriptural arguments to convince an English readership that the abolition of immolation was sanctioned by scripture. It shows how anxious western readers were about any possible violation of Hindu prescription. On the other hand, when he wrote for his Bengali compatriots – first in Bengali, and then translated in English – he went beyond scripture. He wrote on gender prescriptions among Hindus with a passion and a bitterness, with a keenness of observation and with an intensity of language, that was unprecedented in our history. Both these points are ignored by Mani.[27]

In 1818, he published his first tract on sati, as a dialogue between two imaginary adversaries, one supporting and one opposing immolation. He put all the arguments in favour of immolation that obviously circulated among his contemporaries, in the words spoken by the advocate of immolation. In 1819, shortly after he wrote the first tract, Kashinath Tarkabagish, an orthodox pandit, wrote a tract in reply to Roy.[28] In 1820, Roy wrote a second tract in response where after replying to Kashinath, he went on to make larger case, not just against sati, but against Hindu gender prescriptions.[29]

Both agree that the ancient eponymous law-giver Manu is the highest court of authority. That both needed to agree to this suggests that Manu was, indeed, given this authoritative status by Bengali pandits of those times, and that his importance was not something that colonial Indologists had invented. In fact, Roy made so much of Manu's authority that he created some problems for the next generation of reformers who had to search for scriptural endorsement for widow remarriage. While Manu was silent on widow immolation, he was extremely censorious about remarriages.

Roy was, indeed, playing with very poor cards since much of the scripture that was available to him did advocate sati and some of those who criticized the practice – Medhatithi, for instance – were not known to him. In the very early years of print culture, the textual canon had not yet been consolidated and different regions worked with different fragments of traditions. Roy, therefore, depended partly on linguistic play and a subversive translation of a passage from the *Rg Veda* which changed the meaning from a celebration of immolation to one about fire worship.[30] He also conjoined two different scriptural citations from two different contexts, neither of which related to sati. By pulling them together, however, he arrived at a conclusion that would oppose the basis of sati.

He quoted the *Bhagavad Gita*, to claim that action-driven desire was inferior to action performed with desire for a particular end; the first leads to salvation, the second to heaven which is an inferior goal. He then cites from Manu who does not mention sati but who says that ascetic widowhood would lead to salvation. Roy concluded that since satis desire heaven, they are performing a less meritorious act than living as pious widows, and that Manu actually disapproved of immolation since he does not mention it. He argued that widows immolated themselves because they were prevented from reading scripture. They thus were unaware that living widows were promised a better future.[31]

Kashinath argued that heaven was a legitimate aspiration, even if it was inferior to salvation and that Manu's silence did not necessarily imply criticism of immolation. He, moreover, argued that even if immolation was more a custom, at least in the form in which it was practised, ancestral custom was a perfectly valid source of faith, unless it is specifically countermanded by scripture. He used other arguments too. He said ascetic widowhood was impossible, given the innate immorality of women. Roy objected and said that immorality could be corrected with knowledge. Rather mischievously, he used sati to argue against sati: in a land where men dread death, women court it. Who, then, is irresolute?

Kashinath said that women are not entitled to knowledge or education. Indeed, among contemporary Bengali Hindus, female illiteracy was customarily mandatory, on the understanding that widowhood was the fate of educated women. Women, moreover, were not intelligent enough to absorb knowledge. Roy mocked at custom. He also said: 'As to their (women's) inferiority in understanding, when did you ever afford them a fair opportunity of exhibiting their natural capacity? How then can you accuse them of a want of understanding?'

The major point of contention was the form of immolation. The widow was tied to the husband's corpse, then to the pyre. She was then entirely covered with logs of wood and bales of jute. As the flame was lit, loud music played, drowning out all possible cries of distress that could come from the pyre. A constant emission of dense smoke was ensured by a continuous pouring of ghee into the flames. Large bamboo poles held down the pyre so that the widow would not be able to escape. Roy said that this countermanded the scriptural description where the widow walked free into the flames. Kashinath said defensively that this was, indeed, a customary, non-scriptural form, but it was important because otherwise the widow's limbs may fall off and she would ascend to heaven with a deformed body. Roy said this was not shastric immolation; it was murder which was both a criminal and a scriptural offence. Roy never used the conventional terms for immolation: self-immolation, concremation, post-cremation. He preferred a graphic description of the entire act: 'burning alive of the Hindoo widow' or murder.

In his second treatise on sati, Roy moves beyond scripture. He defends the woman's right to life and to knowledge on grounds of her innate goodness and common humanity. He moves to an argument by nature. He also breaks loose of sati and describes the wife: 'At marriage, the wife is recognized as half of her husband, but in after-conduct, they are treated worse than animals. For the woman is employed to do the work of a slave in the house.' He then proceeds to construct a detailed account of domestic labour, from dawn to midnight, for the poor, low caste woman and for the rich, upper caste woman. He describes their incarceration in the kitchen where they are engaged in prodigious feeding but where they starve most of the time and live off leftover food. He talks of the many different kinds of household work they perform, the penalties they receive for the slightest lapse, their insulation from knowledge and from the world outside, contrasting all this with male privileges. He writes:

> We never consider as criminal the misconduct of men towards women. One fault they (women) have is to give their confidence too readily by considering others equally void of duplicity as themselves. . . . What I lament is that seeing the woman thus exposed to every misery, you feel for them no compassion that may exempt them from being tied down and burnt to death.

What he provides in this tract is an ethnography of female lives and labour, a thick description that is structured as a narrative of exploitation. It initiates a new genre for simultaneously describing and exposing social power.

Law, thus, provided the major site for social criticism, for interrogation of scriptural and customary norms, often as unintended consequence. Even as the brahmanical orthodoxy replied with a renewed defence of textual injunctions. They too had to realign them to ethical standards, assuming certain universal ethical properties, in order to meet the force of arguments of compassion and justice that advocates of equality invoked. For instance, in the debates over widow immolation in the early nineteenth century, both defenders and opponents of the practice built their cases on claims to representing the woman's 'own will and pleasure'. Unnoticed and unintended, female consent slipped into the legal regime as a test for the validity of regulations that rule women. The orthodoxy had referred to 'willing satis' who defied all dissuasion and who followed their husbands to the pyre. To meet their claim, Rammohun Roy then needed to critically articulate the entire regime of the woman's socialization that made her internalize a life structured by exploitation, humiliation, inequality.

We have here, in such close and guilty observations of female lifeworlds, the composition of a new male gaze. While classical and folk literature abounded with elaborate and detailed erotic descriptions of the desirable and sexually-emotionally active woman, we now move towards an eye that focuses on her labour, her punishments, but which insists, at the same time, on her intellectual and moral resources, thus saving the female figure from abjection or victimhood. This is linked to the growth of a reformist masculinity that questions its male privileges, denaturalizes norms: a guilty, introspective masculinity. Moreover, in the course of the continuous debates among reformers and orthodoxy, both religious prescription and state law lost their naturalness, givenness. Their ideological underpinnings were clarified as opponents progressively unmasked one another, and as both norms and law became post-conventional, needing elaborate defences in the public sphere. Such non-linear consequences of reformist laws exceeded their immediate and practical effects. Very few widows remarried even in the South where the remarriage issue constituted the exclusive field of reformist campaigns. At the same time, the law opened up discursive and critical possibilities that were larger than itself.

Notes

1 See, for instance, Sarkar (1947).
2 Sarkar (1948).
3 Chatterjee (1986).
4 Sangari and Vaid (1989).
5 Sarkar (2001a; 2001b).
6 Althusser (1971).
7 Thompson (1975).
8 Inden (1990).
9 Gilroy (1993).
10 Cooper (2005).
11 For a superb example of working-class agency that operates within a structure of constraints, see Joshi (2005).
12 Sarkar (2002).
13 Chakrabarty (2000).
14 Bhabha (1994).
15 Fraser (1985).
16 Chatterjee (1994: 116–34).

[17] See, for instance, Nair (1996) or Singha (1998).

[18] On questions of personal laws in colonial times, see Derrett (1968), Parashar (1992), Washbrook (1981), Sinha (1995), Carroll (1989), Kozlowski (1989),   Mani (1998), McGinn (1992), Arunima (2003), Sarkar (2001a; 2001b).

[19] Firminger (1812).

[20] Colebrooke (1797).

[21] Cited in Dalmia–Lüderitz (1992: 58–64).

[22] Minute on Suttee, November, 1829 in Philips (1977: 367–69).

[23] Biswas (1962).

[24] On his writing under many names, see Killingley (1993).

[25] Mani (1989: 88–126).

[26] Roy (1830).

[27] Roy (1818). See also Roy (1945).

[28] Tarkabagish (1819), reprinted in Ghosh (1973).

[29] Roy (1945).

[30] Biswas (1994).

[31] Roy (1945).

References

Althusser, L. (1971), *Lenin and Philosophy and Other Essays*, translated by B. Brewster (London).

Arunima, G. (2003), *There Comes Papa: Colonialism and the Transformation of Matriliny in Kerala* (Hyderabad).

Bhabha, Homi. K. (1994), *The Location of Culture* (London).

Biswas, Dilip Kumar, ed. (1962), *Sophia Dobson Collett, The Life and Letters of Raja Rammohun Roy* (Calcutta).

——— (1994), *Rammohun Sameeksha* (Calcutta).

Carroll, Lucy (1989), 'Law, Custom and Statutory Social Reform: The Hindu Widow Remarriage Act of 1856', in J. Krishnamurty, ed., *Women in Colonial India: Essays on Work, Survival and the State* (Delhi).

Chakrabarty, Dipesh (2000), *Provincializing Europe: Postcolonial Thought and Historical Difference* (Princeton).

Chatterjee, Partha (1986), *Nationalist Thought and the Colonial World: A Derivative Discourse* (Delhi).

——— (1994), 'The Nation and Its Women', in *The Nation and Its Fragments: Colonial and Postcolonial Histories* (Delhi).

Colebrooke, H.T. (1797), 'On the Duties of the Faithful Hindoo Widow', *Asiatic Society Journal* (Calcutta); reprinted in William Jones and others (1798), *Dissertations and Miscellaneous Pieces, Relating to the History and Antiquities, the Arts, Sciences and Literature of Asia* (London: Vernor & Hoob): 215–25.

Cooper, Frederick (2005), *Colonialism in Question: Theory, Knowledge, History* (California).

Dalmia–Lüderitz, Vasudha (1992), 'Sati as a Religious Rite: Parliamentary Papers on Widow Immolation', *Economic and Political Weekly*, Vol. 27, No. 4: 58–64.

Derrett, J.D.M. (1968), *Religion, Law and State in India* (London).

Firminger, Walter, ed. (1812), *Fifth Report from the Select Committee of the House of Commons on the Affairs of the East India Company*, Vol. 1, 28 July.

Fraser, Nancy (1985), 'What's Critical about Critical Theory: The Case of Habermas and Gender', *New German Critique*, No. 35, Spring–Summer: 97–131.

Gilroy, Paul (1993), *The Black Atlantic: Modernity and Double Consciousness* (Harvard).

Inden, Ronald (1990), *Imagining India* (Oxford).

Joshi, Chitra (2005), *Lost Worlds: Indian Labour and Its Forgotten Histories* (Delhi).

Killingley, Dermot (1993), *Rammohun Roy in Hindu and Christian Tradition* (Newcastle upon Tyne).

Kozlowski, G. (1989), 'Muslim Women and the Control of Property in North India', in J. Krishnamurty, ed., *Women in Colonial India: Essays on Work, Survival and the State* (Delhi).

Mani, Lata (1989), 'Contentious Traditions: Debates on Sati in Colonial India', in K. Sangari and S. Vaid, eds, *Recasting Women: Essays in Colonial History* (Delhi).

—— (1998), *Contentious Traditions: The Debate on Sati in Colonial India* (Berkeley).

McGinn, Padma Anagol (1992), 'The Age of Consent Act Reconsidered: Women's Perspectives and Participation in the Child Marriage Controversy', *South Asia Research*, No. 12: 2.

Nair, Janaki (1996), *Women and Law in Colonial India: A Social History* (Delhi).

Parashar, Archana (1992), *Women and Family Law Reform in India* (Delhi).

Philips, C.H., ed. (1977), *The Correspondence of Lord William Cavendish Bentinck, Governor General of India, 1828–1835*, Vol. 1 (Oxford).

Roy, Rammohun (1818), *Conference between an Advocate for and an Opponent of the Practice of Burning Widows Alive* (Calcutta).

—— (1830), *Abstract of Arguments Regarding the Burning of Widows Considered as Religious Life* (Calcutta).

—— (1945), *A Second Conference between an Advocate for and an Opponent of the Practice of Burning Widows Alive*, in Kalidas Nag and Debajyoti Burman, eds, *The English Works of Raja Rammohun Roy*, Part 1 (Calcutta).

Sangari, Kumkum and Sudesh Vaid, eds (1989), *Recasting Women: Essays in Colonial History* (Delhi).

Sarkar, Jadunath, ed. (1948), *The History of Bengal*, Vol. 2 (Dacca).

Sarkar, Sumit (2002), *Beyond Nationalist Frames: Relocating Postmodernism, Hindutva, History* (Delhi).

Sarkar, Susobhan (1947), *Notes On the Bengal Renaissance* (Calcutta).

Sarkar, Tanika (2001a), 'Enfranchised Selves: Women, Culture and Rights in Nineteenth Century Bengal', in *Gender and History*, Vol. 13, No. 3.

—— (2001b), *Hindu Wife, Hindu Nation: Religion, Community, Cultural Nationalism* (Delhi).

Singha, Radhika (1998), *A Despotism of Law: Crime and Justice in Early Colonial India* (Delhi).

Sinha, Mrinalini (1995), *Colonial Masculinity: The Manly Englishman and the Effeminate Bengali in the Late Nineteenth Century* (Manchester).

Tarkabagish, Kashinath (1819), *Bidhayak – Nishedhak Sambad* (Calcutta); reprinted in Ajit Kumar Ghosh, ed. (1973), *Rammohun Rachanabali* (Calcutta).

Thompson, E.P. (1975), 'The Rule of Law', in *Whigs and Hunters: The Origin of the Black Act* (New York).

Washbrook, D.A. (1981), 'Law, State and Society in Colonial India', in G. Johnson Baker and Anil Seal, eds, *Power, Profit and Politics* (Cambridge).

How Indian is Indian Law?

Oliver Mendelsohn

The question in the title of this chapter is impossibly broad but my hope is that struggling to answer it may prove instructive. Let me begin the discussion with another, semi-rhetorical, question I have often been asked in professional or social situations outside India: 'Indian law is basically the common law, is it not?' My standard answer to this question is something like, 'Yes, but there are important differences in the way it works.' Any person with a substantial understanding of Indian law will know that this answer avoids far more than it illuminates. It is reasonable enough to argue that the single most important influence on the character of contemporary Indian law is the legal concepts and overall approach adopted first in Britain and later in other English speaking territories. But equally, the Indian legal system can certainly not be described as simply the common law in an Indian setting. This is what I want to try to unpack in this chapter, through looking at a number of approaches to law in India.

It is easy enough to locate the 'Indianness' of the way in which the official legal system of India works. The organization and characteristics of the legal profession; the subject matter of litigation; the processes of the courts; the behaviour and expectations of litigants – these are some of the matters explored over many years (albeit by too small a group of socio-legal scholars). These studies have illustrated the distinctiveness of the official Indian legal system, which for many decades has been very far from a 'foreign' or 'colonial' system. But these are *not* the perspectives explored in the present chapter, except in passing. Here, I wish to open up some rather more fundamental questions as to the distinctiveness of Indian law.

Legal Pluralism

The system of law established by the British and carried on by independent India holds itself out as the sole legal authority in the country. In this respect, the Indian legal order simply mirrors the official stance of any other modern legal regime. This pretension to legal monopoly is everywhere a myth or a fiction – we know this comprehensively from 30 years of law and society scholarship, and indeed from much earlier thinkers like Henry Maine.[1] In perhaps every developed political society, there is much law-like activity that takes place outside the apparatus of the state and, conversely, within that apparatus, much of the activity resembles processes in the world outside.[2] The decision to name as 'law' only what happens in official institutions reflects the drive of nineteenth-century legal positivism and also the appetites of the modern nation state. In the case of India, the claim to monopoly of law by the state is especially weak.

The practical ambit of Anglo–Indian law was always narrow: aside from the administration of criminal justice, the Indian courts were dominated by issues surrounding landed property.[3] This is not to say that the British project of transferring law to India was not an ambitious one or that there were not important cases in their courts concerning issues other than land; rather, it is to note that, in quantitative terms, litigation over land dwarfed all other civil cases. For the most part, the great flow of social relations went unregulated by the law and the courts of colonial India. And to a large, if now diminishing, extent, this remains true of the post-independence period too.

For example, the British did not seek to bring marriage and its incidents under the umbrella of the state. Births, deaths and marriages were not required to be registered. A limited legislative regime was provided for marriage and divorce among the relatively small Christian and tiny Parsi communities but not for the dominant Hindus or Muslims.[4] The enactment and dissolution of marriage and disputes to do with children and marital property remained overwhelmingly a matter for agencies constituted without reference to the state. After independence, marriage among Hindus was officially regulated for the first time under the *Hindu Marriage Act* 1955 but, until recently, this has changed behaviour very little. Even now only a tiny minority of people, overwhelmingly in urban situations, and probably women more than men, resort to the courts in family matters.

A glimpse of the apparently traditional world of authority in matters of marriage dispute can be found in the following case I collected during field-work in Behror, a sub-division of Alwar district in Rajasthan, in the mid-1970s.

A Dispute among the Dhobis (Washerfolk)[5]

Two sisters, one of them blind, had been married to one dhobi man.[6] Within three years of the wedding, the man had died, leaving the sighted sister with a small child. The two widows returned to their father's household. Widow remarriage is the norm among dhobis and a second marriage was successfully arranged for the sighted sister, while the blind sister and the small child were left with the parents/grandparents. As part of the second marriage arrangement, the new husband paid Rs 350 to the parents of the bride in a transaction witnessed by several men from communities other than the dhobis. When the parents of the deceased first husband found out about this transaction, they became angry. They said that the money was properly theirs as *jagra* or compensation for the loss of their daughter-in-law's services.

The affair was considered serious by the dhobis, since it appeared that the transaction constituted the prohibited practice of bride price (as opposed to the approved practice of dowry payable by the parents of the bride). Accordingly, on the occasion of the next community funeral, a meeting was convened to consider the case. The meeting found that the new husband had indeed paid bride price, tantamount to purchasing the woman, and because of the seriousness of the breach of caste rules, he and several of his relatives were to be outcasted.[7] For their part, the parents of the bride succeeded in avoiding punishment on the grounds that they had accepted the payment as a contribution towards the costs of maintaining their daughter's child and her blind sister rather than as a payment for the woman herself.

The outcastes felt harshly treated and they sought a special meeting to reconsider the affair (my informant used the language of the state in describing the process: he referred to ordinary community meetings at the time of weddings or funerals as the 'lower court' and special meetings as the 'High Court'). The meeting was duly convened on the understanding that the appellants would pay the considerable cost of a meeting at which some 400 people from widely dispersed locations would attend. This time the appellants argued that the sum paid was indeed *jagra* but that the compensation had been paid to the wrong person; it should have been paid to the father of the deceased husband. It could not be maintained, therefore, that the new husband and his father had not paid compensation in defiance of caste rules or that they had paid bride price instead. But the meeting was not satisfied with this argument: why had none of the elders been consulted about the proper practice, and why was payment witnessed by people from other communities and not by dhobis? The matter was turned over to five respected dhobi elders. These men deliberated and issued judgment that the new husband be fined Rs 350, Rs 300 of which was to go to the father of the deceased husband and the remainder to the community representatives for their expenses. The other outcastes were each fined Rs 11. All were readmitted to the caste upon payment of the amounts.

A notable aspect of this dhobi case is the evidence of widow remarriage and polygamy. The former practice has traditionally been forsworn by many high castes or castes pretending to high status, the Brahmins above all. The dhobis' liberal position on widow re-marriage happens to be in line with the *Hindu Widows' Remarriage Act* 1856, one of the few legislative interventions of the British designed to bring about more 'civilized' family practices.[8] Until recently, arguably, the dhobis' tolerance of polygamy was also in conformity with the law. The British made no serious effort to prohibit polygamy among Hindus.[9] It was left to the *Hindu Marriage Act* 1955 to render polygamy clearly unlawful for Hindus, though the effect of this prohibition on practice remains unclear. Beyond the matter of legislation by the colonial and independent authorities, the dhobi case is a simple pointer to the great plurality of Indian practice in family relations.

The dhobi case is also an example of the workings of what is called in the sociological literature, 'the caste *panchayat*'.[10] By the time I collected this and a number of other cases in the early 1970s, only some of the lower castes of

Behror still had any ongoing processes that could address disputes within their community.[11] Many such cases appear to have been taken up because they involved behaviour seen as adverse to the reputation of a caste actively seeking to improve its reputation. In the case among the dhobis, it was the charge of payment of bride price that produced such resolute action. Bride price is an emotive issue throughout Hindu India: there is widespread self-righteousness about families denying themselves the proceeds of 'selling' their daughters. It may be that the latter practice is associated with Muslims, though on the sub-continent Muslims themselves have tended to move towards the Hindu practice of dowry rather than bride price. So this is the context of the dhobis wanting to separate themselves emphatically from the proscribed practice of bride price.

It would be difficult to argue that the above case does not represent a process of 'law' at work, despite the fact that it was conducted outside the institutions of the state. The process was decisional, binding, and has the general appearance of judicial action. The case is also remarkable by the standards of other contemporary nation states possessed of highly developed legal institutions, even if one concedes that law-like activities outside the state apparatus are characteristic of all those societies. This is not a case of tentative decision-making on a matter of family relations while nervously looking over the shoulder at the official legal system – decision-making 'under the shadow of the law', to use Marc Galanter's phrase.[12] Rather, the panchayat of the dhobis was squarely and seemingly with perfect confidence in its own legitimacy resolving a complex and important issue that had arisen in relation to the community's rules for the arrangement of marriage. It is clear from this one small case that the modern legal order of India has left space for legal action by parties outside the state in a way that has no simple analogue in most other nations with a highly developed legal order.[13]

I know of no comparable example to be found in contemporary Britain, France or Germany. Nor could similar examples easily be found in the US, Canada or Australia – except, importantly, among the indigenous people of these settler societies. Among the latter peoples, there may indeed be forms of contemporary legal ordering that are broadly analogous to that of the dhobis of Rajasthan. But what makes India different from these settler societies is that, at least in conceptual terms, the example of the dhobis' tribunal is not exceptional. Thus there is no apparatus of state that could readily have been approached by the dhobis for resolution of their problem, even if they had wanted this. If, inconceivably, the dhobis had gone to court over this matter, just one of their problems would have been the evidence of 'traditional' but now unlawful polygamous marriage. Although there is now a single family law applicable to the dhobis and to all other Hindus in India, we have noted that very few Indians in fact approach the courts for resolution of family problems according to this law. The Indian state is in practice content to leave family law to any body that can assert authority over such issues, though the number of such bodies is declining. True, and whatever the past situation, the Indian state does not now lend legitimacy to the activities of 'customary' bodies like the panchayat of the dhobis. But nor has it taken action to de-legitimate these bodies. It just ignores them, leaving their vitality to be determined by forces other than the legal apparatus of the state.[14]

The dhobi case was not typical of dispute processes in Behror even 30 or 40 years ago, when it took place. At that time, and even more so today, there were very few communities in Behror that had the coherence to resolve a serious dispute surrounding community rules so neatly. Yet this is not to say that the case is an isolated one that lacks any more general relevance. To what extent, then, does the case among the dhobis represent a form of justice that was previously characteristic of Indian village life? Secondly, can we proceed analogously from this case to formulate more general propositions about Indian patterns of 'dispute settlement' or 'law' or 'justice' that hold good for India today? Before we address these questions directly, it will be useful to say something about 'Hindu' law, since this represents another and more celebrated body of law than any legal process to be spelled out of cases such as that of the dhobis above.

The Question of Hindu Law

The most discussed body of distinctively Indian law is generally known by the name 'Hindu law'. Today, Hindu law usually appears as a body of principles of 'personal' or family law embodied in statutes (many of them passed by independent India) and associated case law. 'Muslim law' consists of rules on the same subject matter but the difference is that, for political reasons, there has been no codification of this law, the greater part of it remaining to be found in cases. The courts that interpret and apply Hindu and Muslim law are the ordinary Indian courts. So 'Hindu' and 'Muslim' or 'Islamic' law have in formal terms become simply sets of principles dealing with matters such as marriage, inheritance and adoption. From this perspective, Hindu and Muslim law are two among many classificatory subjects of law within the overall legal system of the state and are thus analogous, say, to criminal law or the law of contract. The relative impact of this Hindu and Muslim law is often seen to be shrinking as other areas of law, concerning direct foreign investment, for example, proliferate and develop greater significance

It is now commonly accepted that the British transformed and – this is perhaps more controversial – substantially degraded Hindu and Muslim law in India, and that this process was considerably furthered by post-Independence codification of Hindu law.[15] Whatever they were before the arrival of the British, Hindu and Muslim law were certainly not a limited set of substantive laws within a far wider state legal order. This said, there is now a stirring of argument to the effect that Muslim and particularly Hindu law are no longer to be seen as mere historical relics. Hindu law, it is argued, is now rising from the ashes of the legal holocaust that was Anglo–Indian law.[16] So one recent work argues at great length that Hindu law is currently undergoing a vigorous 'postmodern' revival.[17] While Menski endorses Derrett's position on the decline of Hindu law under the British and the early post-independence regimes, he suggests that over the last couple of decades, the Indian courts have been engaged in a little noticed reformation of Hindu law which has revived its relevance and utility. We will return to this proposition towards the end of this chapter.

Menski seemingly calls his own position 'postmodern' by virtue of his rejection of what he calls the 'positivism' and 'modernism' brought to bear upon Hindu law for centuries. His argument is that the colonial authorities and early postcolonial elites attempted to create a legal order under the state that was oblivious or contemptuous of practical differences in the customary law followed by different communities in India. The root fallacy underlying the British approach was a complete misunderstanding of the nature of Hindu law. That body of law was never comparable with law in the west. Contrary to what the British policy-makers of the late eighteenth and nineteenth centuries thought, there were no 'codes' of law to be found in Hindu India. Manu, the presumptive author and eponymous title of the most celebrated text of Hindu law, was not a 'code' of law that was ever enforced in pre-colonial India.

Shorn of Menski's language of 'postmodernism', there is general agreement on this central proposition of his work. To borrow a memorable phrase from Robert Lingat, 'the classical legal system of India substitutes the notion of *authority* for that of legality'.[18] The great texts of Hinduism, including the Dharmasastras such as Manu, can be seen to have underpinned the idea of a Hindu legal order, but they did not represent textual codes to be enforced by courts. Lingat and others have argued that the highly variable custom of different communities must have been a more fertile source of social rules than were the great texts. Lingat tries to link these disparate sources (text and custom) in the following summary:

> This conception would have ended in a complete divorce between reality and law, had not the law revealed by the Sages been profoundly based in the traditions and aspirations of the Hindu world. It is careful to explain that wherever it cannot conquer custom remains queen. But custom's triumph by no means diminished the authority of the law. It can only fetter the application of the latter, perhaps only for a time. No rule is really legitimate and finally sanctified until it conforms to that law.[19]

So for Lingat, even highly variable custom derives its ultimate authority from the Hindu text.

Despite his agreement with scholars like Lingat as to the essential unenforceability of the Dharmasastras, Menski's account of the classical Hindu period is somewhat distinctive. He insists that the ideal form of Hindu law involves no external authority at all but consists wholly in self-regulation by individual Hindus. It is only with the breakdown of self-regulation that the morally inferior but more efficacious external legal authority needed to be constructed. For Lingat, by contrast, Hindu law only became truly 'law' once the commentators and digest makers of the medieval period had done their work sufficient for it to be enforced by the institutions of the state. Menski criticizes this approach as 'positivist', by which he means that Lingat has unwarrantedly conceived of law as essentially, indeed exclusively, a creature of the state. This criticism seems to have some validity to it, though Menski himself is sharply vulnerable to criticism that his own account of the classical Hindu approach leaves law completely undefined. If law is self-regulation according to principles derived from revelation and associated traditions, then where does law begin and end? How is law to be distinguished from religion or morality? There is no hint of an answer to these questions in Menski's work.

A different approach again is taken in some recent work by Donald R. Davis Jr. He takes issue with the proposition endorsed by Menski and others to the effect that Hindu law is an example of natural law thinking. In conformity with almost all recent approaches to Hindu law, Davis sees 'the Dharmsastra texts not as codes of black-letter law to be applied by judges'.[20] Rather, they are 'textbooks of materials, hypotheticals, and systematizations pertaining to a legal system'.[21] These materials must be accorded their full weight by the persons authorized to expound them – people trained in the Vedas, not judges – but there is no process of appealing to the authority of the Sastras over any principles applied in actual cases. So complete is the separation between the religious and moral precepts of the scriptures and the content of custom, that Davis categorizes the Hindu system as one of legal positivism rather than natural law:

> Whereas natural law theory is concerned to maintain the superiority of natural law in the face of expedient concessions to social facts in the form of unjust laws, Hindu jurisprudence admits the superiority of social facts in the determination of *dharma* and law, despite any contravention of Vedic 'natural law'. This is the essence of legal positivism.[22]

There is

> legal recognition even of acts that violate rules of Dharmasastra, when those acts have already been accomplished in fact. Part of the legal interpretation here involves taking certain rules as advisory 'oughts' rather than mandatory 'musts'.[23]

Inevitably, Davis faces the objection that the language of legal positivism sits poorly with the unquestionable moral authority of the Dharmasastras within Hindu law. 'Hindu law' cannot exist as an idea or a putative legal system in the absence of the Sastras as ultimate authority within the system. On the other hand, Davis' invocation of the language of legal positivism makes dramatically clear how different the Indian scene was from medieval Christian thinking about the connection of human law and the law of God. He is clearly right to lay such heavy emphasis on the marvellous pragmatism of the Hindu legal system, a pragmatism which operated side-by-side with a powerful set of precepts to which everyone was rigorously subordinate. This is the point of Lingat's statement that the classical Hindu law embodies a conception of 'authority' rather than 'legality'. The core texts and principles of the Hindu order have unquestioned authority, but this does not mean they constitute a black-letter compendium to be applied by courts under the state or the great diversity of tribunals within civil society.

Whether blinded by their own legal tradition or out of deliberate concern to change India – both these outlooks are discernible on different issues and among different policy makers – the British approached Hindu law in a spirit quite alien to its previous development. They assumed that texts such as Manu were enforceable codes of law and set about appointing jurisconsults steeped in such texts to advise the British judges of 'the law' to apply in 'personal' matters that were to be governed by Hindu or Muslim law respectively. Eventually the courts were emboldened to dispense with their advisers and proceed to expound Hindu and Muslim law according to their own understandings. Not the least contradictory aspect of this enterprise was the building of a body of binding judicial precedents of Hindu law, an enterprise previously unknown to India.

But to repeat an observation stated rather than argued above, the material issues of litigation in colonial India were overwhelmingly matters to do with agricultural land. Such material disputes were presumably the context in which most matters of Hindu law arose – issues of inheritance, including adoption, for example – and they cannot have constituted a statistically large part of this litigation over land. In short, the actual impact of 'Hindu law' as manufactured and dispensed by the courts of British India was unlikely to have weighed very heavily on the people of India conceived as a whole. Again, this conclusion can be no more than stated baldly in the present context.

The Question of Customary Law

This short discussion of Hindu law may help frame the case of the dhobis of Behror discussed above. It is clear that the customs of the dhobis are far apart from the ideals enunciated in the Dharmasastras – the dhobis' practice of polygamy and positive endorsement of widow remarriage are examples of this. On the other hand, our discussion suggests that Hindu law left great scope for differentiation of social practice and the development of independent patterns of authority and dispute processing throughout Indian society. So it is not merely the modern Indian state that has been remarkably 'hands off' relative to social practice, but also 'Hindu law' itself.[24]

Thus far we have provided a single example of law-like activity outside the confines of the state, though we have insisted that the courts of the state have been preoccupied with a narrow range of material matters. We have foreshadowed trying to answer the question of whether any generalization can be attempted on the basis of the one case drawn from the dhobis of Behror. In fact, there has been remarkably little attempt to generalize about the whole world of law or legal authority in India. Louis Dumont, with his characteristic clarity and boldness, is an exception. Dumont sums up the situation of post-Independence India thus: 'Contemporary observation shows that there are three main organs of justice: the caste panchayat, the panchayat of the dominant caste, and the official courts.'[25]

Although he uses the term 'justice', it would seem that Dumont is treating this term as a synonym for 'legal authority' or even 'law'. This imprecision in nomenclature is common to those who try to analyse the operations of the legal instruments of the state, chiefly the courts, side-by-side with structures constituted by civil society.

In Dumont's account, the 'official courts' are sufficiently self-explanatory but the other two bodies need brief explication. 'Caste panchayat' is the decision-making council within an individual caste, of which there are many hundreds throughout India. In Dumont's conception the caste panchayat deals with matters internal to the caste and which are conceived to affect the interest or reputation of the caste.[26] Clearly Dumont would regard the dhobi case as an example of the caste panchayat at work.

'The dominant caste' is a term invented in the 1950s by the sociologist M.N. Srinivas, who argued from fieldwork in southern India that there were certain castes that were 'dominant' mainly by virtue of their 'preponderant economic and political power'.[27] For Dumont, it was control of land by a particular caste that was the sole constituent of 'dominance'.[28] This dominance reproduced at the local level the pre-colonial dominance of the king over a more extensive level of territory. While the power of the king has been taken over by the Indian state, the dominant caste retains power in the village. So, in a conceptual and partly practical sense, the dominant landholding communities were and are the 'kings' of their villages. Their power includes the capacity to dispense a certain amount of 'justice': 'the notables of the dominant caste are often entrusted with the arbitration of differences in other castes or between different castes, and they can exact penalties for unimportant offences. . . .'[29]

This is not the place to subject Dumont's argument to close analysis, though it can be said that the schema is outdated (in relation to the idea of the dominant caste) and also insufficiently subtle or complete to be readily accepted.[30] What remains helpful about Dumont's outline is that it points us firmly towards a conception of legal authority in India that is plural rather than unitary; that is part local and part more territorially extensive; and that is composed of institutions and structures that arise both from the state and within civil society. To this complexity we will need to add the fact of historical and to some extent continuing influences exerted by the Hindu and Muslim legal systems.

What is also useful in Dumont's scheme is his avoidance of the term 'customary law' or even 'custom', since my own view is that these concepts often distort, more than they illuminate, the study of Indian society and law. True, this is not always so. Thus there would be no obvious distortion of the dhobis' case to describe it as 'customary law' in operation. I have already stated that the process in that case had all the marks of 'legal' or 'judicial' process, if one leaves aside the fact that it proceeded completely outside the institutions of the state. And it is clear that the decision-making body was 'customary' or 'traditional' in its make-up. Moreover, what was in issue was the apparent 'custom' of compensation being paid by the family of a bridegroom who sought to marry a widow. Where the participants differed was over who was the proper recipient of the compensation. But even in this case there was no readily available body of substantive 'customary law' that could answer the question at issue. Rather, the decision-makers fashioned a judgement of considerably creative jurisprudence. So even here we need to be careful about applying the label 'customary law' so as not to give the impression that there was a cut-and-dried body of principles available for simple application.

The Particular Case of Punjab

The heyday of Indian 'customary law' talk was the second half of the nineteenth century and it flourished particularly in relation to the province of Punjab, finally absorbed into British India in 1849. Punjab was the arena for a revived (from the early decades of the century) contest between the conservative, Romantic and paternalistic school of British administrators and legal reformers influenced by the Utilitarianism of Bentham and James Mill.[31] It might be said that over India as a whole, the winner of this contest was the latter group, since Macaulay's Indian Penal Code was finally enacted in 1860 and a number of other law codes followed. But 'the Punjab system' of administration represented at least a partial victory for the conservatives, who were greatly concerned to prevent the disintegration of 'the village community'.[32] It was largely in relation to this latter concept that the discourse of 'customary law' developed.

Much later, in 1915, the then Lieutenant Governor of Punjab, Michael O'Dwyer, summed up the attitude to 'customary law' in Punjab thus:

> The problem before us in the Punjab is unique. Other Provinces in India have as a rule, the Dharma Shastras and the various commentaries on them for the Hindus and the Shariyat and the Hadis for the Muhammadans. . . . Here we have elected to be governed by custom. We have no body of feeling that condemns our tribal customs as a whole as antiquated or unsuitable. No desire for uniformity, no sense of injustice is involved in the maintenance of the existing system. Our function is therefore to uphold, not to destroy.[33]

The legislative basis of this election to recognize custom was the *Punjab Laws Act* (1872). The critical part was section 5:

> Decision in certain cases to be according to Native law. – In questions regarding succession, special property of females, betrothal, marriage, divorce, dower, adoption, guardianship, minority, bastardy, family relations, wills, legacies, gifts, partitions, or any religious usage or institution, the rule of decision shall be:
> (a) any custom applicable to the parties concerned, which is not contrary to justice, equity or good conscience, and has not been by this or any other enactment altered or abolished and has not been declared to be void by any competent authority;
> (b) the Muhammadan law, in cases where the parties are Muhammadans, and the Hindu law, in cases where the parties are Hindus, except in so far as

such law has been altered or abolished by legislative enactment, or is opposed to the provisions of this Act, or has been modified by any such custom as is above referred to.

By virtue of this section, 'applicable' custom could trump the Hindu and Muslim law as declared by the courts in other regions of India. This was, on the face of it, a momentous change of legal approach for at least this province. It maintained and provided firmer legal foundation for an administrative and judicial approach that had already been pursued in Punjab for at least 20 years. Following the formal annexation of Punjab to British India in 1849, Lord Dalhousie had issued a Despatch in which he stated that as Governor-General he 'would wish to uphold Native institutions and practices so far as they are consistent with the distribution of justice to all classes. . . .' But he also noted that with a couple of exceptions 'there is no portion of the country which will not be benefited by the gradual introduction of the British system at the earliest possible period. . . . (T)hese directives may have been said to have been the ultimate basis of the observance of customary law from 1849 to 1872.'[34]

Punjab was perhaps a particularly favourable case for the recognition of 'customary law'. More than for many parts of India, Punjab could be seen as composed of what were termed 'tribes', albeit these tribes were for the most part settled in villages and practising agriculture. Indeed, recognition of the customary law of the Punjabi villagers proceeded mostly in relation to the principles by which *land* was either shared out or held in common. This preoccupation with land simply echoed the refrain of the British administration throughout India, dependent as it was on the taxation of agriculture. But here, in Punjab, the effort was to attend to the 'customary law' by which land was managed. To this end, and as part of the land settlement operations,[35] the official records were filled out with answers to a set of standard questions about matters such as inheritance rules (affecting women, including widows, for example), tenancy, admission of outsiders to the 'village community' (of landholders, not including tenants), principles for sharing the 'waste' land utilized for grazing and other purposes, rules for the rotation of crops, and so on. In addition to the material collected for individual villages (known as the *wajib-al urz*), a record of tribal customs that affected numbers of villages (called *riwaj-i am*) was also compiled.

This is not the place for a full consideration of the Punjab experiment in the recognition of customary law. What is relevant in the present context is a cluster of deep problems in the British encounter in Punjab. First, we can point to the simplistic and ultimately false notion of 'the village community' implicit in much of the British consideration of 'customary law' in Punjab. When the British administrators/scholars of the period talked in terms of 'the village community', they meant the landholders. These were the only people of regular interest to the administration, except in its criminal jurisdiction, since they were the people from whom land revenue (the principal form of taxation) was levied. Other communities often became virtually invisible in British accounts. A century later

Dumont and other scholars rightly dismissed the notion of 'the village community' with its mute but nonetheless audible denial of differentiation, domination and subordination within the perhaps typically multi-caste villages of India. The 'village community' of British imagination was largely coterminous with the 'dominant caste' of post-independence anthropology, including that of Dumont. This left a great number of subordinate castes out of account, a statistical majority of the population.

There was also a deep contradiction in the British effort to enforce customary law through their own courts. If there were such a thing as customary law, then it must have been enforced by indigenous institutions (whether within civil society or 'the state') prior to the British arrival. Logically the British administrators of Punjab must have known this, but they wasted no effort in puzzling over any mechanisms by which this may have proceeded. There was a sound enough logic to this lack of official curiosity, since in policy terms the issue was irrelevant. The administration of Punjab was not qualitatively different from that elsewhere in British India; it was merely that in Punjab, the British were prepared to recognise custom as the source of law regarding certain issues in their courts, as opposed to the hybrid Hindu and Muslim law they recognized (and partly created) in the other provinces. But from the perspective of society in Punjab, this studied ignorance of the structures of customary lawmaking or enforcement (as opposed to the substantive rules) made for a profound falsification of the whole enterprise of 'customary law'.

The closest the British came to recognizing the problem of how custom was created and sustained was in the debate on the merits of codifying custom in Punjab. Following definitive recognition of custom as a source of law in the *Punjab Laws Act* 1872, there was considerable discussion as to whether the next appropriate step was codification. C.L. Tupper, an official greatly influenced by Maine and his ideas of evolutionary jurisprudence, was the most energetic promoter of codification. Tupper's view was that society in Punjab was not sufficiently evolved to benefit from the systematic application of British law. In order to sustain the prevailing custom he proposed that it be codified where possible and that the code be admitted to the courts as a 'rebuttable presumption'.[36] Such a measure would both preserve custom and simplify the task of the courts. But this was not the view of the then Lieutenant Governor of Punjab, Sir Robert Egerton. His views were presented in a letter from the Secretary of the Government of Punjab to the Government of India in 1881, and are worth quoting at some length:

> [C]ustoms arose under a state of social life governed by many inter-dependent conditions. Tribal customs are appropriate, and should be enforced so long as the conditions remain unimpaired, and so long as they are suited to the expectations and views of justice of the members of the tribe; but the tendency of our administration is to dissolve the tribal bond and to give free scope to individual energy. New conditions are thus created and new expectations raised. The

process is gradual, but sure; and though the Lieutenant-Governor does not desire to hasten the decay, he would not propose any measure which would prolong the existence of a custom for a longer time than is necessary to prevent the dislocation of the society which has been governed by it. . . . (D)irectly any attempt is made to legalize a custom, its virtue as a custom is lost. . . . As soon as the impress of the Legislature is stamped upon such customs, they become to all intents and purposes unalterable records of a state of things which may continue or may change, while a change in the body of substantive law thus formed is very difficult to effect without the pressure of an influence which a social revolution only could exercise. . . . Instead of codifying customary law, Sir Robert Egerton would prefer to leave the enforcement of it to the courts as at present.[37]

This passage offers two connected views of custom. First, Egerton makes clear that his and the British Government's overall preference was 'to dissolve the tribal bond' in favour of unleashing 'individual energy'. Tribal custom was therefore only to be tolerated as an interim measure. Connected to this was his view that codification of custom would freeze it, preventing its change unless it became quite grossly out of kilter with the present constitution of society.

The views of Egerton and others prevailed and the customs of Punjab were never formally codified, though codification was again seriously contemplated as late as 1915. On the other hand, a de facto form of codification gradually asserted itself through a standardization and homogenization of customs as they were recorded in villages and districts of Punjab.[38] And a companion standardization was asserted through the Chief Court of Punjab, which operated from 1866 until 1947. The Court's findings as to applicable custom became precedents for future cases, and inevitably what was created was a new Anglo–customary law for Punjab that paralleled the Anglo–Hindu and Anglo–Muhammadan law throughout India. Whatever customary law in Punjab might have been before the British, it must have been quite different from the creature of the British administration over a period of some 80 years.

This discussion of customary law in Punjab may seem something of an excursus but the reason for it is that this side of the Anglo–Indian law story has been considerably forgotten. And whatever the flaws in the British approach in Punjab, there was more than a kernel of validity in their discovery of customary law there. The British were clearly correct in their recognition that matters of what were called 'personal law' elsewhere in India were largely regulated by the communities of Punjab themselves. Of course, this was true not just for the land-holding communities that monopolized the attention of the British but presumably for all religious categories – Hindu, Sikh or Muslim – and for all castes or tribes.[39] To say this is not to suggest that the communities or the villages were self-governing 'little republics', in Metcalfe's famous phrase – this romantic British depiction left totally out of the account the habitual, not episodic, involvement of regional and even imperial rulers in the lives of the villages.[40] It also incorrectly conflated village and tribe or caste. And it ignored the profound influence exerted by Hindu and Muslim law. But what the Punjab materials do make clear is the plural ways in which authority was asserted prior to and even after the British arrival.

This is a convenient point at which to turn back to the questions posed after the discussion of the dhobis' case. I observed that there were few caste communities in Behror of 30 years ago still capable of taking up disputes within the community, as the dhobis had done in that case. If we put this observation alongside the discussion of the British treatment of customary law in Punjab, it seems clear that over time there has been a major decline in the capacity of communities to govern themselves (or, to use the other language encountered in the literature, administer 'justice' [Dumont's phrase], 'settle disputes', constitute 'juridical' authority,[41] dispense 'customary law', and so on). We lack evidence to verify Dumont's claim that authority in rural India was shared by three parties: the king (and later the courts introduced by the British), the dominant caste and the caste panchayats. It seems almost certain that Dumont has oversimplified a complex and fluid set of social arrangements across both region and time. But equally, Dumont seems to have been travelling in the general right direction in his claims (albeit claims dressed as fact). At, say, the turn of the nineteenth century, the landholding communities of Punjab and most other places of India seem to have been what Srinivas and Dumont much later called the dominant castes, and such communities clearly exercised disproportionate power in the villages. To a considerable extent they governed themselves – the 'customary law' discovered by the British in Punjab comprised some of the understandings and processes whereby these dominant landholding castes managed their own affairs. The landholders also governed their subordinates to a large extent. Sometimes this latter power might well have amounted to 'juridical' authority, in Cohn's language. These same communities were often bolstered in their authority by connections with regional rulers, or kings; sometimes the two came from the same clan or lineage (or 'tribe', as the British tended to call such social formations). But these clans or dominant castes were not omnipotent, and they must often have left space for the inward-looking actions of caste panchayats, such as the dhobis of Behror.

By now, the patterns of social governance in rural India can no longer be epitomized with even approximate accuracy in the short-hand manner attempted by Dumont. To state somewhat baldly what I have argued in detail elsewhere, the dominants have largely lost the capacity to impose anything like 'juridical authority' on their subordinates in the countryside.[42] This does not mean that the dominants have totally lost their power. Rather, the relationships between the most powerful elements in the countryside and their dependents or subordinates have changed. In other words, the subordinates are no longer prepared to accept the domination they once had to. They may still be weak and dependent economically but they are citizens of a democracy with the right to vote. Political competition has often taken the place of oppressive domination. Among the many factors that have brought about change in the relationships in the countryside, perhaps this advent of democratic politics is the most significant.

Alongside the change in power relations between what Srinivas and Dumont called the dominant castes and their subordinates, there has been a prolonged and deep erosion of coherence within seemingly most of the multiple communities of the Indian countryside. Caste communities in the villages, whether dominant or subordinate, habitually report an inability to protect their norms through the imposition of punishments such as outcasteing. Only those at the very bottom of the hierarchy regularly show continuing coherence. This suggests that the example of the dhobis of Behror cannot now be generalized to any great extent. There has clearly been a significant growth of individualism brought about by factors such as temporary and permanent migration to towns and cities, increased education, the spread of mass media and film, the globalization of opportunity, and so on. But do all these changes amount to a complete destruction of the group basis of life in the Indian countryside? And what can we say about such issues in relation to the cities, which contain a fast growing proportion of the Indian population? This is what we need to turn to now, near the end of this chapter.

From 'Customary Law' to Legal Pluralism

The examples in this chapter have been directed to the development of an account of Indian law, authority or dispute settlement – these terms have largely been run together – that emphasizes the vitality of processes outside 'the state' (itself a problematic term in the Indian historical context). This is not because the importance of the official legal system of India is discounted here; it is the great legal system of Asia, and is becoming more significant all the time. Rather, I am concerned to try to locate what I take to be the particular genius of Indian society for authority, sometimes amounting to 'legal' or 'juridical' authority, to be constituted in civil society rather than by the state. But I have argued that some of the old patterns of coherence and group assertion within civil society have been weakening over time. We are certainly long past the time when it would be plausible to talk of rural India as marked by the rule of 'customary law'. A fortiori, presumably, the cities of India cannot be marked by the rule of custom. And yet it seems to me that there remains a profound current of group organization within many areas of Indian social and industrial life, including in the cities. With this perspective in mind I recently conducted some research, scarcely more than preliminary, into patterns of dispute processing in some diverse communities, mainly in Mumbai, but also in Delhi. It may be useful to say something about these inquiries.

The Palanpuri Diamond Merchants

One community I looked at was the diamond merchants. The diamond industry has been a considerable Indian success story over the last several decades. India now processes the overwhelming majority of the world's rough diamonds, and Indian traders have come to be leading players in the global diamond industry. The first Indians began trading in Amsterdam and Antwerp – the latter is still the most important trading centre in the world – as early as the 1930s, and they have now reportedly taken majority control of this trade away from other communities, chiefly Jews.[43] The leaders of the Indian diamond industry come overwhelmingly from one community of some 4000 to 5000 households of Jains in the village of Palanpur in northern Gujarat.[44] These are the people who have come to dominate the Indian and now the whole world's manufacture (cutting and polishing) of diamonds. Latterly, they have leveraged this position into a majority share of the post-mining trade in diamonds.[45] The Palanpuris' success has been so great that by now they can no longer supply sufficient labour even for the trading and management level of the Indian industry, and this has opened up opportunities to others including collaborators/competitors from Kathiawad in southern Gujarat.

The Palanpuris see themselves as a tight-knit community. They compete with each other during the day but have a common social life. Marital alliances between the richest Palanpuri families of the diamond industry are frequent. Their self-image is of a highly functional and ethical community, well able to regulate themselves through a pattern of mutual trust bolstered by the steadying hand of respected figures within the community. They attribute much of their success to this mutual confidence within the community. Naturally, on occasion disputes arise amongst the Palanpuris. There are many points at which such disputes can occur in the diamond trade: substitution of inferior diamonds can take place in physical exchanges; diamonds may be stolen or simply lost; insolvencies occur; and there are often questions as to price payable. Some of the disputes are common to just about all manufacturing and trading industries, whereas others arise from the particular nature of the diamond industry. Thus the physical circumstance of trading in tiny packets of immensely valuable stones leads to great potential opportunity for fraud and theft and, conversely, the demand for high levels of trust between the participants as an alternative to expensive and perhaps ineffective external security measures.

The Palanpuris pride themselves on usually keeping themselves out of court. They are by now quite professional in their dealings, taking care over the drafting of business documents such as approval memoranda and consignment notes. In the event of disputes arising, they are able to enlist pressures including fear of loss of face in order to bring recalcitrant disputants or malefactors to agreement. Given the smallness of the Palanpuri community, they are all specially dependent on retaining the trust of their fellows. This is said to act as a spur to reasonableness and compromise in disputes. On occasion someone (always a man) respected both for his business credentials and as a community figure is enlisted as a third party to help resolve a dispute. Such involvement does not usually take the form of an official third party. For example, in one case, a Palanpuri broker had lost a small packet of diamonds, worth some Rs 150,000, entrusted to him by a Palanpuri trader. This loss was accepted as a genuine misfortune. Although the small-scale broker was willing to make good most of the loss, he wanted to retain Rs 25,000 of his capital to enable him to carry on his livelihood. A respected Palanpuri diamond manufacturer was called in to assist in the settlement, and after some five hours of talk he was able to get the trader to propose the sum of Rs 125,000 compensation as if it was his own suggestion.

In another case a young Palanpuri trader had made significant losses and in an attempt to cover them, he lost more; he could only meet 25–30 per cent of the shortfall. The same business figure as in the case above was consulted, and he managed to get the creditors to see that the statement of remaining assets was genuine. While the trader agreed to sell his wife's ornaments and his house, the majority of the debt could still not be paid. This outcome was accepted by the creditors, not all of whom were Palanpuris.

In a third case involving the same business figure, one of his relatives came to propose that he mediate a dispute in which the relative was himself involved. The prospective third party agreed to assist, but told his relative that he would show him no favour. The relative went away and did not come back. This example was said to illustrate the standards of fairness and honesty that underpin the success of the Palanpuris' management of their business operations in India and now world-wide. The Palanpuris see their industry's standards as now under attack, since they do not see the Kathiawadis as possessing the same high standards of morality as they themselves have. The Kathiawadis were originally employed as diamond cutters, mere workers, and are said not to have attained high levels of education. This gathering diversity within the industry is seen as a challenge to the Palanpuris' preferred way of running affairs.

Of course, self-management of disputes within a particular business community is not peculiar to the Indian diamond industry; we know from Stewart Macaulay's early work on contract enforcement that informal dispute processing is the hallmark of much commercial organization even in the US.[46] And within the world diamond industry, there are more striking examples of self-management of disputes outside India. Thus, the diamond industry of New York is dominated by Orthodox Jews, and Richman notes that these traders 'have systematically rejected the court and state-created law to enforce contracts and police behaviour'.[47] Richman argues that the Jewish merchants of New York have been able to accomplish this despite the high value and portability of the products and also the preference of the trade for credit sales rather than simultaneous exchange. Both the latter circumstances would ordinarily tend to increase theft, fraud and general non-performance of contracts. The critical factor that has offset these temptations is the fear of loss of reputation within the Orthodox Jewish community. In a word, few of the participants in the diamond industry will risk the ostracism within their religious community that would result from any business malfeasance. There appear to be some points of convergence here with the conduct of the Palanpuri Jains.

Some Other Examples from Mumbai and Delhi

The Palanpuri diamond traders are only one among a number of Indian commercial groupings that can be seen to have made attempts to regulate their affairs with a firm eye towards avoiding the courts. For example, there is an active mercantile association among the traders in the wholesale cloth market in Delhi. This association elects office bearers (called *panchas*) and one of their principal tasks is to try to resolve disputes between the traders themselves and between traders and certain customers. There are particular incentives to keep commercial matters out of court, including an incentive that arises from the universal practice of keeping two sets of account books. While the motive for this (as in almost every country on earth) is tax avoidance, one of its by-products in India is to provide a powerful disincentive to going to court. Thus, typically at least, one of the parties cannot afford to produce to the court the evidence locked in different account books – to do so would invite the tax authorities to take action.

Within the association of cotton merchants of Maharashtra based in Mumbai, there are frequent exercises in conciliation and mediation rather than formal arbitration. Disputes can arise over the quality of cotton and the terms of the contract. Such disputes are particularly likely to arise in contracts for 'forwards' and futures, since there may well be a discrepancy between the quality of cotton sought and the quality delivered some time later. There are thousands of agricultural markets across the country at which cotton is sold, as well as smaller marketing centres. Sometimes it is necessary to go to a farm to verify quality. If a dispute does arise, it may be handled in different ways and with the intervention of different third parties. Sometimes the machinery of government – the District Officer (Collector), for example – is enlisted to help settle a dispute. But sometimes higher-level, more formal, dispute resolution within the merchants' association is necessary to sort the matter out.

If we turn from commercial organizations to residential communities in the large cities, it is possible to see similar patterns in village India. For example, in the Dharavi-Matunga Labour Camp complex of Mumbai (often dubbed the world's largest slum) there are communities that replicate caste communities elsewhere in India. Thus, there is a community of some 300 Valmiki or sweeper families in Dharavi, almost all of them originally from Haryana. Some of them have been in Mumbai for more than 50 years. What had led me to look at this community, and to mention it in the present context, was familiarity over many years with the relatively large Valmiki community of Behror, which is geographically close to the area in Haryana from which the Dharavi Valmikis have migrated. 35 years ago in Behror, the Valmikis had the most active caste panchayat of all the castes of the village. Their special motivation arose from their position as the ritually lowest caste in Behror and the ambition to try to improve their status. In Dharavi, the community has a *samiti* or organization comprised of elected (male only) *panchas* and some respected elders. This *samiti* is said to be active in resolving disputes within the community, as well as making representations regarding their living conditions within their oppressively crowded quarter.

The above examples of group organization and actual dispute settlement in urban India, mainly Mumbai, are no more than suggestive. What they suggest to me is continuing patterns of willingness, for various reasons, to organize in groups that to a highly variable extent are prepared and capable of intervening in conflicts within the group. Sometimes the basis of the group is what Geertz called primordial affiliation (the Palanpuris and the Valmikis fall into this category),[48] while at other times the primary basis seems to be a common industrial or commercial situation (the clothsellers of Delhi, the cotton merchants of Maharashtra and, again, the Palanpuri diamond merchants). The motivations of the groups are not always the same either, though desire to avoid the courts is strong among the commercial groups. It may be that these examples are no more than straws in the wind but I have raised them here because I have the impression that they may be connected with patterns of community organization that characterized village India in the past. True, a number of these examples are scarcely unique to India. But this does not of itself falsify the idea that the Indian situation is specially productive of a particular kind of group organization that involves the construction of patterns of authority or, sometimes, pathways to cooperation and compromise. It seems to me to be social structure and material self-interest rather than any psychology of abnegation that might account for such a propensity, if it exists.

Menski, Hindu Law and Legal Pluralism (or 'Customary Law'?)

In the earlier consideration of Hindu law, I foreshadowed returning to Menski's claim that something of a 'postmodern' reformation of Hindu law is at work in India today. Menski's argument is that there has been an effective judicial abandonment of the modernist vision most plainly stated in Article 44 of the Constitution, which looked towards the enactment of a uniform civil code for Indians of all communities and religious traditions. For Menski, enactment of such a code would have spelled the end of Hindu law. The code has not been enacted and conversely, from the late 1970s:

> Hindu law was increasingly reconstructed by an activist judiciary to revert to a more outrightly pluralist shape, emphasizing situation-specific justice over certainty of legal rules, and thereby giving new respect to Hindu law's customary plurality and internal diversity.[49]

From these beginnings a new hybrid postmodern law has gradually emerged, particularly from about 1988:

> Postmodern Hindu law remains at present characterized by the uneasy coexistence of official formal sources of state law and continued adherence to informal value systems which are extremely diverse, are anchored in religion, culture, and social reality, and may be instantly called upon in situations where conflicts

arise. In fact, before any matter goes to court, it may be resolved in the informal sphere. Formal recourse to law is neither the only, nor necessarily the most appropriate method of solving Hindu law disputes.[50]

In Menski's account, the gap between the world of formal state law and the pluralistic social world has increasingly been bridged by the courts. The judges have declined to impose the legislative Hindu law in a mechanistic, modernist, uniform way. They have attended to the specificity of social situation and, in the process, have crafted a far from consistent but more appropriate Hindu law. Menski argues that this postmodern process is proving more favourable to women than did the heedless modernism of the earlier legislative approach of the early post-independence period. In the development of this argument Menski sets his face firmly against the feminist proponents of a uniform civil code; their approach is seen as imported western modernism without useful relevance to Hindu India.

I am not in a position to evaluate the evidence Menski provides for his argument, since I have not read a number of the cases he relies upon. But if this evidence stands up to analysis, it might be said that the contemporary Indian courts are now implementing an evolved version of what the Chief Court of Punjab tried to do in relation to customary law from 1866 until 1947. If Menski's reading of the case law is correct, then the new approach may well represent an appropriate response to the great variability of Indian practices in matters of 'personal law'. One can only speculate on what might have happened if one of the parties in the dhobis' dispute had taken their case to a court operating in the way Menski says Indian courts now do. Would the court have been prepared to come to the same decision as the dhobis' panchayat did, including acceptance of the dhobis' polygamy (contrary to the *Hindu Marriage Act* [1955])? I am attracted to the idea of courts looking patiently and sympathetically at social practices that may be different from modern westernized norms in India, provided that they are not oppressive to women. To that extent, Menski's account of the present judicial approach is consistent with the emphasis in this chapter on the great plurality of legal sources in India both historically and today. Of course, such a judicial approach gives rise to the not so small problem of reconciliation with 'the rule of law'. Which legislative principles is an activist judiciary permitted to enforce, and which to ignore? The field of 'personal law' in India might be specially productive of such dilemmas.

Conclusion

The drift of my argument in this chapter should now be evident. In broad terms, it seems to me that India is unusual for the variety and strength of efforts to manage disputes in civil society without recourse to the institutions of the state. This vitality of processes within civil society is not primarily a function of the weakness of the Indian state either historically or today. Rather, patterns of Indian social organization, ideology, culture, and the historical conception of law have provided a foundation for communities taking more responsibility for their own ordering than in most other societies.

At the centre of this argument is the historical construction of Hindu law. We have seen that there is something of a consensus among contemporary students of Hindu law to the effect that there was no historical demand that the Dharmasastras be enforced by rulers responsible for maintaining order and distributing justice. In short, Hindu India did not develop a body of substantive law fit even presumptively to be enforced in problem cases. And yet the Dharmasastras seem to have retained their authority in the face of countervailing custom as the standard of governance. Conceivably, this pragmatic separation of Dharmic rules and practical governance encouraged the widespread taking of responsibility within diverse social formations in India.

As usual, it is critical to distinguish the problem of maintaining order from the task of administering law or justice. It is true that the Hindu scriptures charge the one body, the king, with both these functions. And there is evidence to suggest that Indian rulers did sometimes dispense justice even to distant villagers as well as to people closer at hand. But any judicial function of the king seems to have been far less prominent than military and other activities associated with the maintenance of order. Given the non-enforceability of the Dharmasastras, this might suggest that India was a society only lightly touched by law. It could more specifically be argued that for the most part order was successfully maintained in India without recourse to law. These last two propositions might be maintained even if it were conceded that Indian civil society is marked by a high degree of self-management by diverse communities formed on the basis of tribe, caste, religion and industrial situation. But while these propositions are plausible enough, they are not subscribed to here. India seems to me to be a society highly imbued with law, in the dual sense of embodying a deep respect for the principles and beliefs underlying the social order and also in a respect for properly constituted authority. That these deep principles and beliefs may be as much 'religious' as 'legal', does not seem to me to falsify this statement.

I am aware that I am being vague as to the conception of law I am employing here. Such vagueness seems to be an almost inescapable result of rejecting a view of law as only constituted by the state. But this rejection does not mean I have also abandoned the idea of distinguishing, at least in principle, processes that embody 'law' or 'legal authority' from those that do not. I have suggested above that the dhobis' dispute had the markings of a law case, despite the non-involvement of the state in that case. On the other hand, the interventions of the third party in the diamond industry seem to have been too tentative and lacking in authority to suggest they had some kind of legal quality. In many instances it may be too difficult or too artificial to bother trying to distinguish the legal from the non-legal, but it seems to me that the principle of the distinction remains of some importance. From a related perspective I need to distinguish my own position from that of someone like Menski, whom I have criticized early in this essay for suggesting that self-rule according to revealed truths in the Hindu tradition can itself constitute 'law'. I would want to say that there has to be some kind of external authority for a 'legal' situation to be formed. But in the end I have to concede that we will not be able to agree on a tightly formulated conception of 'law' so late in the day. We can all agree that the Supreme Court of India is engaged in matters of law, but there will be no unanimity when we consider processes within Indian civil society. Invoking a conception of 'customary law' will not help us resolve this problem.

To sum up, the Indian legal system seems highly distinctive or 'Indian' from a number of perspectives.[51] The most fundamental difference argued here is that India has a rich civil society that has been specially productive of activities that have to do with 'legal' or perhaps 'juridical' authority. In India, both historically and today, the state has asserted less complete a legal dominance over society than in other political formations with highly developed legal systems. I want to suggest that the difference is not primarily an artefact of a weak state in India but of the converse, that is a particularly strong society, in the sense of a society unusually productive of legal authority asserted in the name of community (or, rather, plural communities). The British 'discovery' of customary law in Punjab is the leading example of the colonial state's encounter with this phenomenon. Of course, the underlying British ambition in Punjab was to dissolve the groups that gave rise to 'law' or 'custom' and to substitute a modern, western individualism in their stead. To a great extent many of the nationalist elite both before and after independence have sympathized with this ambition, though this sympathy may now be waning.

My reading of some of the recent English literature on Hindu law suggests that long before the European entry into India, the particular nature of Hindu law may have facilitated the profusion and assertiveness of legal authority within what can loosely be called 'civil society'. I have drawn attention to Lingat's elegant summary of this argument, viz. that the classical legal system of India did not embody a conception of *legality* to which actions had to conform but that the authority of the sacred truths always retained their *authority*. This is said to have freed the king, the designated legal authority, from enforcing any particular dogma derived from the books. Perhaps, by extension, this conception of law also encouraged the kind of legal pluralism discussed in this chapter. But admittedly, these are little more than speculations.

Successive waves of external influence have obviously shaped the Indian legal order quite profoundly – the Aryans, the Mughals and then the British conquerors have left their deep impress upon India. The impress of the British is the latest and in our time by far the most salient of these influences. But the argument of this essay is that there is an Indian legal pluralism that goes considerably beyond the pluralism represented by successive invasions and colonialisms. On the other hand, it might be objected that what I am pointing to could be said to mark a number of other nations in Asia, Africa and perhaps Latin America, too. A number of nations in these regions have had layer upon layer of external legal systems imposed upon indigenous foundations. In so far as the latter

foundations have survived, the composite legal order might be said to resemble
the pluralistic Indian order I have tried to sketch here. But my argument can be
limited to this proposition – I know of no other nation-state that possesses an
official legal system as sophisticated as that of India and which is also composed
of a civil society so marked by patterns of authority and dispute settlement constituted without reference to the state. In terms of the sophistication of its legal
order, India demands comparison with perhaps only one other Asian nation,
Japan, and even more with the developed nations of the west. My current understanding is that those nations do not possess the kind and degree of pluralistic
vigour within civil society that I have argued to exist in India. Perhaps I should
add the value judgment that this seems to me to be one of India's greatest strengths
as a society.

I thank Marika Vicziany, as usual, and Upendra Baxi for commenting on the draft of this
chapter. I am particularly indebted to Professor Baxi, who dissected the piece in his familiar
manner (simultaneously devastating and supportive). I know that this published version has not
met his criticisms but I am still thinking about them!

Notes

[1] Henry Maine's most celebrated work is *Ancient Law*, first published in 1861.

[2] The best statement of this argument is Galanter (1981).

[3] The most developed argument to this effect is Mendelsohn (1981).

[4] See the *Indian Christian Marriage Act* (1872); *Special Marriage Act* (1872); *Parsi
Marriage and Divorce Act* (1865).

[5] My informant was the head of the sole dhobi family in the village (the sub-district
headquarters) of Behror and, indeed, the head of the whole community council cov-
ering a large number of villages. As the principal *panch* or elder he took the leading
role in addressing this matter, the precise date of which is unclear.

[6] Polygamy is unlawful in India but this does not mean that it is not practised among
some communities, some of them Hindu.

[7] Outcasteing involves a total exclusion of the affected person and their closest relatives from all contact with any member of the community – the outcaste is completely
shunned, such that he cannot speak or eat with his community, and his children
cannot marry within the community and therefore effectively at all.

[8] Curiously, this Act was repealed after independence by the *Hindu Widows' Remarriage (Repeal) Act* (1983) (Menski 2003: 176–77).

[9] Menski (2003: 374–426).

[10] 'Panch' is the Sanskrit word for 'five', and panchayat is a council of five or less,
literally, simply a council. The place of *caste* justice more generally is discussed below.

[11] The dhobis are a 'scheduled caste', an official designation given to the old untouchable castes. This quite small community is widely dispersed throughout northern
India, mostly in rural areas (Singh 1993: 442–53). Seemingly there are few large
concentrations of dhobis; typically, and presumably because of their occupation as
washerfolk, individual families are located in villages where their customary work is
valued. In Behror, unlike the other untouchable communities, the sole dhobi family
lived in the middle rather than the outskirts of the settlement. This suggests that their
status was more ambiguous and higher than that of the other untouchable castes. For
a discussion of the history and contemporary status of untouchables, see Mendelsohn
and Vicziany (1998).

[12] Galanter's article (1981) was the first of three widely cited articles of the 1980s that
played a major part in establishing an almost counter-orthodoxy to the hitherto
prevailing conception of law in the west as solely a creature of the state. The other

articles were by Griffiths (1986) and Merry (1988). It was no accident that these authors had all worked on non-western societies, in many of which the state was not so developed as in the west. The phrase 'legal pluralism' came to be a common identifier of this approach to the study of law, and it became an underpinning of much of the 'law and society' approach to studies conducted in universities in the United States and Europe. Recently, Roberts (2005) has been highly critical of the 'law is everywhere' approach to law studies, insisting that law must have something to do with 'government'. Against this, Griffiths (2004) has found the approach applicable to new phenomena in a globalizing world. Clearly the debate over 'legal pluralism' and older conceptions, often somewhat dismissively lumped into the category 'legal positivism', has a long way to run.

[13] I am aware that this is a rather sweeping statement. I should make clear that my proposition is based on a judgement, perhaps contestable, that the official legal system of India is more highly developed than that of other nations in Asia and Africa, a number of which may well have judicial processes outside the state, that are broadly analogous to that of the dhobis of Behror. So what I am drawing attention to is the conjunction of a highly developed and sophisticated state legal system and these other processes. I return to this issue at the end of this chapter.

[14] Upendra Baxi's *The Crisis of the Indian Legal System* (1982) remains the most serious attempt to comprehend the variety of legal phenomena within India as well as discuss their limitations. There is an urgent need to return to the themes that Professor Baxi laid out in that work.

[15] This view has been most thoroughly developed by Professor Duncan M. Derrett. See Derrett (1968).

[16] Primarily for reasons of space, only Hindu and not Muslim law will be considered in what follows.

[17] Menski (2003).

[18] Lingat (1973: 258).

[19] Ibid.

[20] Davis (2006: 290).

[21] Ibid.

[22] Ibid.: 295.

[23] Rocher; cited in Davis (2006: 302).

[24] Menski cites with approval an observation of Dhavan (1992) to the effect that the Dharmasastra was really a part of civil society and not the state.

[25] Dumont (1970: 181).

[26] Ibid.: 179.

[27] Srinivas (1955: 18).

[28] Dumont (1970: 162).

[29] Ibid.

[30] Mendelsohn (1993).

[31] The classic account of the contending British administrative schools of the nineteenth century is Stokes (1959).

[32] Dumont's (1966) article remains a marvellously acute discussion of the career of this concept in the hands of the British and, later, nationalist Indians.

[33] Report on the Codification of Customary Law Conference, Lahore, 1915: 11; quoted in Chakrabarty-Kaul (1996: 212). I am grateful to the Workshop in Political Theory and Policy Analysis, Indiana University, for providing me with a copy of Tupper (1881), and to Dr Minoti Chakrabarty-Kaul for putting me in touch with the Workshop about this rarely available source.

[34] Tupper (1881: 2, 3).

[35] The 'settlement' was the single largest administrative operation carried out by the British provincial administration. Its fundamental objective was to fix the amount of 'land revenue' or land tax payable from villages, and to assign liability for its payment. This entailed compilation of a minute record of 'ownership', since it was from the 'owners' that the revenue was collected. These basic objectives tended to ramify

into the recording of a range of other matters (such as rights to share in common lands) relevant to the taxation and management of villages.

[36] Tupper (1881: 38).

[37] Ibid.: 221–22.

[38] Chakrabarty-Kaul (1996: 187–219).

[39] I am not suggesting that Punjab was fundamentally different in these matters from the rest of India; almost certainly there were historical, ideological and institutional developments more than the distinctiveness of Punjab that accounted for the recognition of 'customary law' in Punjab and not elsewhere.

[40] Metcalfe (1830).

[41] Cohn (1987: 587).

[42] Mendelsohn (1993).

[43] Rajghatta (2004).

[44] Interview with a leading diamond manufacturer in Bombay on 25 November 2004. Given their now geographical spread, this concept of the Palanpuri 'household' may be problematical.

[45] The world's largest centre for the cutting and polishing of diamonds is Surat. Presumably most of the workers, as opposed to the proprietors and traders, in this industry are not Palanpuris.

[46] Macaulay (1963).

[47] Richman (2006: 1).

[48] Geertz (1960).

[49] Menski (2003: 244).

[50] Ibid.: 266.

[51] I have noted above that the present work does not consider the way the official legal system of India actually works – that is, the organization of the legal profession, the characteristics of the courts and litigation, and so on. It is clear from a study of these factors alone that the Indian legal system is highly distinctive. This essay has sought to look at rather deeper factors to try to answer the question posed in the title of this chapter.

References

Baxi, Upendra (1982), *The Crisis of the Indian Legal System* (Delhi: Vikas).

Chakrabarty-Kaul, Minoti (1996), *Common Lands and Customary Law: Institutional Change in North India over the Past Two Centuries* (Delhi: Oxford University Press).

Cohn, Bernard (1987), 'Anthropological Notes on Disputes and Law in India', *American Anthropologist, 67*(6)(2), 1965; reprinted in *An Anthropologist among the Historians and Other Essays* (Delhi: Oxford University Press).

Davis Jr, Donald R. (2006), 'A Realist View of Hindu Law', *Ratio Juris,* 19(3), September: 287–313.

Derrett, J.D.M. (1968), *Religion, Law and the State in India* (London: Faber & Faber).

Dhavan, Rajeev (1992), 'Dharmasastra and Modern Indian Society: A Preliminary Exploration', *Journal of the Indian Law Institute,* 34(4): 515–40.

Dumont, Louis (1966), 'The "Village Community" from Munro to Maine', *Contributions to Indian Sociology,* IX, December: 67–89.

—— (1970), *Homo Hierarchicus: The Caste System and its Implications* (Delhi: Vikas).

Galanter, Marc (1981), 'Justice in Many Rooms: Courts, Private Ordering and Indigenous Law', *Journal of Legal Pluralism,* 19: 1–47.

Geertz, Clifford (1960), *The Religion of Java* (Glencoe: The Free Press).

Griffiths, Anne (2004), 'Customary Law in a Transnational World: Legal Pluralism Revisited', Conference on Customary Law in Polynesia, 12 October.

Griffiths, J. (1986), 'What is Legal Pluralism?', 24 *Journal of Legal Pluralism* 1.

Lingat, Robert (1973), *The Classical Law of India* (Berkeley: University of California Press).

Macaulay, Stewart (1963), 'Non-Contractual Relations in Business: A Preliminary Study', *American Sociological Review* 28(1): 55–67.

Maine, Henry Sumner (1888), *Ancient Law: Its Connection with the Early History of Society and its Relation to Modern Ideas* (London: Murray).

Mendelsohn, Oliver (1981), 'The Pathology of the Indian Legal System', *Modern Asian Studies*, 15(4): 822–63.

——— (1993), 'The Transformation of Authority in Rural India', *Modern Asian Studies*, 27(4): 805–42.

Mendelsohn, Oliver and Marika Vicziany (1998), *The Untouchables: Subordination, Poverty and the State in Modern India* (Cambridge: Cambridge University Press).

Menski, Werner (2003), *Hindu Law: Beyond Tradition and Modernity* (Delhi: Oxford University Press).

Merry, S.E. (1988), 'Legal Pluralism', 22 *Law and Society Review* 869.

Metclafe, Sir Charles (1830), *Report from the Select Committee in the House of Commons, Evidence*, III, Revenue, Appendices (App. 84, 328ff.).

Rajghatta, Chidanand (2004), 'Antwerp Diary', 12 parts, *The Times of India*, 17 November–4 December, http://timesofindia.indiatimes.com/articlesshow/939105

Richman, Barak D. (2006) 'How Community Institutions Create Economic Advantage: Jewish Diamond Merchants in New York', *Law and Social Inquiry*, 31(2), Spring.

Roberts, Simon (2005), 'After Government?: On Representing Law Without the State', *Modern Law Review*, 68(1): 1–24.

Singh, K.S. (1993), *The Scheduled Castes* (Delhi: Oxford University Press).

Srinivas, M.N. (1955), 'The Social System of a Mysore Village', in McKim Marriott, ed., *Village India* (Chicago: University of Chicago Press): 1–35.

Stokes, Eric (1959), *The English Utilitarians and India* (Oxford: Oxford University Press).

Tupper, C.L., ed. (1881), *Punjab Customary Law* (Volumes 1, 2 and 3) (Calcutta: Government of India).

State Control and Sexual Morality

The Case of the Bar Dancers of Mumbai

Flavia Agnes

Historical Ruling

I begin this essay on a positive note – the historical Bombay High Court ruling which upheld the dancers right to dance in bars and earn a living.[1] It was a morale booster for the pro-dancer lobby which had been fighting an uphill battle against extreme odds, countering the norms of middle-class, Maharashtrian, sexual morality. For the last several months, it seemed that the ground was steadily slipping from under our feet and we were left with only a slender hope of the judiciary deciding in our favour. Since the ban was couched in a language of cleansing the city of sex and sleaze, our hopes were indeed slender, considering that our courts are known for their Victorian 'stiff upper lip' moral sensibilities. But when we had all but given up hope, the High Court ruling came as a bolt out of the blue or rather a ray of hope for the lowly bar dancer who lives at the margins and our stand was vindicated.

The judgement striking down the dance bar ban as unconstitutional was pronounced on 12 April 2006 to a packed court room by a Division Bench comprising of Justices F.I. Rebello and Mrs Roshan Dalvi and made national headlines. The concerned statute, an amendment to the Bombay Police Act, 1951, was passed by both Houses of the Maharashtra State legislature in July 2005 and the ban had come into effect on 15 August 2005 to coincide with the Independence Day celebrations. The decision to ban dance performances was part of a drive to cleanse the state of immorality. But the statute exempted hotels with three stars or above as well as gymkhanas and clubs so that they could hold such performances to 'promote culture' and 'boost tourism'. As the state celebrated Independence Day, an estimated 75,000 girls, mainly from the lower economic strata, lost their means of livelihood.

Soon thereafter, petitions were filed in the Bombay High Court challenging the constitutionality of the Act by three different segments – the bar owners' associations, the Bar Girls' Union and social organizations. After months of legal battle, finally, the High Court struck down the ban as unconstitutional on the following two grounds:

- The exemption (given to certain categories of hotels as well as clubs etc.) has no reasonable nexus to the aims and objects which the statute is supposed to achieve and hence it is arbitrary and violative of Article 14 of the Constitution of India (the clause of equality and non-discrimination).

- It violates the fundamental freedom of the bar owners and the bar dancers to practise an occupation or profession and is violative of Article 19 (1)(g) of the Constitution.

Regarding the exemption given to starred hotels, gymkhanas, clubs etc. the Court held as follows: '. . . *the financial capacity of an individual to pay or his social status is repugnant to what the founding fathers believed when they enacted Article 14 and enshrined the immortal words, that the State shall not discriminate.*'

But if this was the only ground of violation of fundamental rights, then the provision granting exemption to a certain category of establishments, which is contained in a separate section, i.e., Section 33B[2] of the amended statute, could easily have been struck down; the ban could have been retained and made uniformly applicable to all establishments to remedy the Act of its discriminatory aspect. But the fact that the judgement goes much beyond this and deals elaborately with yet another fundamental right seemed to have missed the media attention.

The Court struck down the dance bar ban on the ground that it violates a fundamental freedom guaranteed under Article 19(1)(g) of the Constitution. This is a significant development and nearly half the pages of the extensive 257 page judgment deals with this concern. '*Are our fundamental rights so fickle that a citizen has to dance to the State's tune?*' was the caustic comment.[3] Further the court held:

> The State does not find it offensive to the morals or dignity of women and/or their presence in the place of public entertainment being derogatory, as long as they do not dance. The State's case for prohibiting dance in dance bars is that it is dancing which arouses the physical lust amongst the customers present. There is no arousing of lust when women serve the customers liquor or beer in the eating house, but that happens only when the women start dancing. . . . The right to dance has been recognized by the Apex Court as part of the fundamental right of speech and expression. If that be so, it will be open to a citizen to commercially benefit from the exercise of the fundamental right. This could be by a bar owner having a dance performance or by bar dancers themselves using their creative talent to carry on an occupation or profession. In other words, using their skills to make a living . . . .[4]

While contextualizing the High Court ruling, this essay attempts to locate the bar dancer within a larger framework of state policies and the entertainment industry of the colonial and post-colonial period and examine the hypocritical and contradictory moral postures of the state administration and the politics of police raids in recent times. Of particular interest are the concerns of morality and obscenity which surround the bar dancers, the construction of their sexuality by social organizations supporting and opposing the ban and their own agency in negotiating their sexuality in an industry confined within the traditional binaries of a male patron and female seductress. It also traces my own journey into the world of sexual erotica and dwells upon the personal challenges it posed to my notions of sexual morality.

Entertainment Industry and Liquor Policy

The female dancer/entertainer has been an integral part of the city's thriving nightlife, the Bombay that never sleeps. The city is hailed as the crowning glory of the nation's entertainment industry. Her history is also linked to the migrant workers who were brought in to build this city.

From the time when the East India Company developed Bombay as a port and built a fort in the seventeenth century, Bombay has been a city of migrants. Migrant workers have flocked to the city for over three hundred years in search of livelihood, and with the workers have come entertainers.

The traders, the sailors, the dockworkers, the construction labour and the mill hands – all needed to be 'entertained'. So the government marked areas for entertainment called 'play houses' which are referred to in the local parlance even today as 'peela house' areas. Folk theatre, dance and music performances and, later, silent movie theatres all grew around the 'play houses' and so did the sex trade. Hence Kamathipura – a name which denoted the dwelling place of a community of construction labourers, the *Kamtis* of Andhra Pradesh, later came to signal the sex trade or 'red light' district of the old Bombay city. Within the red light district, there were also places for the performance of traditional and classical dance and music, and the *mujra* houses. (Sometime in the seventies, when the then Prime Minister, Indira Gandhi, visited the area and saw the dilapidated status of the dwellings of the performers, she sanctioned a grant to construct modern buildings under the banner of Lalit Kala Akademi. This did not bring much change in the social status of the performers or their dwelling places which continue to be dilapidated except for a change of nomenclature. The area is now ironically referred to as 'Congress House'.)

The prevalence of dance bars is linked not only to the restaurant industry and the entertainment business, but also to the state policy on the sale of liquor. After independence, during the fifties, when Morarji Desai was the Chief Minister, the state of Bombay was under prohibition and restaurants could not serve liquor. But after Maharashtra severed its links with the Gujarat side of the erstwhile Bombay Presidency, the newly formed state reviewed its liquor policy and the prohibition era was transformed into the 'permit' era. A place where beer was served was called a 'permit room'. Only a person who had obtained a 'permit' could sit in a permit room and drink beer.

But, gradually, the term 'permit room' lost its meaning and the government went all out to promote liquor sale in hotels and restaurants. It is during this period that the beer bars introduced innovative devices to beat their competitors – live orchestra, mimicry and 'ladies' service bars' where women from the red light district were employed as waitresses. In the early 1906s, the state started issuing entertainment licences,[5] and some bars introduced live dance performances to boost up their liquor sales. Hindi films also started introducing sexy 'item numbers' and the dancers in the bars imitated these popular dances. The government also issued licenses for the performance of 'cabaret shows'. A place that was notorious for its lewd and obscene cabaret performances is 'Blue Nile' which was constantly raided and was entangled in a lengthy litigation. It is this litigation that forced the High Court to examine the notion of obscenity under Section 294 of the Indian Penal Code (IPC), an issue I will deal with more elaborately later in this essay.

Soon the sale of liquor and consequently the profit margins of the owners recorded an upward trend. This encouraged the owners of other Irani 'permit room' restaurants, South Indian eateries and Punjabi *dhabas* to convert their places into dance bars. Coincidentally, during the same period, the *mujra* culture in Bombay was on the decline due to loss of patronage. The dance bars opened up a new and modern avenue of earning a livelihood to these traditional *mujra* dancers.

Soon the 'dance bar' phenomenon spread from south to central Bombay, to the western and central suburbs, to the satellite cities of New Bombay and Panvel, and from there, along the arterial roads, to other smaller cities and towns of Maharashtra. From a mere 24 in 1985–86, the number increased tenfold within a decade to around 210. The next decade 1995–2005 witnessed yet another phenomenal increase and according to one estimate, just before the ban there were around 2,500 dance bars in Maharashtra.

As the demand grew, women from traditional dancing/performance communities of different parts of India, who were facing a decline in patronage of their age-old profession, flocked to Bombay (and later to the smaller cities) to work in dance bars. These women from traditional communities have been victims of the conflicting forces of modernization. Women are the primary breadwinners in these communities. But after the zamindari system introduced by the British was abolished, they lost their zamindar patrons and were reduced to penury. Even the few developmental schemes and welfare policies of the government bypassed many of these communities. From their villages, many moved to cities, towns and along national highways in search of a livelihood. The dance bars provided women from these communities an opportunity to adapt their strategies to suit the demands of the new economy.

Apart from these traditional dancing communities, women from other poor communities also began to seek work in these bars as dancers. These women are mainly daughters of mill workers. With the sole earner having lost his job after the closure of the textile mills, young girls entered the job market to support their families. Similarly, women who had worked as domestic maids, or in other exploitative conditions as piece-rate workers, or as door-to-door sales girls, as well as women workers who had been retrenched from factories and the industrial units, found work in dance bars. For children of sex workers, dancing in bars provided an opportunity to escape from the exploitative conditions of brothel prostitution in which their mothers had been trapped.

Tax Revenue and Police Raids

Paucity of jobs in other sectors and the boost given by the Maharashtra government to the active promotion of liquor sales led to the proliferation of dance bars. Each ruling power provided additional boost to this industry. The maximum gain to the state government was the 20 per cent sales tax on liquor. As the liquor sales increased, so did the coffers of the bar owners and the revenue for the state. But while the business of dance bars flourished in the state, until 2001, the state administration did not frame any rules to regulate the performances.[6]

The official charge for police protection was a mere Rs 25 per night and the stipulated period for closing the bars was 12.30 am. But in this *hafta raj* (corrupt state administration), most bars remained open till the wee hours of morning. Only when the *haftas* (bribes) did not reach the officials in time would the bars be raided. The grounds for raiding the bars were:

> (a) the owner had violated the license terms by keeping the place open beyond 12.30 am; (b) the dance bar caused 'annoyance' through obscene and vulgar display under Section 294 of the IPC; and (c) caused a public nuisance under Section 110 of the Bombay Police Act.

After a raid, licenses were sometimes either suspended or revoked. But the bar owners say that the government always came to their rescue. They could approach the Home Department for cancellation of the suspension orders issued by the police or for getting the revoked licenses re-issued, all this for a fee!

But something went wrong in late 1998. A large number of bars were raided. The state government also declared a hike of 300 percent in the annual excise fee, raising it from Rs 80,000 to Rs 240,000. It was at this point that the bar owners decided to organize themselves. Around 400 bar owners responded to a call given by one Mr Manjeet Singh Sethi; later they formed an association called 'Fight for the Rights of Bar Owners Association' which organized an impressive rally on 19 February 1999.

In order to work out a compromise, the Association approached the then Commissioner of Police (CP), assured him of their cooperation and sought his intervention to end the *hafta raj*. They claim that they had evolved an internal monitoring mechanism to ensure that all bars would abide by the stipulated time for closing down. But the local police stations were most unhappy at their potential loss of bribes. They tried to break the unity among the members of the Association. The police benefit when the bar owners violate the rules and consequently pay regular *haftas*. Over a period the regular *haftas* paid by each bar owner to the police increased, and just before the recent ban, each bar owner was allegedly paying Rs 75,000 per month to the Deputy Police Commissioner (DCP) of their zone. The money then trickles down the police ladder from the DCP to the lowest ranking constable in pre-determined proportions.

The right-wing BJP–Sena alliance lost the 1999 Assembly elections and there was a change of regime. The Association started fresh negotiations with the ruling National Congress Party (NCP). They greased the palms of high ranking politicians to extend the timings from 12.30 am to 3.30 am so that there would be no need to pay regular *haftas* for this particular violation. After much negotiation, on 3 January 2001, the first ever regulation regarding dance bars came through a government notification. The bars were granted permission to keep their places open till 1.30 am. But somewhere the negotiations backfired, or perhaps the right palms were not sufficiently greased. The government decided to increase the police protection charges from Rs 25 to Rs 1500 per day per dance floor. The angry bar owners held rallies and approached the courts. Due to court intervention, the hiked fees were brought down to Rs 500 per night.

Bar owners claim that the police raids increased after a National Congress Party (NCP) worker was beaten up by a security guard, outside a bar, late at night in February 2004. Following this, 52 bars were raided in February, and 62 in March 2004. The bar owners alleged that the raids were politically motivated and were connected to the forthcoming state Assembly elections. The NCP denied these charges and accused the bar owners of indulging in trafficking of minors. The bar owners approached the High Courts and several FIRs filed by the police were quashed. Again, in July, 30 bars were raided. This time, the bar owners filed a Writ Petition in the Bombay High Court and sought protection against constant police harassment. They also organized a huge rally at Azad Maidan on 20 August 2004. An important feature of this rally was the emergence of the Bar Girls' Union on this public platform.

Women Activists and Differing Perceptions

The mushrooming of an entire industry called the 'dance bars' had escaped the notice of the women's movement in the city despite the fact that several groups and NGOs had been working on issues such as domestic violence, dowry harassment, rape and sexual harassment. Everyone in Bombay was aware that there are some exclusive 'ladies bars'. But, usually, women, especially those unaccompanied by men, are stopped at the entrance. Occasionally, when a bar dancer was raped and/or murdered, women's groups had participated in protest rallies organized by local groups, more as an issue of violence against women than as a specific engagement with the day-to-day problems of bar dancers.

The 20 August 2004 rally in which thousands of bar dancers participated received wide media publicity. The newspapers reported that there were about 75,000 bar girls. Soon thereafter, Ms Varsha Kale, the President of the Bar Girls' Union, approached us (the legal centre of Majlis) to represent them through an 'Intervener Application' in the Writ Petition filed by the bar owners. Varsha is not a bar dancer; she was part of a women's group in Dombvili (in the Central suburbs of Bombay), which had left leanings.

During the discussion with the bar dancers, it emerged that while for the bar owners it was a question of business losses, for the bar girls it was an issue of human dignity and the right to livelihood. When the bars are raided, it is the girls who are arrested, the owners are let off. During the raids, the police molest them, tear their clothes and abuse them in filthy language. At times, the girls are retained in the police station for the whole night and subjected to further indignities. But in the litigation, their concerns are not reflected. It is essential that they be heard and they become part of the negotiations with the state regarding the code of conduct to be followed during the raids.

As far as the abuse of power by the police was concerned, we were clear. But what about the vulgar and obscene display of the female body for the pleasure of drunken male customers, promoted by the bar owners with the sole intention of jacking up their profits? It is here that I lacked clarity. I had been part of the women's movement that has protested against fashion parades and beauty contests and the semi-nude depiction of women in Hindi films. But the younger lawyers within Majlis had a different perspective. They belonged to a later generation which had a different perspective an sexual agency and sex worker rights.

Finally after much discussion, we decided to take on the challenge and represent the Bar Girls' Union in the litigation. We invited some of the girls who had been molested to meet with us. Around 35 to 40 girls turned up. We talked to them at length. We also decided to visit some bars. This was my first visit to a dance bar. Though I was uncomfortable in an environment of palpable erotica, I realized that there is a substantial difference between a bar and a brothel. An NGO, Prerana, which works on anti-trafficking issues, had filed an intervenor application, alleging the contrary – that bars are in fact brothels and that they are dens of prostitution where minors are trafficked. While the police had raided the bars on the ground of obscenity, the Prerana intervention added a new twist to the litigation because they submitted that regular police raids are essential for controlling trafficking and for rescuing minors. The fact that the police had not abided by the strict guidelines in anti-trafficking laws and had molested the women did not seem to matter to them.

Opposing a fellow organization with which I had a long association was not easy. Prerana had been working with sex workers and had started an innovative project of night crèches for children of sex workers in Kamathipura way back in 1986–87. I had conducted several legal workshops with sex workers to explain to them their basic legal rights. During these workshops, the main concerns for the sex workers was police harassment and arbitrary arrests. I viewed my intervention on behalf of bar girls as an extension of the work I had done with Prerana. But members of Prerana felt otherwise. At times, after the court proceedings, we ended up being extremely confrontational and emotionally charged, with Prerana representatives accusing us of legitimizing trafficking by bar owners and us retaliating by accusing them of acting at the behest of the police.

Under the Garb of Morality

From September 2004 to March 2005, the case went through the usual delays. In March, when the case came up for arguments, the lawyer for the Bar

Owners produced an affidavit by the complainant, upon whose complaint the police had conducted the raids. The same person had filed the complaint against nine bars in one night. The police themselves admitted that he was a 'professional' *pancha* (police witness). The second person who had filed the complaint was a petty criminal. In the affidavit produced by the bar owners, the professional *pancha* stated that he was not present at any of the bars against whom he had filed the complaints and the complaints were filed at the behest of the police.

This rocked the boat for the police and invited the wrath of the judges against them. They were asked to file an affidavit explaining this new development. This turned out to be the last day of the court hearing. Before the next date, the Deputy Chief Minister (DCM) who also happens to be the Home Minister, Shri R.R. Patil had already announced the ban. So in view of this, according to the police prosecutor, the case had become infructuous.

Rather ironically, just around the time when the DCM's announcement regarding the dance bar ban was making headlines, the Nagpur Bench of the Bombay High Court gave a ruling on the issue of obscenity in dance bars. While according to the Home Minister the dances in bars are obscene and have a morally corrupting influence on society, the High Court held that dances in bars do not come within the ambit of Section 294 of the IPC.

The police had conducted raids on a dance bar in Nagpur and initiated criminal proceedings against the owners as well as the dancers on grounds of obscenity and immorality. The bar owners had approached the High Court for quashing the proceedings on the ground that the raids were conducted with a malafide intention by two IPS officers who had a grudge against them. In his affidavit filed before the High Court, the Joint Commissioner of Police, Nagpur stated as follows: 'It is found that certain girls were dancing on the floor and were making indecent gestures. The girls were mingling with the customers, touching their bodies, and the customers were paying money to them.'

On 4 April 2005, Justice A.H. Joshi presiding over the Nagpur Bench of the Bombay High Court quashed the criminal proceedings initiated by the police on the ground that the case made out by the police does not attract the ingredients of Section 294 of the IPC. Section 294 is attracted only when annoyance is caused to another, due to obscene acts in a public place. The court held that the affidavit filed by the Joint Commissioner of Police did not reveal that annoyance was caused to him personally or to any other viewer due to the alleged obscene dancing.

This ruling followed several earlier decisions by the Bombay High Court, which had addressed the issue of obscenity in dance bars. One of the earliest rulings on this issue is by Justice Vaidhya in the *State of Maharashtra v. Joyce Zee alias Temiko* in 1978, where the court examined whether cabaret shows constitute obscenity. The police had conducted raids in Blue Nile and had filed a case against a Chinese cabaret artist, Temiko, on grounds of obscenity.

While dismissing the appeal filed by the state, the Bombay High Court held as follows: 'An adult person, who pays and attends a cabaret show in a hotel runs the risk of being annoyed by the obscenity. . . .' Interestingly, prior to the raid, the policemen had sat through the performance and enjoyed the same. Only when the show was complete did they venture to arrest the dancer. The court posed a relevant question – when and how was annoyance caused to the police, who had gone in to witness a cabaret performance? Regarding notions of morality and obscenity, the judge commented: 'A cabaret performance may or may not be obscene according to the time, place, circumstances and the age, tastes and attitude of the people before whom such a dance is performed.'

Out of the Closet – Into the Public Domain

The DCM's statement announcing the ban was followed by unprecedented media glare and we found ourselves in the centre of the controversy as lawyers representing the Bar Girls' Union. The controversy had all the right ingredients – titillating sexuality, a hint of the underworld, a faintly visible crack in the ruling Congress–NCP alliance and polarized positions among social activists. Ironically, the entire controversy and the media glare helped to bring the bar girl out of her closeted existence. It made the dance bars more transparent and accessible to women activists.

The controversy was not of our own making but we could not retract now. We threw in our lot with that of the Bar Girls' Union. The bar girls petitioned the Chief Minister, the National and State Women's Commissions, Commissions for Backward Castes, Scheduled Castes and Scheduled Tribes, the Human Rights Commissions and the Governor, Shri S.M. Krishna. We even met Sonia Gandhi, the Congress President, and sought her intervention. Other women's groups joined in and issued a statement opposing the ban.

An equal or even greater number of NGOs and social activists issued statements supporting the ban. The child-rights and anti-trafficking groups led by Prerana issued a congratulatory message to the DCM and claimed that they had won. Then women members of the NCP came on the street brandishing the banner of depraved morality. The Socialists and Gandhians joined them with endorsements from stalwarts of the women's movement like Mrinal Gore and Ahilya Rangnekar to aid them. These statements had the blessings of a retired High Court judge – Justice Dharmadhikari. Paid advertisements appeared in newspapers and signature campaigns were held at railway stations. 'Sweety and Savithri – who will you choose?' goaded the leaflets distributed door to door, along with the morning newspaper. The term 'Savithri', denoted the traditional *pativrata,* an ideal for Indian womanhood, while 'Sweety' denoted the woman of easy virtue, the wrecker of middle-class homes.

Suddenly the dancer from the city's sleazy bars and shadowy existence had spilled over into the public domain. Her photographs were splashed across the tabloids and television screens. She had become the topic of conversation at street corners and market places; in ladies' compartments of local trains and at dinner tables in middle-class homes. Everyone had an opinion and a strong one at that. Saint or sinner? Worker or whore? Spinner of easy money and wrecker of homes or victim of patriarchal structures and market economy? The debate on sexual morality and debasement of metropolitan Bombay seemed to be revolving around the bar girl's existence.

Interestingly, the Gandhians seemed to be only against the dancers and not against the bars that have proliferated. Nor have they done much to oppose the liquor policy of the state, which had encouraged bar dancing. The anti-trafficking groups which had been working in the red light districts had not succeeded in making a dent in child trafficking in brothels that continue to thrive. But in this controversy, brothel prostitution and trafficking of minors had been relegated to the sidelines. The sex worker was viewed with more compassion than the bar dancer, who may or may not resort to sex work.

The bar dancer was made out to be the cause of all social evils and depravity. Even the blame for the Telgi scam was laid at her door; the news story that Telgi spent Rs 9,300,000 on a bar dancer in one night was cited as an example of their pernicious influence. The criminal means through which Telgi amassed wealth faded into oblivion in the fury of the controversy. Was it her earning capacity, the legitimacy awarded to her profession and the higher status she enjoyed in comparison to a sex worker that invited the fury from the middle-class Maharashtrian moralists?

Hypocritical Morality

While the proposed ban adversely impacted bar owners and bar dancers from the lower economic rungs, the state proposed an exemption to hotels which hold three or more 'stars', or clubs and gymkhanas. Those of us who opposed the ban raised some uncomfortable questions. Could the state impose arbitrary and varying standards of vulgarity, indecency and obscenity for different sections of society or classes of people? If an 'item number' of a Hindi film can be screened in public theatres, then how can an imitation of the same be termed 'vulgar'? The bar dancers imitate what they see in Indian films, television serials, fashion shows and advertisements. All these industries use women's bodies for commercial gain. There is sexual exploitation of women in these and many other industries. But no one has ever suggested that an entire industry be close down because there is sexual exploitation of women. Bars employ women as waitresses and the proposed ban would not affect this category. Waitresses mingle with the customers more than the dancers who are confined to the dance floor. If the anti-trafficking laws had not succeeded in preventing trafficking, how could the ban on bar dancing prevent it? If certain bars were functioning as brothels, why were the licenses issued to them not revoked? These were several contradictions and hypocrisies in the stand adopted by the ruling party and the pro-ban lobby but no one was willing to listen.

While the hue and cry about the morality of dance bars was raging, in Sangli district, the home constituency of the DCM, a dance performance entitled 'Temptation' by Isha Koppikar, the 'item girl' of Bollywood, was being organized to raise money for the Police Welfare Fund. The bar girls flocked to Sangli to hold a protest march. This received even more publicity than the performance by Isha Koppikar who, due to the adverse publicity, was compelled to dress modestly and could not perform in her usual flamboyant style. The disappointed public felt it was more value for their money to see the protest of the bar girls than to witness a lacklustre performance by the 'item girl'. The bar girls raised the pertinent question about whether different rules of morality apply to the police and to the Home Minister.

All this was heady news for the television channels and the tabloids. From April to July 2005, the city was abuzz with the dance bar ban controversy. In June, the state tried to bring in the ban through an ordinance. But to everyone's surprise, the Governor Shri S.M. Krishna returned the ordinance and insisted that the ruling party should introduce a Bill in the state Legislature. The pro-ban lobby raised a stink and accused him of taking bribes from the bar owners, the majority of whom come from the southern state of Karnataka and from the beer baron Vijay Mallya, who also hails from Karnataka. Interestingly, before being appointed as Governor of Maharashtra, Shri S.M. Krishna was the Chief Minister of Karnataka and he had been accused of safeguarding the Kannadiga interests.

Legislative Conspiracy

Finally, a Bill was drafted and presented to the Assembly. It was an amendment to the Bombay Police Act, 1951, inserting certain additional sections. On 21 July 2005, the Bill was passed at the end of a marathon debate. Since the demand for the ban was shrouded with the mantle of sexual morality, it was passed unanimously. The debate was prolonged not because there was opposition, but every legislature wanted to prove his moral credentials. No legislator would risk sticking his neck out to defend a lowly bar dancer and tarnish his own image. In the visitors gallery, we were far outnumbered by the pro-ban lobby, the 'Dance Bar Virodhi Manch', who had submitted 150,000 signatures to the Maharashtra state assembly insisting on the closure of dance bars.

It was a sad day for some of us, a paltry group of women activists, who had supported the bar dancers and opposed the ban. We were sad not because we were outnumbered, not even because the Bill was passed unanimously, but because of the manner in which an important issue relating to women's livelihoods, which would render thousands of women destitute, was discussed. We were shocked at the derogatory comments that were passed on the floor of the House by our elected representatives, who are under the constitutional mandate to protect the dignity of women. Not just the bar dancers but even those who spoke out in their defence became the butt of ridicule during the Assembly discussions.

One of the comments was aimed at us. *'These women who are opposing the ban, we will make their mothers dance . . .'* (the comments have to be translated into Marathi to gauge their impact.) During the campaign we had been asked, 'will you send your daughter to dance in a bar?' But on the floor of the House, the situation had regressed, from our daughters to our mothers. *Isha Koppikar . . . she is an atom bomb, attttom bomb . . .* laughter and cheer . . . *the dancers wear only 20% clothes* . . . more laughter and cheering . . . *these women who dance naked* (nanga nach), *they don't deserve any sympathy* . . . a round of applause.

An esteemed member narrated an incident of his friend's daughter who had committed suicide because she did not get a job. He said it was more dignified to commit suicide than dance in bars. And the house applauded! Yet another congratulated the Deputy Chief Minister, Shri R.R. Patil, for taking this bold and revolutionary (*krantikari*) step but this was not enough. 'Hotels with three stars . . . five stars . . . disco dancing . . . belly dancing . . . all that is vulgar . . . every thing should be banned', he urged.

Another esteemed member was anecdotal. He had gone to dinner with a friend to a posh restaurant in South Mumbai which has a live orchestra. Not a dance bar – he clarified. But women there were dressed in an even more obscene manner than the bar dancers. (Comments: 'why had you gone there?' [laughter] 'Was it part of a study tour?' [more laughter]). When licenses were given to bars, the understanding was that it would promote art – performing art. But what actually happens is vulgar dancing, a total destruction of our culture. Belly dancing in five star hotels is also vulgar. That should be stopped too. This Bill deals with the dignity of women. So, all dancing, except *bharatanatyam* and *kathak* should be banned. Schools and colleges are full of vulgarity. We need a dress code for schools and colleges. The bill needs to be made more effective so that it can deal with issues like MMS and pornography.

Then there were comments about films – 'western . . . English . . . Tamil – all are obscene', they argued. But not a word about Hindi and Marathi films. That is '*amchi Mumbai, amchi Marathi*', I guess!

Then another esteemed member commented, 'we are not Taliban but somewhere we have to put a stop. The moral policing we do, it is a good thing, but it is not enough . . . we need to do even more of this moral policing. . . .' Suddenly the term 'moral policing' had been turned into a hallowed phrase!

These comments were not from the ruling party members who had tabled the Bill. They were from the opposition. Their traditional role is to criticize the Bill, to puncture holes in it, to counter the argument, to present a counter viewpoint. But, on that day, the House was united, across party lines and all were playing to the gallery with their moral one-upmanship. No one wanted to be left out. Even the Shiv Sena, whose party high command is linked to a couple of dance bars in the city, supported the ban on 'moral' grounds. And the Marxists were one with the Shiv Sainiks. The speech by the CPI(M) member, Narsayya Adam, was more scathing than the rest. He went to the extent of casting aspersions on the Governor for returning the bill. To return a bill passed by the cabinet is an insult to the Maharashtra state, he declared. The women members, though a small minority, happily cheered the barrage against bar dancers.

It was a moral victory to the Deputy Chief Minister (DCM), Shri R.R. Patil. In his first announcement in the last week of March 2005, he had said that only bars outside Mumbai will be banned. A week later, came the next announcement. The state shall not discriminate! All bars, including the ones in Mumbai, would be banned. What had transpired in the intervening period one does not know. But what was deemed as moral, legal and legitimate, suddenly a week later, came to be regarded as immoral, vulgar and obscene.

At this time, the idea of a ban did not go down well even with NCP MLAs, let alone others. It took more than two months to get the Ordinance drafted and approved by the cabinet. Finally, when it was sent to the Governor, he had returned it on technical grounds. By then, it was mid-June. But even thereafter, the Congress Party Chief in Maharashtra stated that the Congress Party had not discussed the ban. In fact, the media hinted that this indicated a rift within the ruling alliance over the dance bar issue.

But gradually everything got ironed out. Not only was the ruling alliance cemented, even the opposition had been won over. Rarely does a bill gets passed without even a whimper of protest. But this bill was showered with accolades. All had done their bit in this endeavour of 'protecting the dignity of women'.

The 'morality' issue had won. The 'livelihood' issue had lost. It was indeed shocking that in this era of liberalization and globalization dominated by market forces, morality had superceded all other concerns, even of revenue for the cash-strapped state.

The demand for the ban was grounded on two premises which are contradictory to each other. The first is that the bar dancers are evil and immoral, they corrupt the youth and wreck middle class homes; they hanker after easy money and amass a fortune each night by goading innocent and gullible young men into sex and sleaze. The second is that bars in fact are brothels and bar owners are traffickers who sexually exploit the girls for commercial gains. This premise refused to grant any agency to the women dancers. Rather unfortunately, both these populist premises appealed to the parochial, middle-class Maharashtrian sense of morality. What was even worse, the demand for a ban was framed in the language of 'women's liberation' and the economic disempowerment of this vulnerable class of women came to be projected as a plank which would liberate them from sexual bondage.

On 14 August 2005, at the midnight hour, as the music blared in bars packed to capacity in and around the city of Bombay, the disco lights were turned off and the dancers took their final bow and faded into oblivion.

Some left the city in search of options, others fell by the wayside. Some became homeless. Some let their ailing parents die. Some pulled their children out of school. Some were battered and bruised by drunken husbands as they could not bring in the money to make ends meet. Some put their pre-teen daughters out for sale in the flesh market. And some committed suicide. Just names in police diaries – Meena Raju, Bilquis Shahu, Kajol. In the intervening months, there were more to follow. A few stuck on and begged for work as waitresses in the same bars.

The exit of the dancer brought the dance bar industry to a grinding halt.

Devoid of glamour and fanfare, the profit margins plummeted and many bars closed down. A few others braved the storm and worked around the ban by transforming themselves into 'silent bars' or 'pick up points' – slang used for the sex trade industry. Left with few options, women accepted the paltry sums thrown at them by customers, to make ends meet. Groups working for prevention of HIV/AIDS rang a warning bell at the increasing number of girls turning up for STD check ups.

Malafide Motives

Why was the dance bar ban struck down by the court? To understand this, first we must examine the Statement of Objects and Reasons (SOR) of the amendment. The SOR claimed the following:

- The dance performances in eating houses, permit rooms and beer bars are indecent, obscene or vulgar.
- The performances are giving rise to exploitation of women.
- Several complaints regarding the manner of holding such dance performances have been registered.
- The Government considers that the performance of dances in an indecent manner is derogatory to the dignity of women and is likely to deprave, corrupt or injure the public morality or morals.

The court overruled each of these reasons stated by the Government on the ground that there is no rational nexus between the amendment and its aims and objectives. Some relevant comments from the judgement are summarized below:

> Entry into bars is restricted to an adult audience and is voluntary. The test, therefore would be whether the dances can be said to have a tendency to deprave and corrupt this audience. The test of obscenity and vulgarity has to be judged from the standards of adult persons who voluntarily visit these bars.[7]
>
> If the dances which are permitted in the exempted establishments are also permitted in the banned establishments then, considering the stand of the State, they should not be derogatory to women and on account of exploitation of women and are unlikely to deprave or corrupt public morals. The expression western classical or Indian classical which are used by the State in the affidavit is of no consequence, as the Act and the rules recognize no such distinction. All applicants for a performance licence have to meet the same requirements and are subject to the same restrictions. . . . If the test is now applied as to whether the classification has a nexus with the object, we are clearly of the opinion that there is no nexus whatsoever with the object.[8]
>
> Dancing is one of the earliest form of human expression and recognized by the Apex Court as a fundamental right. If it is sought to be contended that a particular form of dance performed by a particular class of dancers is immoral or obscene that by itself cannot be a test to hold that the activity is *res extra*

commercium. It can never be inherently pernicious or invariably or inevitably pernicious. If the notions of the State as to the dancing are to be accepted, we would have reached a stage where skimpy dressing and belly gyrations which today is the Bollywood norm for dance, will have to be banned as inherently or invariably pernicious. We think as a nation we have outgrown that, considering our past approach to dancing, whether displayed as sculpture on monuments or in its real form. Dancing of any type, if it becomes obscene or immoral, can be prohibited or restricted. Dancing however would continue to be a part of the fundamental right of expression, occupation or profession protected by our Constitution.[9]

The right to dance has been recognized by the Apex Court as part of the fundamental right of speech and expression. If that be so, it will be open to a citizen to commercially benefit from the exercise of the fundamental right. This could be by a bar owner having dance performance or by bar dancers themselves using their creative talent to carry on an occupation or profession. In other words, using their skills to make a living.

Does the material relied upon by the state make out a case that the manner of conducting places having bar dances constitute a threat to public order? The case of the State can be summarized as: 'Complaints were received by wives relating to illicit relationships with bar dancers.' This by itself cannot amount to a threat to public order considering the number of complaints which the State has produced on record.

The bar girls had to suffer commercial exploitation and were forced into a situation that used to leave them with no other option than to continue in the indecent sector. It is true that there is material on record to show that many of those who perform dance in these bars are young girls, a large section being less than 21 years of age and with only a primary education. Can that by itself be a ground to hold that they constitute a threat to public order? Can a girl who may be semi-literate or even illiterate, beautiful, knows to dance or tries to dance be prohibited from earning a better livelihood or should such a girl, because of poverty and want of literacy, be condemned to a life of only doing menial jobs?

It is normal in the hospitality and tourist related industries to engage young girls. Inability of the State to provide employment or to take care of those women who had to take to the profession of dancing on account of being widowed, or part of failed marriages or poverty at home and/or the like cannot result in holding that their working for a livelihood by itself constitutes a threat to public order. There is no sufficient data to show that the women were forced into that profession and had no choice to leave it.

It is then set out that in or around places where there are dance bars, there are more instances of murder, firing, thefts, chain snatches and that the public in general and women in the locality feel unsafe. In what manner does dancing by women in dance bars result in increase in crime which would constitute a threat to public order? Inebriated men, whether in dance bars or other bars are a known source of nuisance. The State has not cancelled the liquor permits to remove the basic cause of the problem. Maintenance of law and order is the duty of the State. *If drunk men fight or involve themselves in criminal activity, it cannot result in denying livelihood to those who make a living out of dance.* It is not the case of the State that apart from these places, in the rest of the State the same kind of offences do not take place.

The state has produced the record that 17403 cases have been registered under section 110 of the Bombay Police Act. These are incidents within the establishments and in front of an audience who have taken no objection to the dresses worn by the dancers or the kind of dancing. The public at large are not directly involved. A learned Judge of this Court, Justice Srikrishna (as he then was) in *Girija Timappa Shetty* v. *Assistant Commissioner of Police*, 1977 (1) All M.R. 256, has taken note of the fact that in order to inflate the figures, the police would register a separate case against every customer and employee present. Even otherwise we are unable to understand as to how, if there is a breach of rule by an establishment, that would constitute a threat to public order. An illustration has been given of one Tarannum as having links with the underworld. At the time of hearing of this petition, the police had not even filed a charge sheet. Even otherwise, a solitary case cannot constitute a threat to public order.

It has also been pointed out that the Legislature has noted that the dance bars are used as meeting places for criminals. This defies logic: why criminals should meet at the dance bars where they could easily be noted by the police. Criminals, we presume, meet secretly or stealthily to avoid the police unless they are confident that they can meet openly as the law enforcement itself has collapsed or they have friends amongst the enforcement officers. Even otherwise, how does a mere meeting of persons who are charged or accused for criminal offence constitute a threat to public order? Do they not meet in other places? It is then pointed out that the nature of business of dance bar is such that it is safe for criminals and immoral activities and this constitutes a serious threat to public order.

It was on the State to show that the dance bars were being conducted in the manner which was a threat to public order. The bars continue to operate with all activities except dancing. The State has been unable to establish a nexus between dancing and threat to public order.[10]

It was pointed out that though the State has initiated action under Section 294 of I.P.C. it was not possible to secure a conviction as the State had to prove obscenity and annoyance to customers. This by itself would indicate that the dance performance inside the premises are not obscene or immoral as to cause annoyance amongst those who gathered to watch the performance. How that could cause annoyance to those who do not watch it or affect public order is not understood. It is like saying that watching a Hindi movie which has dance sequence and the dancers are skimpily dressed, would result in affecting public order.

It is then submitted that though the Police were prompt in taking action under the prevailing enactments, the accused, being successful in getting around the law, continued to indulge in the same activities again. Failure of the police to secure a conviction cannot be a valid ground to impose a restriction on fundamental rights. The pronouncement of this Court under Section 294 would be the law. How then can the State still insist that the performance of dance was obscene or vulgar and caused annoyance to the public?[11]

Constructing the Sexual Subject

A glaring discrepancy in the arguments advanced by the state was in the realm of the agency of the sexual woman. At one level, the state and the pro-ban lobby advanced an argument that the dancers are evil women who come to the bars to earn 'easy money' and corrupt the morals of the society by luring and enticing young and gullible men. This argument granted an agency to women dancers. But after the ban, the government tried to justify the ban on the ground of trafficking and argued that these women lack an agency and need state intervention to free them from this world of sexual depravity in which they are trapped.

Refuting the argument of trafficking, the Court commented:

No material has been brought on record from those cases that the women working in the bars were forced or lured into working in the bars. The statement of Objects and Reasons does not so indicate this. . . . To support the charge of trafficking in order to prohibit or restrict the exercise of a fundamental right, the State had to place reliable material which was available when the amending Act was enacted or even thereafter to justify it. A Constitutional Court in considering an act directly affecting the fundamental rights of citizens, has to look beyond narrow confines to ensure protection of those rights. In answer to the call attention Motion, an admission was made by the Home Minister and it is also stated in the Statement of Objects and Reasons that young girls were going to the dance bars because of the easy money they earned and that resulted also in immoral activities. There was no mention of trafficking.[12]

Rather ironically, the anti-ban lobby also framed its arguments within this accepted 'victim' mould: single mothers, traditional dancers with no other options. It was important for the anti-ban lobby to make a clear distinction between the dancer/entertainer and the street walker, and base the arguments squarely upon the fundamental right to dancing. The eroticism inherent in dancing had to be carefully crafted and squarely located within 'Indian traditions' and the accepted norm of 'Bollywood gyrations' and not slip beyond into sexual advances. The emphasis had to be for a right to livelihood only through dancing and not beyond.

During the entire campaign, the world of the bar dancer beyond these confines lay hidden from the feminist activists campaigning their cause and was carefully guarded by the bar dancer. Only now and then would it spill over as a defiant statement. So while we were exposed to one aspect of their lives which had all the problems – of parenting, poverty, pain and police harassment – we must admit that this was only a partial projection, an incomplete picture. We could not enter the other part of their world in which they are constantly negotiating their sexuality, the dizzy heights they scale while they dance draped in gorgeous chiffons studded with sequins.

Did the problem lie with us and the picture that we wanted to paint for them? Well, perhaps yes. But for now as the state prepares to file its appeal in the Supreme Court, aided with the best legal minds in the country, to defend its stand on sexual morality, we would be content, if we are able to safeguard the advantages we have gained in the Bombay High Court.

Notes

[1] Writ Petition No. 2450/2005 – *Indian Hotel & Restaurants Association (AHAR) and others v. State of Maharashtra and others.*

[2] As per the amended statute, the concerned Section, i.e., Section 33B of the Bombay Police Act, 1951 is worded as follows: 'Nothing in section 33A shall apply to the holding of a dance performance in a drama theatre, cinema theatre and auditorium or sport club or gymkhana where entry is restricted to its members only or a three starred or above hotel or in any other establishment or class of establishment. Which having regarding to (a) the tourism activities in the State or (b) cultural activities, the State Government may by special or general order, specify in this behalf'.

[3] Para. 61 at page 163.

[4] Para. 68 at page 183.

[5] *Rules for Licensing and Controlling Places of Public Amusement (other than Cinemas) and performances for Public Amusement including Melas and Thamashas, 1960.*

[6] The bar owners functioned under regular licenses issued to restaurants and bars. They paid Rs 55,000 per month for the various permits and licenses to the Municipal Corporation. They also paid an annual excise fee of Rs 80,000. In addition, the bar owners also pay Rs 30,000 per month to the Collector by way of 'entertainment fee'.

[7] Para. 49 at page 130.

[8] Para. 52 at page 135.

[9] Para. 58 at page 155.

[10] Para. 83, pages 222–25.

[11] Para. 84 at page 232.

[12] Para. 86 at page 235.

'You Can See Without Looking'

The Cinematic 'Author' and

Freedom of Expression in the Cinema

Ashish Rajadhyaksha

The Controversy

• Report in *The Times of India*: 'The controversy around the film *Fire* took a new turn on Sunday with Shiv Sena chief Bal Thackeray stating that he would withdraw his objection to the movie if the names of the main protagonists were changed.

'Let them change (the names) from Radha and Sita to Shabana and Saira or Najma', he said in a tersely worded statement.

'Why is the entire film shown against the backdrop of a Hindu family? Why have the names Radha and Sita been given to the lesbian partners in the film?'

Mr Thackeray's son Uddhav said, 'None of those who are now crying hoarse about freedom of expression protested when the government banned Salman Rushdie's *Satanic Verses* and a 'fatwa' was issued. . . This double standard exposes the hypocrisy of those opposing us for our stand on *Fire*', he observed ('Change Radha-Sita to Shabana-Saira: Thackeray Sets Condition for Allowing Fire to Be Screened', 1998).

• Shabana Azmi: 'Mr Bal Thackeray must be chuckling with glee at how cleverly he has taken the wind out of the sails of those stupid few clamouring for the right to freedom of expression with his latest diatribes against the film, *Fire*. [B]y attempting to communalize the debate on *Fire*, Mr Bal Thackeray wants to take the spotlight away from the main issue – the vandalism by the Shiv Sainiks, the use of force and violence as premeditated acts to disrupt the screening of a film running to full houses for three weeks, duly passed by the Central Board of Censor Certification. And the subsequent endorsement of violence by the Maharashtra Chief Minister, Mr Manohar Joshi' (Azmi 1998).

• Report in *The Hindu*: 'Declining to go into the merits of *Fire*, Mr Mukhtar Abbas Naqvi (Minister of State for Information & Broadcasting) said he could unhesitatingly say that lesbianism may be a subject for discussion among liberated and progressive women but not among the large body of Indian women. Mr Naqvi indicated that he did not give much importance to the views of the National Commission for Women because it was not a representative body. He declined to discuss the reported unhappiness of Ms Asha Parekh, Chairperson of the Censor Board, over the Government's stand. He denied that the authorities had failed to curb graphic scenes of rape in Indian films. To another question, he said he did not support attacks on cinema theatres by the Shiv Sena followers' ('Naqvi Assails Opposition to Saraswati Vandana/Decision on Fire Justified', 1998).

The Film

Opening shot: a slow track left over vivid yellow mustard fields, to A.R. Rehman's score evidently borrowed from the film *Bombay*. It dissolves on an MCU of a woman telling a singsong story to little Radha:

> A long time ago there were people who lived high up on the mountains.
> They had never seen the sea.
> They were very sad.
> Then an old woman in the village said don't be sad.
> You can see. You just have to see without looking.
> Radha, do you understand?
> [This is an exact quote.]

Opening surprise: the film was in English. Convent school, nursery rhyme. Moment of wonder: can one element within realist construction, if suppressed, serve to heighten every other effect? The language? The intonation? Not here: the fields evoked *Dilwale Dulhaniya Le Jayenge* (*DDLJ*), everything was rhetorically, externally, addressed with little diegetic integrity – the score and the postcard, the hill men, the old woman and the sea. The English was just another uncritical addition to the film's assembly of bits and pieces of referenced data. Next shot: man eating apple at (slow pan right) full frontal shot of Taj Mahal (!). Wife enjoying story of tourist guide in pidgin telling the love legend of Mumtaz. Husband is clearly not interested in wife. The legend is a commentary on their domestic relationship. Each sentence in this list uhammered home like a caption on a photograph. This film is not subtle. If it wants you to know something it makes sure. A few shots later: wife dances in solitude performing for camera (surface of star), husband goes off to see his girlfriend.

Fire offers no great challenge as to what it is trying to do. It was somewhat bizarre, then, to have this most 'obvious' of all films get elected for the intense war of words between different interest groups on what it was, or was not, saying. In terms of the argument around symbolic textuality that I am trying to build here, the film offers itself as a classic candidate.

The story is about a young bride who enters a new home, one representative of the values of the new Hindu middle-class, and finds – amid a quarrelsome family and an uncaring husband – solace in a lesbian relationship with her sister-in-law. The bride is played by Nandita Das, introduced in the film as a star attraction clearly in her launch vehicle, and the sister-in-law by the diva of India's independent cinema, Shabana Azmi. Both the women are 'complex' characters in the literary sense, and they are surrounded by unidimensional people each illustrating a particular character trait. From the casting device of two stars surrounded by bit actors, to various actorial strategies including naturalist performative gestures, speeded up into comical effect (e.g., with the brother-in-law, or with the voyeurist masturbating servant) and 'slowed down' into meaningful pauses and naturalist gesture when these two women are shown, a clear storytelling strategy develops.

It appears that the film's realism will exist in its fullness only when the two women are present: it is condensed into the performative idiom of these two stars.[1] Surrounding this realism is a mélange of purely symbolic eruptions: 'individuals' periodically used to disrupt the narrative through behaviour illustrating their particular disposition.

The display of crude symbolism that surrounds the actions of the lead duo has been discussed by critics including those involved in the ensuing controversy.[2] My argument is more concerned with the disputes around its narrative *purpose*. I suggest that the production of what we might call a threatened, or fugitive realism, incarnated by the two women in their privacy, a 'realism' within quotes surrounded by articulate (if admittedly crude) symbolic constructions, invokes, even if unintentionally, the entire history of what we have called a statist-symbolic textuality: for it invokes the precise role of a 'realist' text lying, as a spectatorial production, at the core of the story and from there seeking to incorporate, *interpret*, all the crude stuff that lies about at its edges. Such a production is, apparently, intended to facilitate, not so much a successful transition of the crude stuff into properly realist interpretability but, in actual fact, the reverse of that: it seeks to enable *realism's* entry into the zone of a purely *symbolic* structure, or 'effect', even as it keeps intact its major asset of incarnating the gaze of the citizen-spectator.

In fact, we may say from hindsight that such a restaging of realism itself may well be seen, in hindsight given our knowledge of Mehta's future career as the maker of films like *Bollywood/Hollywood* (2002), as taking place primarily at the service of Bollywood and its free-associative usurpation of a particular history of spectatorial right.

So far, so good: Mehta is functioning within the almost classic terms of a theatrical or cinematic propaganda or direct spectator address, where naturalism, or the capacity for the character to doubt (and for the spectator to disavow), is attributed only to the good guys, surrounded by uniconceptual baddies.[3]

What Mehta was unable to predict however, and indeed what caught everyone unprepared, was the vociferous presence of an articulate audience who now wanted a say in how the film's realism would be interpreted. *This* debate, repeatedly evidenced by a 'surprised Deepa Mehta',[4] went way beyond the film itself or its self-understanding of what it was doing. It hit, at a historically significant moment in the Indian state's negotiations with globalization, at the very basis of state-endorsed – and we shall see below, *legally* endorsed – cinematic realism. In opening up for questioning the very validity of textual endorsement, and what such authentication could mean in the present, the film went to the very heart of spectatorial rights.

We shall use the example of this film to open up the spectatorial question further. I want to explore[5] the role played by the major Marathi, anti-Communist and Hindutva icon, Bal Thackeray, and the opportunity *he* created for himself in this. Of the many disputes that took place over spectatorship, it appeared that *his* were the actions that consciously resonated with the history we are seeking to identify here in terms of the administration of the symbols of authenticity.

The Spectatorial Crisis

In the period after Independence, a major restructuring took place around the cinema: contextualized by a larger programme of technologized cultural production on behalf of the Indian state. It was further proposed that such a restructuring also assembled a particular textuality, extending into a reading competence underwritten by the legally endorsed authority of the apparatus. The present argument, exploring the problematic nature of both the competence and its legal endorsement, will suggest that, for perhaps the first time in independent India, there may have emerged an unintended degree of clarity – and perhaps some consensus – around what we might call the *aesthetic–textual* interpretations of Articles 19(1)(a) ('All citizens shall have the right to freedom of speech and expression') and 19(2) ('reasonable restrictions on the exercise of the right . . . in the interests of the sovereignty and integrity of India'[6]) of the Indian constitution, at the very time that saw fierce battles raging around what such a right may mean in the cinema. An ensuing legal consensus, shared by political positions that were, at one point, historically opposed, has also opened up a whole new field for working out old questions of artistic freedom versus state regulation. This moment also therefore opens up a 'restrictive' reading – an 'it means this and nothing else' reading – of symbolic productions on behalf of the independent Indian state, and as such, may be a direct contribution of the cinema, and of cinematic realism, to an important terrain of political functioning in India.

Consider this: the very icon of threatened freedom in the late 1990s, Deepa Mehta's film, and the symbol historically enshrining that threat, the Censor Board, were, for the duration of the controversy, for the first time ever in India on the same side of the fence: both united, if unwillingly, against the Hindu right represented by Bal Thackeray. When Shabana Azmi argued – justifiably – that the film had been 'duly passed' by the CBFC and thereby received the right to be publicly screened, she was also pointing to the seriously compromised nature of what *should* have been, in the prevailing political arena, an ally. It was well known that in numerous instances during the nefarious reign of a previous CBFC chief, film producer Shakti Samanta, the Board would routinely abdicate its own right to be the sole arbiter of what may or may not be publicly screened by asking the police, the Home Ministry and, in at least one extreme instance, Bal Thackeray himself (Mani Ratnam's *Bombay*, 1995), to decide on its behalf. And in the controversy at hand, when the then BJP government asked the CBFC to 'review' its earlier decision on *Fire*, Samanta's successor, Asha Parekh, was clearly, and embarrassingly, incapable of asserting that she stood by the Board's first decision and that the film – whatever we, or anyone else, might think of it – continued to remain fit for public screening.

Now consider Thackeray's own position in all this. You needed only to equate the word 'state' in Article 19(2) with the concept 'Bal Thackeray' (and then the concept 'spectator') for much of the confusion to be apparently resolved. Indeed, it was impossible to arrive at a coherent explanation of what went on in the tumultuous months that followed *Fire*'s Indian release, or to account for the helplessness or embarrassment Thackeray caused as much to previous Congress governments as to his own ruling SS–BJP coalition, if one did not recognize that Thackeray was speaking as though he *were* the Indian state. If he *had* been, things might have been conceptually easier: he would then, in his comments on *Fire*, be simply following explicitly stated constitutional procedures in imposing 'reasonable restrictions' on the right to freedom of speech and expression, bearing in mind the problems the film might cause to 'public order, decency or morality'. It seems to me that the explanation for this shift in authority was not to be found in Azmi's sarcastic allusion to the mundane fact that Thackeray effectively ran the government of Maharashtra at the time, or that the Shiv Sena was part of the then ruling coalition in New Delhi. The answer has to be cast over a longer time frame, has to address his claim that he represented the *authentic* Indian state (note how mutually hurled accusations around authenticity dominated much of the *Fire* controversy)[7] and therefore spoke as a 'true' pre-Independence nationalist might have in the face of discredited colonial authority, or as a film protagonist might who rejects the law of a state represented by corrupt judges or khakhi-clad extras who arrive in the last shot of the film, in favour of a more primordial law of the kin. How, in the late 1990s, Thackeray got round to doing *that* – in the sheer mechanics of his mode of functioning – was, I believe, an integral part of the overall debate that *Fire* generated around constitutional rights.

Whose freedom were we talking about in those days, and what form of *expression* was it then that this *freedom* was expected to *guarantee*? – these, surely, continue to be important questions in any debate around how Article 19 might make itself available on such occasions. Let me suggest, in getting to what I consider to be the core issue that *Fire* raised, that what was at stake here was not so much the freedom of *expression* – although *Fire* did evoke a long line of recent legal judgments explicitly around Articles 19(1a) and 19(2) – but had, rather, to do with the freedom of *representation*; and that there is a fine line of distinction which was particularly relevant to the issues. In making this suggestion, and in emphasizing its critical importance to cinema, I shall invoke a conceptual tradition in which the linguistic and political senses of the term 'representation' intersect with each other. I shall suggest that there is a necessary caveat built into the Article itself which allows a *transference* of some kind, one that has suddenly acquired a critical political meaning: that here the real right at stake, as many judgments on the issue showed, was not so much Deepa Mehta's right to express *her* ideas on film – contrary then to Azmi's, and the broad secular front's, defence of Mehta – but rather the Indian *people's* right to *receive* this expression once it had been sanctioned by the Indian state as fit for its public. I shall propose that we need to explore the link between the freedom of expression and its manifestations in terms of *representation* and *reception*, and perhaps address just how Indian law allows, and accounts for, this transition if we are to comprehend the legality of the cinematic 'speaking subject'.

For what follows is controversial. In all this, the re-positioning of the symbolic right of the *public* to free expression is precisely the field that, through a series of peculiar slippages, has also made a Bal Thackeray possible. *L'état, c'est moi* – Thackeray was clearly making and underscoring a set of his *own* representations here, which included, first, his much trumpeted personal right; second, his moral right as the 'true' Indian state, and finally the rights bestowed upon him by the presumed mandate of the people on whose behalf he claimed to speak. Given that each is supposedly an independent field of operation, the question arises as to how, and by what sleight of hand, Thackeray could now *bring these together* to assemble his own *speaking subject*. The deeply vexed problematic that has riven at least the Left movement in India in much of this century, of how explicitly *representational* practices as in any form of artistic expression may be mapped onto ideological, institutional or political modes of *organization* was, it seems, poised to enter a new era, as we were to see the often uncannily similar ways in which a secular, modernist and internationalist filmmaker and film star defended their work and a Hindutva zealot defended his rights to impose control. Also, it would take us to the very heart of the question of spectatorial speech.

The Explosively Expanding Cinema Menace

We need to proceed here with caution; examine, with some care, the consequences of these shifts upon authorial practice. Freedom of speech, at its most basic, of course, invokes an individual right; a standard textbook on the Indian Constitution defines it as the 'right to express one's convictions and opinions freely'.[8] Through the twentieth century, this individuated right extended into a series of add-ons which logically furthered this right into a public arena and, in the process, defined the on-the-ground meaning of a *second* set of rights: those of the recipients of someone's expression, or the public's right to be protected from the consequences of that expression.

So Durga Das Basu's *Constitutional Law* textbook goes on to show how this right would extend to the 'expression of one's ideas by any visible representation, such as by gestures and the like. [E]xpression, naturally, presupposes a second party to whom the ideas are expressed or communicated.' And so, to express oneself meant, for instance, to publish one's views, to put them out into the market, or to mechanically de-link the *thing expressed* – by 'mouth, printing, picture or in any other manner addressed to the eyes or ears' – from the *one who speaks*. And as the matter moves away from the individuated speaker who is expressing his/her thoughts into the category of the public sphere where a second set of contrary rights emerge (of those who receive this speech), I think two distinct issues emerge, which need to be discussed, especially in today's times.

First, and critically, this system functions best when the 'thing expressed' – notwithstanding its autonomous legal existence as an object-in-itself – traces a logical and visible relation to its *source* of expression. In other words, the thing expressed owes its expressibility, so to say, to someone who can be held responsible for it. As such, the *source* of expression is best understood, in the sense of Article 19(1)(a), as one that replicates the individuated paradigm of one expressing one's convictions 'freely': in other words, when the speech invents, or somehow traces a link to, an *author*. On the other hand, the *recipient* of the speech can and should demonstrate no transgressive capacity to share authorial responsibility with the speaker. The recipient of speech may perform no discursive actions other than to receive. The vast bulk of the restrictions placed upon the Act are, precisely, restrictions placed upon the actions of those who receive someone else's speech: where any published expression is proscribed precisely for its tendency to, for example, incite violence amongst recipients, or to 'deprave and corrupt those whose minds are open to . . . immoral influences'.[9] In other words, the Act presumes that reception is consequential to speech, and following this assumption, places its key restrictions not upon speech itself but upon the reception.

While this may not be a major issue in most matters, in the cinema such matters cut to the bone. A restrictive law emphasizing restraint upon the actions of those who receive and interpret someone else's speech, cannot, in its liberal-humanist tradition, easily account for forms of representation that do not yield an ideologically coherent source of speech. It cannot, therefore, account for a representation that 'does not re-present an "original"' but instead 're-presents that which is *always already represented*'.[10] It is not for nothing that both actions of reception, and recipient's action, evoke in legal matters primarily a colonial legacy, with the ancestor of this Act being in the Defence of India rules (1939), geared primarily to address questions of sedition[11] or the Penal Code of 1860 used for obscene literature.[12]

And it has been with this law, and this history, that we have come to the cinema. The cinema: the quintessential mode resisting 'objective reality' and thus also resisting a speech mode relating the recipient to the object. The cinema has always had a difficulty with defining the speaking subject in what one theorist calls its 'biographism' – its production of a 'Deepa Mehta', a 'Satyajit Ray' or a 'K.A. Abbas': a full blown author, whose films are mere secondary manifestations 'from which it is possible to 'work back' to the neurosis of the filmmaker' as we provide a '*diagnosis* applied to *persons*, thus explicitly proclaiming (our) indifference both to the textual and the social'[13] – and thereby to the person whose threatened rights we would automatically gather together to protect. The author then is the most convenient incarnation of the speaking subject of the cinema, so much so that legal practice has found it difficult to introduce any category of the subject that might reside elsewhere than in an authorial *persona*.[14]

The cinema has, from this position of legal visibility, posed not only the most spectacular legal cases invoking Article 19(1) but also presented key obstacles to the deployment of the freedom of expression principle in Indian law. It has, in the process, effectively devised a way of making sense of the constitutional right that usefully allows us to understand not only the processes by which the cinema gets institutionalized, but also related political moves, including, here, Thackeray's own discursive *coup d'état*.

Several efforts have been made to define over the years the difference the cinema makes to the legal deployment of Article 19(1). So Chief Justice M. Hidayatullah, passing judgment on what is still the landmark case on freedom of expression in the cinema, *K.A. Abbas v. Union of India*, says:

> . . . it has been almost universally recognized that the treatment of motion pictures must be *different from that of other forms of art and expression*. This arises from the *instant appeal* of the motion picture, its versatility, realism (often surrealism), and its coordination of the visual and aural senses. The art of the cameraman, with trick photography, Vistavision and three-dimensional representation thrown in, has made the cinema picture *more true to life* than even the theatre or indeed any other form of representative art. The motion picture is able to stir up emotions more deeply than any other product of art. Its effect particularly on children and adolescents is very great since their immaturity makes them more willingly suspend their belief than mature men and women. They also remember the action in the picture and try to emulate or imitate what they have seen.[15]

More 'true to life' *and therefore* 'able to stir up emotions'. This was the first instance in Indian cinema where legal language succeeded in finding a definition for issues that have been only more recently explored in Indian film theory: issues arising out of the growing perception of the cinematic institution as primarily geared to the organization of *spectatorial* activity. The legal acknowledgement of a spectator more emotionally stirred by the cinema than by any other mode of address, and further, of the spectator who can 'emulate or imitate' – who, in short, acts upon what is received and is, therefore, no more restricted to being a passive recipient, has had major consequences upon how the law has understood spectatorial behaviour. From gay-rights groups such as the Campaign for Lesbian Rights[16] to 'crackpot litigation' by people with 'hurt feelings' to Shiv Sena vandalism, this field of action has become the dominant location for locating spectatorial agency. It has also been legally circumscribed by the Article 19(2), defining the zone in which the author's freedom of speech is sought to be restricted.

Let us return to the Abbas judgment to see what this and subsequent judgments have done to the first part of the Freedom of Expression tug-of-war, i.e., Article 19(1a) itself: to the speech emanating from a speaker, and to the inevitable *authorial* underpinnings of this category.

As he notes in his autobiography, Abbas had made *A Tale of Four Cities* (*Char Shaher Ek Kahani*, 1968) – the censorship of which was the crux of the petition – for a specific purpose. It appears that, in a meeting of the G.D. Khosla

Enquiry Committee on Film Censorship (1968), of which Abbas was a member, the Chairman of the Censor Board denied that there was any political censorship: 'They never had any social or political themes to which anyone might object. They only knew dancing, singing and hip-swinging. That provoked me to challenge the statement', he writes.[17] The twists and turns by which the challenge was assembled are worth noting: Abbas made the documentary, screened it for the Khosla Committee and the Censor Board and when, as expected, his brothel scene was objected to by the latter, he filed a petition with the Supreme Court.[18] When the government relented and offered an unchanged version of the Universal certificate, Abbas further amended his petition to be 'able to challenge pre-censorship itself as offensive to freedom of speech and expression and alternatively the provisions of the (Indian Cinematography) Act and the rules, orders and directions under this Act, as vague and arbitrary'.[19] He did this, he says, because he 'wanted to put the censorship machinery in the docks'.[20]

What did Abbas achieve? Concretely, as it happens, a great deal: the judgment led to the instituting of a Censorship Appellate tribunal consisting of 'eminent persons' to exist independent of the government, a landmark in the history of film censorship in India. There are, however, a series of less obvious consequences of Abbas' intervention, which are mostly evident in the later legal deployments of this judgment.

To begin with, the Abbas intervention itself, and the manner in which it was made, was clearly intended to resuscitate a particular, and rather special, concept of the cinematic author: as something resembling what Habermas calls the 'moral person'.[21] This category bears scant relation to, say, Robert Bresson's use of the term 'cinematographer',[22] since in its flawed, inaugural definition – the one that Abbas was now about to change – it appeared to be valid only for certain kinds of ('art'?) films. It is well known that in several official film bodies, filmic authors function in given ways, work with certain kinds of budgets, are backed by organizations like the 'script committee' of the National Film Development Corporation (NFDC), and lend their names and their genius to certain causes. A number of India's independent filmmakers have been able to function precisely because of these mechanisms. And while the Abbas move certainly went far towards substantiating this definition, its truly important aspect was the expansion of the 'author' (our 'Deepa Mehta' making films about loneliness) *to incorporate in its entirety the category of the speaking subject*, and thus to track a retroactive trajectory from film to speaker within the full definition of Article 19.

Critical to the manoeuvre was the success with which the 'author' became an interim proxy for the true speaking subject of the law: the fictitious 'average viewer'. Indeed, Hidayatullah responds with gratitude to Abbas' voluntary effort to legally manufacture an author entirely suited to the classic conditions under which Article 19 functions at its best, by showing how the manoeuvre allowed the court to overcome what he calls the 'void for vagueness' doctrine. This doctrine has taken censorship 'to the verge of extinction' in the press, art and literature 'except in the ever-shrinking area of obscenity'. 'Regulations containing such words as 'obscene', 'indecent', immoral', 'prejudicial to the best interests of the people', 'tending to corrupt morals', 'harmful' were considered vague criteria:

> If the law is open to diverse construction, that construction which accords best with the intention of the legislature and advances the purpose of legislation, is to be preferred. Where however the law admits of no such construction and the persons applying it are in a boundless sea of uncertainty and the law prima facie takes away a guaranteed freedom, the law must be held to offend the Constitution. . .[23]

How then to revalidate the category? In one of the most remarkable expansions of the issue, Hidayatullah takes the matter to the very heart of realism. Having made the first move, of naming the speaking subject as the film's spectator, whose speech – in the spectator's own interest – has to be taken away from him/her and invested in the filmic author, the judgement makes the further discursive move: into the further production of the commonsensical object of interpretation that the author will now both oversee and stand as guarantee:

> (Nevertheless Article 19(1)(a) uses words which) are *in the common understanding* of the average man. For example the word 'rape' indicates what the word is, ordinarily, understood to mean.[24]

Who guarantees that a word may mean only what it is intended to mean? Jean Mitry's contention that the cinematic *representation* is always, to the 'reasonable person' at least, identical to the 'common understanding' of the *object represented*, now turns out to be so because the law says so. You only get the full force of Hidayatullah's argument, and its foundational place in this debate, in a considerably later judgment. This is the Supreme Court sitting on Govind Nihalani's *Tamas* (1987), a famous film based on the novel of the same name by Bhisham Sahni which too had faced Hindutva ire and an attack on Doordarshan's Bombay office while it was being telecast in serial format.

The legal writ petition on the film, and its earlier version in the Bombay High Court, had been filed by one Javed Ahmad Siddique arguing that the film 'is likely to promote . . . on grounds of religion, caste or community, disharmony or feelings of enmity, hatred or ill-will among different religious, racial, language or regional groups or castes (and) is prejudicial to the maintenance of harmony'.[25] Particular offence had been taken to the sequence in which an elderly Hindu tries to teach a young boy how to kill. On the other hand, the Additional Solicitor General asked for an order from the Supreme Court 'to the government to exhibit the film again and again'.

In his judgment, Chief Justice Sabhyasachi Mukharji too asserted that the case should be judged from the view of the reasonable 'common man' or what he (quoting English law) calls 'the man on top of the Clapham omnibus':

the effect . . . must be judged from the standards of reasonable, strongminded, firm and courageous men and not those of vacillating minds, nor of those who scent danger in every point of view.[26]

Going on to a summary of the film's intentions, Mukharji expands this 'courageous man' to the author proper. He ruled as follows:

The *attempt of the author in this film is* to draw a lesson from our country's past history, to expose the motives of persons who operate behind the scenes to generate and foment conflicts and to emphasize the desire of persons to live in amity and the need for them to rise above religious barriers and treat one another with kindness, sympathy and affection. It is possible only for a motion picture to convey such a message in depth and if it is able to do this, it will be an achievement of great social value.[27]

Who decides that this is so? Both Mukharji and his predecessors in the Bombay High Court, Justices Lentin and Sujata Manohar, went to some length to explain on whose behalf they spoke:

The learned Judges found that the message of the film was good. They have stated that the film shows how realization ultimately dawns as to the futility of violence and hatred, and how the inherent goodness in human nature triumphs. Dr Chitale submitted that the Judges have viewed the film from their point of view but the average persons in the country are not as sober and experienced as Judges of the High Court. But the Judges of the High Court of Bombay have viewed it, as they said, from the point of view of 'how the average person for whom the film is intended will view it' and the learned Judges have come to the conclusion that the average person will learn from the mistakes of the past and realize the machinations of the fundamentalists and will not perhaps commit those mistakes again.[28]

I think it is worth repeating in its entirety, Hidayatullah's judgment on *A Tale of Four Cities*:

She sits at the dressing table, combs her hair, glances at the two love-birds in a cage and looks around the room as if it were a cage. Then she goes behind a screen and emerges in other clothes and prepares for bed. She sleeps and dreams of her life before she took the present path. The film then passes on to its previous theme of contrasts mentioned above, often repeating the earlier shots in juxtaposition as stills. *There is nothing else in the film to be noticed either by us or by the public for which it is intended.*[29]

We can of course argue, as many, including A.G. Noorani, have done,[30] that judges are not film critics, that they see films only in the ways by which film narratives may be brought under the purview of the law. When the *Tamas* judgment reforged the link between the controversial filmic object and speaking voice – ('the attempt of the author of this film is . . .') – and in turn extended it to the average member of the public, then went on to reiterate the characteristics of this receiver as well as his/her legal identity exclusively in terms of the *limits* placed upon his action by Article 19(2); when both Hidayatullah and Mukharji imposed a given way, and no other, by which a film may be seen by this viewer, it would seem that they were aware that all this could not be sustained through ethical-humanist thematics of 'kindness, sympathy and affection' alone. So Mukharji invokes, and not for the last time, *the special responsibility of the author*, reinforced by the Indian Cinematograph Act, 1952, as being one of

> meeting the explosively expanding cinema menace if it were not strictly policed. No doubt the cinema is a great instrument for public good if geared to social ends and can be a public curse if directed to anti-social objectives.[31]

The argument can be made that a forcible legal curtailing of the viewer's right to respond to a film with the complexity that we, film theorists, know any film to be capable of, and indeed a further 'policing' (Mukharji's phrase) of such a *way* of seeing films, might well be the only possible means by which Article 19 can at all be implemented in the cinema.

Cinema, Broadcast Media and the New 'Public'

What made the argument difficult to sustain, in the face of the onslaught that *Fire* encountered, were two major problems that the controversy sharply revealed. The first was the graphic demonstration of the growing roadblocks that the cinema and the cinematic spectator were presenting to a seemingly straightforward application of Article 19 to the media. As it appeared that the cinema had its own spin on the freedom of speech and expression doctrine and its implications, a second problem arose through an increasingly widespread invocation, in the 1990s, of 'the filmmaker' – or more precisely the independent filmmaker – as incarnating the very epitome of the victim threatened by loss of free speech. This invocation, and eventual misuse, of the cinematic author is most directly evident in its use in broadcast media committed to new globalized policies in the name of Article 19.

We have already noted some of the characteristics of the cinematic viewer, the viewer desirous of belief in the 'reality effects' of cinema while not being deluded in the least by the fiction machine; the viewer who is a 'player, accomplice, master of the game' involving the cinema's 'fictional deceit'.[32] While such a film viewer does derive from, for example, the reader of print journalism, the cinematic variant can often severely undermine the fairly straightforward nexus between author/publisher and reader-citizen, with each being able to adequately represent the interests of the other in Indian case law.[33]

Through the 1990s, on the one hand, we see a spate of judgments that induct the increasingly visible film spectator at the service of a new, refurbished 'public', and further see many new rights being attributed to an increasingly bloated category of 'author' claiming protection under Article 19; and, on the other hand, a growing legal crisis caused by the cinematic spectator's inability to be spoken for by the author. In 1989, lawyer Indira Jaising, complaining at the manner in which her interview on Doordarshan was edited so as to misrepresent her views, invoked Article 19 to demand that her freedom of speech expand into her right to speak on Doordarshan, to which the Judge Sujata Manohar said:

> Under Art 19(1)(a) of the Constitution all citizens have a right to freedom of speech and expression. This right protects freedom of speech on television as much as anywhere else. It was contended by Mr Nilkanth, learned advocate for the respondents that there is no right of free speech on TV. He said that Art. 19 does not apply to television programmes. Mr Nilkanth has not cited any authority of law in support of this somewhat alarming proposition.[34]

Around the same time and in an argument that that barely differs from this one, some filmmaker-'citizens' similarly argued that they had a *constitutional right* to show their films on Doordarshan.[35] When Cinemart Foundation, makers of the documentary *Bhopal: Beyond Genocide*,[36] had their film rejected by Doordarshan on the grounds that the film had lost its relevance, lacked moderation and restraint, dealt with sub-judice issues, criticized the State government etc., Cinemart too filed and won a case under the freedom of speech doctrine.[37]

And then came the cricket case. When the Cricket Association of Bengal (CAB) filed a case claiming their right, and that of the Board of Control for Cricket in India (BCCI), to sell telecast rights to multinational telecasting outfits, and demanded that they be allowed to use Intelsat and to allow uplinking equipment to be imported, no guesses on what category of law was deployed. The CAB/BCCI claimed that if they could not do all of these things, *their* citizen's right to freedom of expression would be violated. Justice P.B. Sawant, in the most extensive summary of the history of Article 19(1) available, quoted all of the above precedents drawn, among other sources, from the independent documentary cinema. He then based his argument on the fact that 'sport is an expression of self'. As such, in constructing such a self it too adheres to the basic canons of speech production:

> [T]he right of freedom of speech and expression also includes the right to educate, to inform and to entertain and also the right to be educated, informed and entertained. The former is the right of the telecaster and the latter that of the viewers. The right to telecast a sporting event will therefore include the right to educate and inform the present and prospective sportsmen interested in the particular game. . . An organizer such as the BCCI or CAB which are indisputably devoted to the promotion of the game of cricket cannot be placed in the same scale as the business organizations whose only intention is to make as large a profit as can be made.[38]

Leaving aside the irony of India's biggest and most avowedly commercial sports organization pretending to be an independent filmmaker who in turn pretends to be an ordinary citizen, let us address instead the more abstract notion of what *kind* of 'public' speaker such a judgment puts in place. It is well known that this judgment's historic declaration, that 'air waves are public property', deployed the term 'public' in a wide-ranging but, nevertheless, rather specific way:

> The airwaves or frequencies are a public property. Their use has to be controlled and regulated by a public authority in the interests of the public and to prevent the invasion of their rights. . . The right to impart and receive information is a species of the right of freedom of speech and expression guaranteed by Art. 19(1a) of the Constitution. A citizen has a fundamental right to use the best means of imparting and receiving information and as such to have an access to telecasting for the purpose.[39]

By the late 1990s, as the term 'public' more or less blew apart because of the sheer number of legal rights being sucked out the speaking subject, it was increasingly clear that a new location was gradually emerging upon which to work out the limits of Article 19(1). In the short-lived 1977 Broadcast Bill, the first effort to put the cricket judgement into legislative effect, it was widely accepted that the new locus that would provide for the new citizen, as a member of the new public, had to be the *viewer* of a technology that was creating the new public par excellence: the broadcast media. The new rights of this public, whose membership we can now see as descending directly from the old cinematic spectator, were to be defined primarily by the circumstances of their *spectatorial access to, and ability to use, such media*. And so in the numerous representations made to the Sharad Pawar Joint Parliament Committee, and subsequently in the controversy surrounding the Prasar Bharati Board, a refurbished use of the term 'public' was implicated in at least four areas:

1. *As being 'in the public interest'*. In contrast to relatively more familiar legal definitions of the term, such as those surrounding the debates on public interest litigation, here the concept split up into two further categories. One invoked democratic language: for example, I&B Minister S. Jaipal Reddy's preface to the Bill arguing that it is 'our great democratic traditions' which make it 'imperative that our citizens are well informed and given wider choice in matters of information, education and entertainment', or the Asian Media Information and Communication Centre's (AMIC's) suggested basic guidelines for transnational programming and advertising, which went further in equating 'concepts of democracy, peace and cooperation' with 'recognizing and projecting the family as the basic unit of society'.[40] A related use, in bureaucratic short-hand, seemed to imply that the term could be adequately equated with 'non-commercial', as exemplified by the UGC-sponsored educational TV service in the afternoons on Doordarshan. The question 'non-commercial for whom?' was answered by the further assumption that anything that was not explicitly pay-TV – anything that the *public* apparently didn't have to pay for – could well be characterized as non-commercial in the future. Democracy and commerce now came together to open up an area of negotiation on just how suppliers of 'public interest' material could reap financial benefits, or at least incentives, from this service.

2. *As having 'access to the public'*. In terms of providing a *representa-tion* for the public. Legally, this was precisely the aspect explored by the Jaising case, and the Sawant judgment too had named the public representation of views *on* broadcast media as a critical function of such media. However, in pragmatic terms, spectatorial access to representation on television came to simply mean the access of political parties to express their views on Doordarshan. Still more commonly, 'access' was translated into the far more easily comprehended right to 'have access to' – i.e., to *receive* – electronic media.

3. In a new kind of use, as literally *'public property'*, and, therefore, 'in the service of what the public wants'. Given the fact that, by the late 1990s, it was virtually impossible to assume that 'the public' could want anything other than entertainment, this definition clearly overrode the first: for if we shall re-strict software to what the public actually *wants*, then why on earth should it remain non-commercial? This was indeed the stand taken by numerous advo-cates of both the temporarily banned DTH (direct-to-home) service as well as commercial broadcasters wishing in the late 1990s to enter the still off-limits category of news broadcasting.

4. As a 'public service', widely and commonly interpreted as *'not what the public wants but what the State thinks the public should have'*. Categories 3 and 4 were virtually written into both judgment and Bill as innately contradic-tory, subscribing to the commonly held assumption that the concept of 'public service' clashed with that of 'public property'. While Jaipal Reddy's preface acknowledged that 'it is felt that the public service broadcaster alone will not be able to meet the needs and urges of the people in terms of variety and plurality', the Bill nevertheless explicitly exempted a 'public service broadcaster' from be-ing subject to the licensing process – a major concession – while offering no new clarification as to what such a service should do in these times, given its ac-knowledged limitations.

Through the entire debate, it remained unclear as to just what the status of Doordarshan was likely to be in the eyes of the proposed Broadcast Authority of India (BAI), and the already-existing Telecom Regulatory Authority of India (TRAI) if the Prasar Bharati Bill had been rushed through parliament as the then-government intended to do. If Doordarshan were corporatized as an autonomous entity, the question of whether it could validly claim a status significantly differ-ent from any of the other competing channels turned out to be, across the precise domain of 19(1), more negotiable than one might have thought![41]

A new category of 'public' was clearly being put in place in all this. This new 'property-owning public' was, at first glance anyway, a somewhat different entity – a different negotiating ground – from what we have known, and in much recent theory analysed, as the relationship between the post-Independence Indian State and its citizens in the past five decades. This wasn't the old pluralist every-body-entitled-to-what-they-want formulation. Rather, I suggest, this notion of active reception-as-production – of *citizen–spectator as author* – can only be understood as the furthest, and final, transference of the nexus of object tracing itself back to speaker – a concept of audience as author/producer derived from the cinema and updated to become more compatible with the mode of television broadcasting.[42]

The New Spectator: No Longer Merely the Recipient of Speech

In such a situation, how were we to arrive at valid arguments around the right to both expression and reception that could validly counter threats such as *Fire* faced in the 1990s from the Shiv Sena? By describing it as a great movie, as Lentin and Manohar did with *Tamas*? More fundamentally, why was the *cinema* to suddenly find itself so *centrally pivotal to* a judgment on one of the foundational rights of Indian democracy?

How were the two sets of rights which we have seen – 19(1), or speaker/object, and its proxy in various categories including filmmaker/film/ plot/idealized viewer versus 19(2): viewer emotionally stirred up recipient capable of action – now expected to square up? Or was it that, far from equating with each other as the Hidayatullah and Mukharji judgements had intended them to, the divisions were now virtually unbridgeable? If so, was there something that the cinema could once again uniquely offer this divide?

Justice Sawant, too, acknowledges, as Hidayatullah once did, that there is something special going on when the doctrine of free speech is applied to the cinema. He tries to address the issue as follows:

> The court's commitment to freedom of expression demands that it cannot be suppressed unless the situations created by allowing the freedom are pressing and the community interest is endangered. (However), though the movie enjoys the guarantee under Article 19(1)(a) there is one significant difference between the movie and other modes of communication. Movie motivates thought and action and assures a high degree of attention and retention. . . It has a unique capacity to arouse and disturb feelings . . .
>
> [H]owever the producer may project his own message which the others may not approve of . . . he has a right to 'think out' the counter-appeals to reason. It is a part of democratic give-and-take. . . The democratic form of government itself demands of its citizens an active and intelligent participation in the affairs of the community.[43]

We have finally come to the second half of the tug-of-war: the *recipient* of speech, and the long history of describing such a category, ranging from Hidayatullah's 'average viewer' of 1971 to Sawant's 'public' of 1995.

There is an irony involved in this. Legal judgments bringing Article 19 into the cinema – via its specifically cinematic variant, Section 5B(1) of the Cinematograph Act, 1952 – primarily recognize the carrier of the cinematic, the 'speaker-of-conviction', as the film's author. On the other hand, we have seen, the primary addressee in these judgments is almost inevitably the film's *spectator*. There is a repeated, and insistent, attention that judgments draw to the film-going spectator that may well make legal understandings of spectatorship far more aligned to film theory's understanding of the term than, say, the much more antagonistic relationship of the cinematic *auteur* to the law's production of 'film-maker'. But there are also particular conditions that the law places upon spectatorship that need to be noticed.

The Khosla Committee had, for example, creditably assumed that the filmic spectator was a rather wider category than merely that of 'reasonable, strong-minded, firm and courageous men', and had gone on to inquire into how spectatorial activity may be comprehended as something existing rather than invented for purposes of providing a POV for legally authorized film watching:

> The impact of the film is so vivid, so immediate and so penetrating and the extent of identification with the episodes displayed on screen so complete that all but a few of the more cultured and balanced of individuals can discount the compulsive or persuasive force of what they see. . . The written word is understood only by a small fraction of our people, the spoken word reaches even fewer persons, but the film contains an immediate appeal for everyone, men, women and children, whether literate or illiterate, intelligent or unintelligent. . . . This circumstance places the film medium in a class by itself . . .[44]

However, having stated the problem for itself, its further inquiry into a definition of the cinema's audience led to unexpected roadblocks as the audience proved to be *elusive* – an elusiveness that was to launch a trajectory of argument all of its own. In a chapter entitled 'Audience Reaction', Khosla used a 1957 Bombay-based survey carried out by the CBFC with the help of the Tata Institute of Social Sciences (TISS), and another carried out by the Indian Institute of Mass Communication (IIMC) for the Committee. Neither had got very far in addressing the elusiveness problem – the CBFC found that over 80 per cent of the people questioned saw Hindi films, over half of them at least once a month or more. It also discovered that people were often not honest about admitting that they liked films, or why they liked them. The strange problem was encountered of young people asserting that they 'dislike films dealing with love and romance': probably, said the study, 'due to (their) reluctance . . . to admit their liking for erotic subjects'.[45] The IIMC, on its part, went into the question of how patterns of spectatorial behaviour depended on age and gender: in general, it was recognized that the cinema affects people's habits and behaviour, manners, fashion, and, sometimes, gives rise to immoral practices.

By the mid-1990s, there was a growing chasm – indeed a political crisis of some magnitude – between the textualized spectator, the average individual whose view Messrs Lentin and Manohar claim to adequately and confidently represent, and the increasingly elusive actual viewer who continued to remain frustratingly unavailable for comment. The legal imposition of Hidayatullah's average viewer upon the entire mass of India's film audiences went alongside a normative textual imposition, both impositions explicitly policed by the Cinematograph Act. The 'realist imperative' (as Madhava Prasad names it) developed a harder edge as the policing process extended Hidayatullah's chilling line:

'There is nothing else in the film to be noticed ... by the public for which it is intended'. This imperative consisted, says Prasad:

> in according primacy to the features of a rationally-ordered society – relations of causality, progression along a linear continuum marked by motivation, credibility, and action submitted, in the ultimate instance, to the narrative possibilities arising from the operation of the rule of law.[46]

Prasad draws attention to a realism that exists in its marked contrast to the melodrama of the standard Hindi film, indeed exists *in* its promise to bestow an 'immanent unity (as opposed to a unity that derives from a transcendental plane) on its content'. This account of the 'realist imperative' performs the useful function of outlining the mechanics of how textual reading joins with the emphasis upon a new perceptual field exemplified by the spectator's gaze; and while it can explain the privileged role of certain actual realist films (*Tamas* itself being a classic instance), it can go further to demonstrate how this rule of law might be applied to the reading of *all* films independently of their textual specificities.

Through the 1980s, Indian law adhered steadfastly to such a reading of the cinema: and of even constructing a particular condition of the spectator in whose name, and on whose behalf, the cinematically constructed 'author' existed. Importantly, therefore, Indian law also possessed an honourable record for defending authorial rights of which it was justly proud. This happened in judgment after judgment and in films ranging from Raj Kapoor's *Satyam Shivam Sundaram* (1978) (*Raj Kapoor and Others, Appellants v. State [Delhi Administration] and Others, Respondents*, 1980 hereafter referred to as *Kapoor v. Laxman*) to Anand Patwardhan's *In Memory of Friends* (*Una Mitterandi Yaad Pyari*, 1989) (*Anand Patwardhan, Petitioner v. The Union of India and Others, Respondents*, 1997). However, the growing gap between a textualized spectator functioning under what Prasad calls a legally enforced condition of viewing[47] – the condition reinforced by both the Abbas and *Tamas* judgments' explicit recounting of what these films are about, or who is supposed to be watching them – and the elusive 'actual viewer' only grew, became unbridgeable. With *Fire*, it erupted. And the spectatorial high ground was precisely the one opportunistically seized by Bal Thackeray.

There was some recognition that legal representation of spectatorial rights may well be less than ideal. Many opinions were presented of what the problem may be. In the *Tamas* instance itself, Justice Mukharji had wondered whether the Censor appellate tribunal, designed to address the grievances of filmmakers, could also include spectator grievances:

> It is true that the remedy of an approach to the Appellate Tribunal is available only to persons aggrieved by the *refusal* of the Board to grant a certificate or the cuts and modifications proposed by it. It is for the consideration of the Central Government whether the scope of this section should be expanded to permit appeals to the Tribunals even by persons who are aggrieved by the *grant* of

certificate of exhibition to a film on the ground that the principles laid down for
the grant of certificates in Section 5B have not been fulfilled.[48]

The closest that any case got to placing the spectatorship problem squarely
in the foreground was *Raj Kapoor v. Laxman*, dealing with his *Satyam Shivam
Sundaram*. There the petitioner, a spectator who had objected to the religious-
sounding title, had filed a case that the 'fascinating title was misleading, foul and
beguiled the guileless into degeneracy'. The Magistrate's court, in an unprecedented departure that even the High Court endorsed, had overturned the Censor
Board's clearance and asked that the film be withdrawn from circulation. In the
Supreme Court, Kapoor – who evidently didn't withdraw the film – claimed that,
in assuming that he had been protected by the Censor Board's giving him an A
certificate, he 'did not know' that he was committing a crime. Eventually, things
went Kapoor's way, but, in conclusion, Krishna Iyer went on to say that:

> Prosecutions like this may well be symptomatic of public dissatisfaction with
> the Board of Censors. . . The ultimate censorious power over the censors be-
> longs to the people and by indifference, laxity or abetment, pictures which
> pollute public morals are liberally certificated, the legislation, meant by Parlia-
> ment to protect people's good morals, may be sabotaged by statutory enemies
> within. Corruption at that level must be stamped out.[49]

To recapitulate: as in the Broadcast Bill debate, where the question was
primarily one of people's 'access' to (express their views on versus rights to
receive) television, in the cinema, too, it appeared that the field of spectatorship
could shift, acquire various kinds of citizenship privileges, provided they were
only seen as *receivers* of someone else's speech, from which speech they may at
best receive legal protection. The prior question, of how 19(1)(a) could accord
speech to spectators *in the first place*, has remained an ever-increasing problem.
For the most part, it can only function under certain conditions, enable only
certain readings of films. At its most extreme, it becomes eventually an expro-
priation, as a fictional construct of an author – ranging from Abbas to the Cricket
Board – is incarnated, *in the name of the spectator*, as the bearer of 19(1)(a). This
is the way by which the legally privileged perception of the cinematic institution
inscribes its narratively constructed speaking subject. This non-variable category
was what spectators of the cinema now had necessarily to assume, and to replicate, if they were to become legally visible at all. For the most part then,
spectatorial right to free speech could occur only in conflict with the film's maker.

Postscript
After the news came that the Censor Board had passed *Fire* a second time
round without cuts, the nationwide distributor of the film, Harish Sugandh of
Friends India, was quoted as saying, 'We will only release the film again in India
if the Shiv Sena allows us to do so', and that the decision of the CBFC was 'not
enough'.[50]

Notes

1 Susie Tharu describes this performative tradition perfectly in another instance of the display of a 'realist' female character: that of Sulabha (played by Smita Patil, Azmi's legendary contemporary and a direct actorial predecessor to Das) in Jabbar Patel's *Umbartha/Subah* (1981). Tharu says, 'The filmic focus, emphasized by several close-ups of Sulabha, sitting, toying with her glasses, looking up, walking, sitting again (e)stablishes her as the central character as well as the problem (the disruption, the enigma) the film will explore and resolve. In *Umbartha*, it is clear that to search herself is, for a woman, a tragic enterprise. An enterprise in which she is doomed to fail, but can fail bravely and heroically' (Tharu 1986).

2 Madhu Kishwar writes: 'If one were to take (Deepa Mehta's) version of the *Ramayan* a seriously, we would be led to believe that there are only two purposes behind the writing of this popular Hindu epic: (a) to condition women into accepting servility and even death by torture without protest and (b) to encourage men to be crude and insensitive in their relationship to women. . . Deepa Mehta also let it be known that her ire is not just confined to icons from the epics, but that she also aims to show up poor Mahatma Gandhi as a sexual-moral hypocrite. Gandhi is brought under her critical scrutiny through the character of Radha's husband Ashok. After Radha fails to bear children, Ashok takes a vow of celibacy under the influence of his guru in his pursuit of moksha. . . You don't have to be a Shiv Sainik to feel offended and hurt by the gratuitous insults aimed at Indian culture in this crude caricature' (Kishwar 1998).

3 The stridently 'instructional', pamphleteering style of the film may well allow *Fire* to be seen within a long tradition of stage and film propaganda – in the tradition one would most directly associate with, say, Utpal Dutt's (1994) idea of 'heroic cinema'. This curious and, it appears, largely unintended legacy may also arguably have allowed the film to lend itself so easily to political use, much to Mehta's surprise. (On Dutt, also see Bharucha 1983.)

4 In their important essay on the film, Mary John and Tejaswini Niranjana draw attention to the difficulties that such spectatorship caused to the filmmaker and to critics. Deepa Mehta, fighting to maintain her own understanding of the film's realist career, claimed that the film was not about lesbianism but about 'loneliness', and most film critics too, say the authors, have generally chosen to see the lesbian content as incidental. 'Taking their cue from Mehta's attitude, Madhu Jain and Sheela Raval in *India Today* speak about placard-waving lesbians during the candlelight protest outside the Regal cinema in Delhi. The "broader issue of freedom of expression and tolerance had got derailed by the lesbian debate", they say, A "surprised Mehta", according to them, declares: "I can't have my film hijacked by any one organization. It's not about lesbianism, it's about loneliness, about choices."' (John and Niranjana 1999). Perhaps the most far-out statement on Mehta's fuzzy understanding of the issues was, 'If I'm entitled to my freedom of expression, then why can't others be allowed the same privilege? What I really hated was when people pretended to love *Fire* in front of me, only to turn around later and say they hated it' (Jha 1999).

5 For an account of this battle, of the intense debates that accompanied its clearance by the Censor Board, the opposition to the film by the Hindu right, within feminist and gay-rights organizations, see John and Niranjana (2000) and http://www.cscsarchive.org for an extensive news dossier.

6 Article 19(2) includes eight explicit categories under which restrictions can be imposed on speech and expression: 1. State security, 2. Friendly relations with foreign States, 3. Public order, 4. Decency or morality, 5. Contempt of court, 6. Defamation, 7. Incitement to an offence, 8. Sovereignty and integrity of India.

7 So in response to Thackeray's question on why the film uses a Hindu milieu, Deepa Mehta was quoted by Shabana Azmi as saying, 'The majority of films made in India are set in Hindu households. Besides, I am a Hindu and the particular milieu of *Fire* is a milieu with which I am familiar and feel comfortable portraying. It is like asking Ismat Chughtai (posthumously) to change the milieu of *Lihaaf* from a Muslim household into a Hindu one' (Azmi 1998).

8 Basu (1995/98: 47).

[9] *Ranjit D. Udeshi v. State of Maharashtra*, 1965.

[10] Niranjana (1992: 9).

[11] See for example *Emperor v. Sadashiv Narayan Bhalerao – Respondent*, 1947 (full text available at: http://www.cscsarchive.org:8081/__e52568520028b5fe.nsf/0/3cf9f66015992bb1e525685200375d32?OpenDocument&Highlight=0,Bhalerao).

[12] *Emperor v. Harnam Das and Another – Accused Respondents*, 1947 (full text available at: http://www.cscsarchive.org:8081/__e52568520028b5fe.nsf/0/3efae49bcdf90ac0e525685200375d41?OpenDocument).

[13] Christian Metz attacks what he calls the 'nosographic' approach as an ideology of 'pure creation' that tends to 'neglect everything in a film which escapes the conscious and unconscious psychism of the filmmaker as an individual, everything that is a direct social imprint and ensures that no one is ever the 'author' of his 'works': influences and pressures of an ideological kind, the objective state of the cinematic codes and techniques at the moment of shooting, etc.' (Metz 1982: 26–27).

[14] Liang (2004).

[15] *K.A. Abbas* v. *The Union of India and Another, Respondents*, 1971, hereafter referred to as the Abbas judgement; emphases mine.

[16] Part II, John and Niranjana (2000: 519–20).

[17] Abbas (1977: 477).

[18] *Abbas: The Short and Long of It* – K.A. Abbas (a 16-minute film called *A Tale of Four Cities* became a Long Feature titled *A Tale of Censorship*, with a running time of 11 months, from Close Up).

[19] Abbas judgement, paragraph 7.

[20] Abbas (1977: 480).

[21] Each member of the 'public' is, individually, a 'human being, that is, a moral person'; further, such human beings have basically a 'private existence' which they have to by no means abandon in order to 'exercise their public role. For the private person, there was no break between *homme* and *citoyen*, as long as the *homme* was simultaneously an owner of private property who as *citoyen* was simultaneously to protect the stability of the property order as a private one' (Habermas 1991/1995: 79–87).

[22] Bresson (1977).

[23] Abbas judgement, paragraph 48.

[24] Abbas judgement, paragraphs 48, 49.

[25] *Ramesh Chhotalal Dalal, Petitioner v. Union of India and Others, Respondents*, 1988, paragraph 4; hereafter referred to as the *Tamas* judgment.

[26] *Tamas* judgement, paragraph 13.

[27] *Tamas* judgement, paragraph 21; emphasis mine.

[28] *Tamas* judgement, paragraph 20.

[29] Abbas judgment, paragraph 4, emphasis mine.

[30] Noorani (1988).

[31] *Tamas* judgement, paragraph 17. Interestingly, any symptomatic reading of this film would entirely eliminate such meaningless textual data before the film's frontal address, its sledgehammer-like intention, given its primarily political (rather than humanist) existence, to challenge the Censor Board. Abbas himself arguably recognizes this in the way he gestures towards the 'knowing' audience by putting suspense music over the film's opening Censor Certificate! A similar reading may well be made for the next film that briefly threatened to challenge the very validity of the Indian Cinematograph Act, 1952: Rakesh Sharma's cause célèbre documentary *Final Solution* (2004). See the nationwide petition against the ban on the film (http://www.petitiononline.com/FilmBan/petition.html).

[32] Comolli (1980: 124).

[33] See *Romesh Thapar v. State of Madras*, 1950 SCR 594 (AIR 1950 SC 124), involving the ban upon the entry and circulation of the petitioner's journal *Cross Roads*, where it was held that the freedom of speech and expression includes freedom of propagation of ideas and that freedom is ensured by the freedom of circulation. Also *Sakal Papers (P) Ltd. v. Union of India*, (1962) 3 SCR 842 (AIR 1962 SC 305), where it was held that for 'propagating his ideas a citizen had the right to publish them, to dissemi-

nate them and to circulate them, either by word of mouth or by writing. The right extended not merely to the matter which he was entitled to circulate but also to the volume of circulation'. Also see *Bennett Coleman and Company v. Union of India* (1972)2 SCC 788 (AIR 1973 SC 106), where the majority of the Constitution Bench held that newspapers should be left free to determine their pages, their circulation and their new edition within their quota which has been fixed fairly. And finally *Indian Express Newspapers (Bombay) Pvt. Ltd. v. Union of India* (1985) 1 SCC 641 (AIR 1986 SC 515) which said that the 'purpose of the press is to advance the public interest by publishing facts and opinions without which democratic electorate cannot make responsible judgments'.

[34] *Indira Jaising, Petitioner v. Union of India and Others, Respondents*, 1989, paragraph 13.

[35] As happened to the TV serial *Honi Anhonee* (*Odyssey Communications Pvt. Ltd. v. Lokvidayan Sanghatana*, 1988).

[36] Directed by Tapan Bose (1986).

[37] *Secretary, Ministry of I&B and Others, Appellants v. Cricket Association of Bengal and Others, Respondents, along with CAB and Another, Petitioners v. Union of India and Others, Respondents*, 1995; referred to here as the Air Waves judgement, paragraph 4.

[38] Air Waves judgement, paragraph 17.

[39] Air Waves judgement, paragraph 24.

[40] Also see AMIC (1999).

[41] The specific issue first rose when Star TV, during I.K. Gujral's brief tenure as India's Prime Minister, made an unsuccessful bid to be the official broadcaster of the Republic Day parade. Television commentator Sevanti Ninan (1998) reported on how Gujral, inaugurating Star TV's 24-hour news channel, 'gushed unreservedly about what a great step forward it was for Indian democracy and what a great turning point for the media. Rupert Murdoch would have loved that'; going further, he stated his hope that 'Prasar Bharati would emulate Star TV'. Star's offer to give free broadcast time to political parties and, even more, to allow itself to be arbitrated by the Election Commission, were all pointers to its ambitions. The question of whether Doordarshan could survive as India's national broadcaster, in the BBC sense, was further complicated with the privately owned NDTV, incubated by Star, approximating more and more closely to that role in Indian television.

[42] For example, private cable television's own production of what Sue Browner calls 'tastemakers' which she explores through a group in Britain named VQT (or 'Viewers for Quality Television'), a variant of televisual fans who are 'devotees of prime time network television' but specifically reproduce the tasks of responsible citizen-viewing. See Browner (1992).

[43] Air Waves judgement, paragraph 4.

[44] Khosla (1968).

[45] Ibid.: 70–71.

[46] Prasad (1998: 62).

[47] Ibid.: 62–63.

[48] *Tamas* judgement, paragraph 19; emphasis mine.

[49] *Kapoor v. Laxman*, paragraph 10.

[50] Kazmi (1999).

References

Abbas, K.A. (1977), *I Am Not an Island: An Experiment in Autobiography* (New Delhi: Vikas Publishing).

AMIC, ed. (1999), *Public Service Broadcasting in Asia: Surviving in the New Information Age* (Singapore: Asian Media Information and Communication Centre).

Anand Patwardhan, Petitioner v. The Union of India and Others, Respondents, A.P. Shah, J, AIR 1997 Bombay 25.

Azmi, Shabana (1998), 'Smokescreen for Hidden Agenda', *The Times of India* (17 December).

Basu, Durga Das (1995/98), *Constitutional Law of India*, seventh edn (New Delhi: Prentice-Hall).

Bharucha, Rustom (1983), *Rehearsals of Revolution: The Political Theatre of Bengal* (Calcutta: Seagull Books).

Bresson, Robert (1977), *Notes on Cinematography* (New York: Urizen Books).

Browner, Sue (1992), 'Fans as Tastemakers: Viewers for Quality Television', in Lisa A. Lewis, ed., *The Adoring Audience: Fan Culture and Popular Media* (London and New York: Routledge): 163–84.

Comolli, Jean-Louis (1980), 'Machines of the Visible', in Stephen Heath and Teresa de Lauretis, eds, *The Cinematic Apparatus* (London: Macmillan).

Emperor v. Harnam Das and Another – Accused Respondents, Cornelius and Falshaw JJ. (1947), AIR (34) 1947 Lahore 383 [C. N. 97.]

Emperor v. Sadashiv Narayan Bhalerao – Respondent, Lords Thankerton Porter and Simonds, Sir Madhavan Nair and Sir John Beaumont (1947), AIR (34) 1947 Privy Council 82 Bombay 31 AIR 1944, Bombay, 255.

Habermas, Jürgen (1991/1995), *The Structural Transformation of the Public Sphere: An Inquiry into a Category of Bourgeois Society*, translated by Thomas Burger (Cambridge, MA: The MIT Press).

Indira Jaising, Petitioner, v. Union of India and Others, Respondents, Sujata Manohar J (1989), AIR 1989, Bombay 25.

Jha, Subhash K. (1999), 'Setting Water on Fire', *The Times of India*, 13 September.

John, Mary E. and Tejaswini Niranjana (2000), 'The Controversy over *Fire*: A Select Dossier Parts 1/2', *Inter-Asia Cultural Studies*, Vol. 1, Nos 2–3, August/December.

——— (1999), 'Mirror Politics: *Fire*, Hindutva and Indian Culture', *Economic and Political Weekly*, Vol. 6, No. 13, March.

K.A. Abbas v. The Union of India and Another, Respondents, Supreme Court, M. Hidayatullah, J (1971), AIR 1971 Supreme Court 481.

Kazmi, Nikhat (1999), '*Fire*: Mumbai Awaits Sen Nod', *The Times of India*, 17 February.

Kishwar, Madhu (1998), 'Naive Outpourings of a Self-Hating Indian: Deepa Mehta's *Fire*', *Manushi*, No. 109.

Liang, Lawrence (2004), *Copyright, Cultural Production and Open Content Licensing* (Rotterdam: Piet Zwart Institute); http://pzwart.wdka.hro.nl/mdr/pubsfolder/liangessay/view.

Metz, Christian (1982), *The Imaginary Signifier: Psychoanalysis and the Cinema* (Bloomington: Indiana University Press).

Niranjana, Tejaswini (1992), *Siting Translation: History, Post-Structuralism, and the Colonial Text* (Berkeley: University of California Press).

Noorani, A.G. (1988), 'Should Judges Judge Movies?', *Sunday Observer*, 1 May.

Odyssey Communications Pvt. Ltd. v. Lokvidayan Sanghatana (1988), 3 SCC 410 AIR 1988 SC 1642.

Prasad, M. Madhava (1998), *Ideology of the Hindi Film: A Historical Construction* (New Delhi: Oxford University Press).

Raj Kapoor and Others, Appellants v. State (Delhi Administration) and Others, Respondents, V.R. Krishna Iyer and R.S. Pathak JJ (1980), AIR 1980 Supreme Court 258.

Ramesh Chhotalal Dalal, Petitioner v. Union of India and Others, Respondents, Sabhyasachi Mukharji and S. Ranganathan, JJ (1988), AIR 1988 Supreme Court 775.

Ranjit D. Udeshi v. State of Maharashtra, Gajendragadkar, P.B.:CJ and K.N. Wanchoo, M. Hidayatullah, N. Rajagopala Ayyangar and J.C. Shah: J (1965), AIR 1965 Supreme Court 881.

'Report of the Enquiry Committee on Film Censorship' (1968), G.D. Khosla (Chairman), New Delhi: Ministry of Information and Broadcasting, Government of India.

Secretary, Ministry of I&B and Others, Appellants v. Cricket Association of Bengal and Others, Respondents, Along with Cab and Another, Petitioners v. Union of India and Others, Respondents, P.B. Sawant, S. Mohan and B.P. Jeevan Reddy, JJ (1995), AIR 1995 Supreme Court 1236.

Tharu, Susie (1986), 'Third World Women's Cinema: Notes on Narrative, Reflections on Opacity', *Economic and Political Weekly*, Vol. 21, No. 20, 17 May.

Times of India, The (1998), 'Change Radha-Sita to Shabana-Saira: Thackeray Sets Condition for Allowing Fire to Be Screened', 14 December.

Index